Railways around Worksop

Volume 2: The Midland Railway
Worksop to Mansfield and connecting branches

Chris Booth

PLATFORM 5

www.platform5.com

Above: On 22 February 1969 Flying Scotsman Enterprises ran the No. 1 Mystery Tour from London St. Pancras to Cleethorpes, seen here at Elmton & Creswell Junction. No. 4472 "Flying Scotsman" paused for water from 12.21 to 12.46 and, as can be seen, locals and the passengers took a look around – something unlikely to happen these days. The mystery train reached Cleethorpes considerably late, where the locomotive was declared a failure with a leaking smokebox steam pipe. The train returned to London King's Cross behind Brush Type 4 No. 1869. ***(Robin Webster/Creative Commons Attribution 4.0 International License)***

Front cover top: The fireman of 16A Nottingham-based 1936-built Stanier Class 4P 2-6-4T No. 42588 climbs onto the running board to begin watering the loco at Worksop, prior to its departure for Nottingham in 1962. ***(Author's collection)***

Front cover bottom left: "Black 5" 4-6-0 No. 45270, allocated to 5B Crewe South, passes Langwith Station 'box with the final Blackpool North to Radford summer Saturday train on 18 August 1962. ***(Author's collection)***

Front cover bottom right: Stanier 3P 2-6-2T 40088 is seen at Mansfield Town on 7 September 1961 with the 3.31pm Worksop to Nottingham, this being due into Mansfield at 4.24pm. ***(Alan Smalley)***

Back cover: On 21 August 2002, 58047 passes the semaphore signals at Creswell with 6A20 Harworth Colliery to Ratcliffe Power Station. The semaphores, loco, HAA wagons, colliery and power station have all now gone. ***(Author)***

Published by Platform 5 Publishing Ltd, 52 Broadfield Road, Sheffield, S8 0XJ. England.

Printed in England by The Amadeus Press, Cleckheaton, West Yorkshire
ISBN: 978 1915984 41 8

Contents

Introduction

The start of being a lifelong railway enthusiast began when my cousin Brian took me on the crossbar of his bike, the seven miles from Worksop to Retford Station to watch the trains pass. I distinctly remember the first time I saw a streamlined A4 come screeching through to the shouts of "Streak" from the gathered spotters. This was no other than the fastest of them all, 60022 Mallard, and that was the beginnings of my love for the railways.

Leaving school I was initially unable to get a job on the railways, but eventually in June 1975 I began work with British Rail as a signalman at Dinnington Colliery Junction, on the former South Yorkshire Joint Railway line between Brancliffe East Junction and Maltby. Moving to Worksop Sidings signal box in 1977, I then moved to Worksop West Junction in 1981, staying there until it closed in 1997. After that I moved to my final position at Worksop Power Signal Box, retiring from there in 2019.

In 1994 I wrote my first article for the railway press and have since had many more features published, I also have several books to my name, beginning with the self-published 40 Years of Sheffield Power Signal Box, with co-authors Andrew K Overton and Mick Charlesworth. This was followed by two self-published books about the Lancashire Derbyshire & East Coast Railway, which were later republished by Fonthill Media in three volumes. Fonthill Media also published my Pit to Power Station book, and I also co-authored Tinsley and the Modernisation of Sheffield's Railways through Platform 5 Publishing. It was whilst working in Worksop Power Signal Box (PSB) that the idea came to me for this book.

As explained in Volume 1, opened in 1997, Worksop PSB's area of control spreads from Kiveton Park Station in the west, to Checker House near Retford in the east, Maltby in the north and Shirebrook to the south. However, the signalman on duty is aware of trains coming towards the area of control as they pass Woodhouse Junction in the west, Retford Thrumpton in the east, St Catherine's Junction near Doncaster in the north and Shirebrook Station to the south. So with this in mind I decided that the book should cover as much of the signalman's knowledge of trains in his area as possible, with a little extra on top. Therefore Volume 1 covered the former Great Central Railway line between Sheffield Victoria and Gainsborough Central, and the Clarborough Junction to Sykes Junction route, which was part of the original plans for a line between Sheffield and Lincoln.

Volume 2 will now cover the former Midland Railway (MR) lines from Shireoaks East Junction to Mansfield and branches off this, and the long gone Killamarsh Branch to Kiveton.

There have been many changes on the former MR routes through the years, and so we will look at those lines through the lenses of photographers spanning many decades, from steam days through to modern diesels.

Map of the route as it was in 1900.

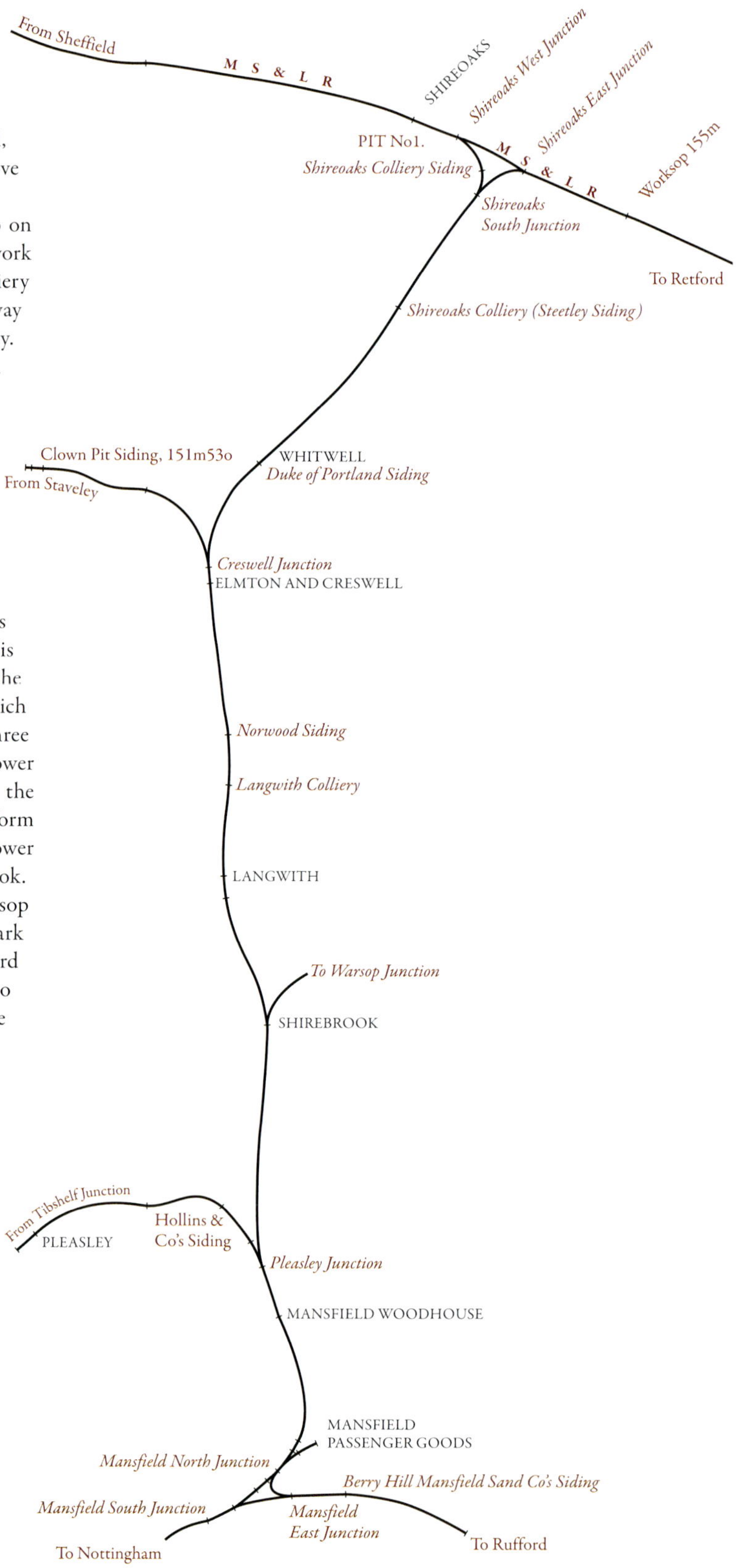

Acknowledgements

This book could not have been completed without the help of other people, and I am indebted to those who have allowed me to use photographs from their collections, some of whom are no longer with us. In no particular order they are:

Adrian Stretton, Adrian Wynne, Alan Padley, Andrew K. Overton, Andy Bailey, Anthony Guppy, Ash Edwards, Barry Taylor, Bill Taylor, Bill Wright, Bob Pixton, Brian Bates, Clyde Hatter, Corwin Bainbridge, Dave Peachey, Dave Phillips, David Horton, Derek Bucket, Derek Talbot, Derek Wilson, Edna Molesworth, Eric Willoughby, Edward Downs, Frank Ashley, Frankie Spowart, Gary Sansom, Geoff Warnes, Gordon Bennett, Ivan Stewart, Jack Cupit, Jim Hatcher, John Alsop, John Gibson, John Law, John Lawrie, John Marsh, John Midcalf, John Miller, John Peck, John Spencer Gilks, John Ward, Ken Milner, Ken Whinfrey, M. Fowler, Malcolm Rush, Mick Nicholson, Mike King, Milespost 92½, Neil Baker, Nigel Thompson, Nigel Tout, Paul Lindley, Pete Churchman, Peter Hawkins, Peter Snell, Peter Stanyard, Phil Sangwell, R. J. Buckley, Ray Richardson, Ray Williams, Richard Bywater, Richard Paget, Robin Stewart Smith, Roger Wainwright, S & A Warnes, Simon Turner, Steve Godman, Steven Allison, Steven Bennett, Steven Gay, Tom Grey, Tony James, Tony Soulby, Val Fowler, W. Ashton.

Special thanks go to Greg Sherlock for editing the text and making it flow better, without his help it would have been much poorer.

I would also like to thank the following organisations for help with photographs diagrams and maps, Great Northern Railway Society, Tickhill & District local history society, Inspire Picture Archive, Colour-Rail, National Library of Scotland, Midland Railway Study Centre Derby, Chesterfield Canal Trust, Stations UK, Historic England, Transport Treasury, RCTS, HMRS and the Old Warsop Society. Thanks also to John Hinson for signalling diagrams and Simon Turner of GW Railwayana Auctions.

My late childhood friend Alan Hazell gifted me his entire photo collection and his help is also acknowledged. If I have forgotten anyone else I apologise, but they are also thanked.

I would like to dedicate this book to my late wife Linda who passed away in April 2024. She always encouraged my writing and never complained about me disappearing upstairs to write the many articles and books on my computer. She was always proud of the results of the time spent on the publications, and will be greatly missed by myself and all who knew her.

◊ **Above**: Self portrait of the author at work in Worksop West in 1996. ***(Author)***

Chapter 1

The main line Worksop to Mansfield

The former Midland Railway (MR) line from Nottingham to Shireoaks East Junction is today known as the "Robin Hood Line"; however, as mentioned in the introduction, Worksop PSB gained knowledge of trains approaching from Shirebrook when they were in the Mansfield Woodhouse area, so in this book we will only be looking at the section from Mansfield to Worksop, along with the branches that connected.

First proposals

The MR plans for a line along the Leen Valley received Royal Assent in July 1846, with the first section from Nottingham to Kirkby-in-Ashfield opening on 2 October 1848. Building continued along the route of the Mansfield & Pinxton Railway, which had opened as far back as 1819 (and was later purchased by the MR) opening through to Mansfield on 9 October 1849. Stations were provided at Lenton, Radford, Basford Vernon, Bulwell Market, Hucknall and Mansfield; with further stations later added at Linby, Newstead, Annesley and Sutton-in-Ashfield.

Not resting on its laurels, in November 1860 the MR next pursued the aim to extend its territory into North Nottinghamshire, by proposing a Mansfield and Worksop railway. It was intended that the extension to Worksop should diverge from the Nottingham and Mansfield line at a point some distance south of Mansfield; that it should bend to the west, and that there should be a second station at Mansfield. It was proposed to pass round the western edge of Mansfield, crossing Stockwell Gate and head northeast towards Mansfield Woodhouse. Passing close to the hamlet of Spion Cop, it would skirt past Langwith Mill, Belph, Steetley and Haggonfields to join the Manchester, Sheffield & Lincolnshire Railway (MS&LR) with a triangular junction just east of Shireoaks.

These plans did not take into account the two major landowners that the route would affect, the Dukes of Newcastle and Portland who, like a lot of the gentry of the time, objected to them. Rather than carry on with the proposals in the face of possible intense opposition, the MR initially abandoned the project.

A second proposal

However, the MR didn't give up and began to survey a different route, this time further to the west along the boundary between Derbyshire and Nottinghamshire, but the issue of a tunnel being required at Whitwell saw them look at a route through the scenic, and historically important, Creswell Crags. This was again objected to by the 5th Duke of Portland, and so a tunnel it was.

In November 1864 the MR thus once again submitted plans to parliament for a Mansfield and Worksop Railway, and the Mansfield Railways Act of 5 July 1865 empowered the following works:

Above: A view of Creswell Crags, if the MR had got their way a railway would probably have run where the road is. ***(Author's collection)***

Railway No. 4 commencing in the Parish of Mansfield with a junction with the Midland Railway and terminating in the Township and Parish of Worksop, by a junction with Manchester, Sheffield and Lincolnshire Railway.

Railway No. 5, wholly in the Township of Shireoaks, Parish of Worksop, commencing with a junction with Railway No. 4, terminating by a junction with the Manchester, Sheffield and Lincolnshire Railway.

This Act also provided running powers to the MS&LR as far as Mansfield in return for that company not proceeding with its own bill for a railway to Mansfield. The MS&LR had proposed their line in the summer of 1860, and with the backing of the Great Northern Railway (GNR), deposited Bills for the 1861 Session. However, the GNR also proposed their own railway from Mansfield to Retford, and in his book The Midland Railway: Its Rise and Progress published in 1878, Frederick S Williams states:

It was contended that Retford was the second largest cattle market in the kingdom; that the Mansfield limestone quarries would be benefited by the Retford route as well as by the other; that whatever went north-east of Retford should be carried direct to Retford; though it was admitted that whatever went westward or north-west would go better by Worksop, and that delay in the transit of minerals did not much matter. It was of little consequence, someone humorously suggested, if a load of pig iron was detained; but if a truck of pigs were starved to death in winter weather, or if fish or fruit coming from Hull were delayed en route at midsummer, the consequences might be unpleasant to all concerned. The Midland replied that theirs was the better route, because they passed through a population twice as numerous as on the line to Retford, and because the latter ran through a purely agricultural country without minerals.

The decision of Parliament was given in favour of the Midland bill and with the MR promising that they would allow the MS&LR equal rights and powers in any future scheme for the district, the MS&LR thus dropped their plans.

The MR's Act authorised the construction of three public level crossings in the Parishes of Pleasley, Bolsover and Elmton, the latter on Mags Lane also later had a siding and became known as Norwood Siding.

It was estimated that the line would cost £137,257 to build; offers for tenders were placed and on 31 January 1869 were received. Thomas Oliver of Horsham bid £147,188 16s 4d and this was approved by the MR Board, even though it was almost £10,000 more.

Construction starts

Preparation work along the route had begun by the end of 1869, houses in Mansfield were demolished to make way for the huge 250-yard long, 82-foot high, 15-arch viaduct to come, and felled trees were being put up for auction in Worksop on 17 January 1870. Building the line required labourers and the local newspapers began to run advertisements for labourers and quarrymen from May 1870. The area is on limestone hence the requirement of quarrymen to make the cuttings and dress stone for bridges and viaducts.

Work on building the line officially commenced in June 1870 and by April 1871 census records showed that at least 21 men were working on the construction at Langwith, 57 around Shirebrook and 70 around Creswell and Whitwell, as work progressed around 1000 men could be found at work along the route.

The construction of the route was not without its disputes, initially the contractors experienced problems with the MS&LR over access rights at Shireoaks; however, the problem was later resolved. Another dispute arising was that Thomas Oliver (the contractor) had an issue with the MR about the construction of the five stations along the route. His claim was that the cost of these was not in the original contract but (although the details went unrecorded), this was resolved in an agreement between the contractor and John S. Crossley the MR's Engineer. It was determined that the MR would pay for the stations at Mansfield Woodhouse, Shirebrook, Langwith and Creswell, while the Duke of Portland would pay for the construction of Whitwell.

Apart from Mansfield Woodhouse, which was of wooden construction, and Whitwell which was designed to suit the Duke of Portland, the stations were built of limestone in the Midland Gothic style, as designed by the MR's Chief Architect, John Holloway Sanders.

There were 51 bridges in total along the route, the only tunnel, 538 yards in length, was through the limestone ridge at Whitwell, but as almost the entire route was on limestone the 1¼ mile long cutting between Shirebrook and Langwith would be the most problematical. With an average depth of 26 feet and at its deepest point, 50 feet deep, it entailed the blasting out of 400,000 tons of limestone with almost two tons of gunpowder, and took around three years to complete. With the inevitable slow work ongoing on the cutting Whitwell tunnel was also causing problems, so much so that the tunnel lining was not finished until the end of 1874.

Inspection

The local press were by then complaining that as far as they could see the line was complete and were querying why it had not opened. Although various works still had to completed, including the station building at Langwith, the line was inspected by Board of Trade Inspector, Colonel William Yolland, on 2 December 1874, his report reading:

The line was covered in light snow; the rails are laid with 80lb 20 feet lengths, fencing made up of larch posts 4½ feet above ground, with stone walls 5 feet high. The maximum incline of the line being 1 in 72, with a minimum curve of 15 chains. No turntables are to be found on the line as the engines will not go to and fro but in a circuit. There are no unauthorised level crossings. Five stations are located along the line. There is only one tunnel of 538 yards. Over and underbridges built of stone, all works and bridges well executed, girders are of sufficient theoretical strength to withstand the weight of the stock. One bridge located at 13 miles 15 chains from Mansfield agreed by the Engineer to be strengthened. Line well-constructed and only one embankment near Worksop seemed to require attention, as it is made with different kind of material to other embankments. Proper instruments are provided. The station buildings and shelters not complete at Whitwell, Langwith and Mansfield Woodhouse. The numbers should be painted on the side of the levers, showing the order in which different levers must be moved to alter the points and signals, with a diagram showing the position of the points and signals. Clocks required in the signal boxes and at all stations in a position to be seen from the platform. There are a few blind signals at the stations and stop blocks are required at the end of the sidings. Company regulations for working the line say that "clear" is given back to the last station as soon as the train has passed home and in many instances signals are only a few yards from the end of the platform, any train stopping would foul the signal. In my opinion, not sufficient provision against collision at the station platform, I requested that the stop signals be placed 100 yards along the line from the rear end of the platform. The MS&LR junction at Shireoaks, the MS&LR signal is contrary to Midland Railway which have specific and distinct distant signal, in my opinion this is very objectionable, as on the London and North Western Railway their signals have a circular disc. The line is incomplete, therefore I cannot open it as it would be a danger to the public, however if the MS&LR would alter the signal at Shireoaks then I would allow Goods traffic.

Initially the west curve from Woodend Junction (originally known as Shireoaks South Junction) was built as a single line, primarily to serve just Shireoaks Colliery; however, a second track would be laid when the connection to the MS&LR was made at Shireoaks West Junction.

And the line opens

The Nottinghamshire Guardian of Friday 22 January 1875 ran a small paragraph that stated:

The goods traffic on the new line of railway from Mansfield to Worksop has been opened, and it is stated that the passenger traffic will be commenced on the 1 February.

The same day's edition of the Mansfield Advertiser ran a report about an inspection train traversing the line on Monday 18 January, conveying MR Inspectors Henry Herbert Loveday and James Anderson. This was used to take signalmen to their respective locations and was followed later that day by the first train of loaded and empty wagons to be taken to their customers.

Passenger traffic did not commence from 1 February as the line was placed in the hands of the Works and Ways Committee on 3 February 1875, and on 19 March an Inspector from the Board of Trade visited. His approval for use of the line from 30 March 1875 came with the proviso that an embankment close to Worksop should be observed during wet weather. The first timetabled freight trains commenced from that date, initially this being a daily 9.20am Nottingham to Shireoaks Colliery train arriving at 1.10pm and returning as a pick-up goods at 2.0pm.

Passengers had to wait until Tuesday 1 June 1875 for the chance to utilise the services between Mansfield and Worksop, with the local press relating the event to the readers. The Worksop Guardian reported the following:

The 7.10am left Mansfield for Worksop with 160 enthusiastic people (90 booked to Mansfield Woodhouse) who gave many cheers as the train quitted the station. Flags were attached to the carriages and the engine driver and, guard appeared in all the glory of their new uniforms, as the train dashed along, there was an incessant waving of handkerchiefs from the carriage windows and responding shouts from the inhabitants who lived along the route. A passenger train seemed to be the most novel of all novelties in the vicinity and everybody appeared to be mentally promising themselves a ride in it as early as possible. At every station along the line crowds of people assembled to watch the train pass and at Whitwell a very energetic brass band made more noise than the engine whistle, in its anxiety to honour the enterprise of the company. Passenger stations have been erected at Mansfield Woodhouse, Shirebrook, Langwith, Creswell and Whitwell.

The Nottingham Journal had a scoop as they actually reported about the opening of the route in their late Tuesday 1 June 1875 edition, saying:

QUIET OPENING OF THE MIDLAND RAILWAY EXTENSION from MANSFIELD TO WORKSOP AND RETFORD FOR PASSENGER TRAFFIC.

At last, to-day, and after many and long delays which have put merchants and traders of wide district no little inconvenience, this line railway is opened for passenger traffic. The goods traffic, will be remembered, was opened some weeks ago, and since then one or two goods trains have run each way per day. The passenger service, provided by the Midland, shows three trains from Mansfield to Retford each day and similar number from Retford to Mansfield. There will, however, less than six trains each way along the line, for the Manchester, Sheffield and Lincolnshire Company start this morning a service of three passenger trains each way between Sheffield and Mansfield, which will run on the Mansfield line at the Shireoaks Junction.

The opening of this line is of each Importance that deem special notice, in which some description of the country through which the new line runs, will be of interest to our readers, and also give idea, so far can be, of the new industries likely be opened out along Its length. The old terminus at Mansfield gave place, about four years ago, a more handsome and commodious structure, which was built so soon as it was decided to push on the extension to Worksop. Just outside Mansfield station the new line begins with lofty and handsome viaduct, which presents a very impressive appearance. To make room for the building of this, some of the wont houses in Mansfield were removed, much to the improvement of that part the town. From the viaduct some splendid bird's eye views of Mansfield with the immediately near country are obtained. The viaduct divides the town in two parts, giving each part one of the churches, and the effect is good.

Leaving the station towards Mansfield Woodhouse we are struck with the high range of hills on the right crowned with half-a dozen old and new-fashioned windmills, the sight of which calls mind the old tale of The King and Miller of Mansfield. None of these mills are any way connected with that old tale, the original mill having long since been pulled down. Its exact site being a matter for doubt. We must not omit to mention standing out this same range hills a queer, weird tree, – a land mark, which we can see for a many miles, – which appears to be a sort of ghostly finger post pointing out the direction of the six windmills. It has also a strange resemblance, in dim light a gibbet and requires only a slight stretch of imagination to fancy there's a criminal dangling from its arm.

There can be little doubt that the principal industries of Mansfield will receive a stimulus from the opening of this important branch of railway, and the local trade of stockings, lace, iron, stone, sand, are considerably augmented. Distant from Mansfield a little over a mile, is Mansfield Woodhouse, a charming, thriving village, in the centre of a district well-watered and wooded. The station here – the first from Mansfield—is situated on rising ground, just outside the village, and from the station the clusters of houses round and about the old church show to great advantage. The new line will not greatly benefit Mansfield Woodhouse (because of its closeness to Mansfield) it will those nearer Worksop, but that the local traffic here already by no means insignificant ample accommodation for growing traffic has been made, and everything here, as well as along the whole line, has been carried out that happy manner which is a characteristic feature of the Midland Company. The chief trade of this village has been for a many years in excellent limestone. It is quarried in huge quantities, and this will no doubt be largely augmented now that railway facilities for transit are at hand. The old quarries, as seen from the railway, give the village a peculiar appearance. The tourist who may be inclined to do this new line will find not a little in the village and neighbourhood to interest him, – especially if is antiquarian turn of mind. First there is the old Early English church, which has some interesting features, and is well worth a visit.

At Pleasley, Derbyshire, some three miles northwest of Mansfield Woodhouse, the Stanton Iron Company are engaged in sinking a pit, and from this place a branch line is in progress, which will join the main line at Woodhouse. This will, in course of time, throw a quantity of traffic to the new line. This short branch will also pick up traffic from Butcherwood Colliery. The line will also open out to the tourists the lovely Pleasley Vale, which lies about three miles from Mansfield on the Chesterfield road, and if but little sought after, a more romantic and pretty valley cannot found in the neighbourhood; its extent is a mile and a half. The worst features of railways are the deep cuttings. A cutting means very limited view indeed. One of these begins soon after leaving Mansfield Woodhouse, and for long portion of the distance to the next station, Shirebrook, in Derbyshire, the travelling train runs between limestone walls, and thus some capital bits of hill and dale scenery are lost.

From Shirebrook station it is easy of access to Hardwick Hall and Park, noted resort touriste (sic). Langwith station is the next come to, and between this and Shireoaks is another long and deep cutting. The station details for traffic accommodation are of the best, and are very much excess of the requirements for a long time to come. The line here is at the top of a very high and massive embankment, right above the level of the top of the houses and mill. The view is very pleasant and interesting. Here the Sheepbridge Iron and Coal Company are just beginning to sink the shafts of a colliery; and brickyards, which are fair to extensive, and were opened only a couple of weeks back by Messrs. Birkett and Co., of Chesterfield.

Bolsover, with its famous Castle, is very easy visited from Langwith station. The Castle, and the ruins near it, will repay the trouble of a visit. It stands on a high ridge of hill, and can be seen from a long distance. It was originally built either at the latter end of the 11th century, or the beginning of the 12th by William Peveril, and it was restored in 1613 by Bess of Hardwick. The Castle is in good repair, but a range of buildings built by the Marquis of Newcastle in the reign of Charles are ruins.

The whole neighbourhood of Langwith abounds with coal, iron, and lime, and there is every prospect that ultimately an extensive trade will arise in this interesting part of East Derbyshire.

About three miles further on Creswell station is pleasantly situated, and the straggling village extends either side of the line. Creswell Derbyshire, will no doubt be the most important station on the whole line, for a branch line has been made, for coal traffic only, which runs through the village of Clown, thence Staveley, to join the Midland system there. Already about here there is a steadily Increasing traffic, and on this branch several collieries are being sunk – one by the Shireoaks Colliery Company, called the Clown colliery. The Staveley Iron and Coal Company have a colliery on this branch.

Creswell station will be found to be the key to several of the moot noted spots in this part of Derbyshire and Notts. Close by are Creswell Crags a deep rocky glen, with steep ragged sides, in which are caves supposed to have once formed one of the haunts of Robin Hood and his merry men. The whole spot is most romantic.

Passing from Creswell station, along the line, we come to the only tunnel on the whole line. This, known as "Creswell Tunnel," is work which took an Immense lot of time and labour in the construction of it, something like four years being spent in making a six hundred yards long tunnel, some hundreds of men were one time employed upon it. The difficulties which had to be against were the extreme hardness of the rock and the fact that it was full of fissures, which, in hundreds of cases, rendered the blasting shots powerless, by letting the force waste itself. The tunnel, its completed state, is fine piece of work. It was found unnecessary to line the tunnel with brickwork throughout, and so the inside has a curious appearance of smooth bricks and at Intervals, with black rugged rock.

Whitwell station is distant about a mile from Creswell, and is only a few hundred yards from the mouth of the tunnel. Here, also, is very siding room, for it is here that the greater bulk of the material for Welbeck will be delivered instead of going to Worksop station. A short line, a mile a half long, is being constructed by the Duke of Portland from Whitwell station towards Welbeck, and it is also the intention of the Duke to use this short branch when he is himself a passenger.

Within a short distance of Whitwell is the beautiful little Norman church at Steetley, which no visitor to the neighbourhood ought to miss. It was built between the year 1150 and of the Britons, and though without a tool, is a gem of architecture. Faring particulars see Mr. White's "Worksop and Sherwood Forest". Close are the Steetley stone quarries, and by the side of line nearer Worksop, and about one mile from the junction of this line with the Sheffield railway, is Steetley colliery, a new venture of the Shireoaks Colliery Company, which is rapidly progressing towards that period when coal will be arrived.

After crossing the Chesterfield canal, line divides into two portions, one of which runs so as form a junction for Worksop and Retford, the other forming the junction for Sheffield close by the Shireoaks Colliery.

We have traced the whole fourteen miles of railway known as the Mansfield and the attractions of Worksop and the district are thus placed within easy access of places south of Mansfield and Nottingham.

Worksop, it is well known, is the door to which everybody and his wife "do" the Dukery, and inspect the grand old oaks of Sherwood Forest, or visit the sylvan retreats of Roche Abbey. We would recommend those who visit this district for the sake of its varied beauties, to possess themselves of Mr. Robert White's valuable "History of Worksop, the Dukery, and Sherwood Forest," for not only is most entertaining, but is a capital guide book in an extended form to this whole district.

It only remains to add that business men of Nottingham and Mansfield will find the new railway most advantageous them when they have business to transact the north. We venture, to predict that this Midland extension will, in a few years' time, be a valuable paying concern, and look forward to the time when the line will be carried on through the northernmost part of North Nott's, and on to Doncaster, catching some important village which very much need railway influence to awaken them and bring them to the level of now a-days.

The following day's Wednesday 2 June 1875 issue of the Sheffield Daily Telegraph supported the words of a reporter who travelled from Sheffield to Mansfield:

OPENING OF THE RAILWAY FROM WORKSOP TO MANSFIELD. [From our own reporter.]

A train embellished with Union Jacks, starting to the music of a feu de joie (French: "fire of joy") of fog signals, is rather unusual at the Sheffield Station of the Manchester, Sheffield, and Lincolnshire Railway. Such a train made its first journey yesterday morning from the Victoria Station to Mansfield, but excited only the minimum curiosity. For many months back the people of Worksop and Mansfield have been looking and longing for some speedier means of communication, with the great industrial and commercial centres of the country. The completion of the project, undertaken by the Midland Company about half a dozen years ago, has been so long delayed that the residents in the quarter through which the new line runs, have fancied that the enterprising Company have been possessed in this instance by the idea which influenced Bess of Hardwick, never to make end of any of her work. There were reasons – good and sufficient themselves, if not to the people of Worksop and Mansfield – why a Company so noted for energy and so successful in catering for the public were in this instance liable to an accusation of dilatoriness. But on this point it is not necessary to enlarge. Let the dead past bury its dead. The line is now open. Mansfield cotton spinners may now rush backwards and forwards to Manchester or London at their own sweet will. Worksop maltsters may interest themselves in practically every Nottingham ale without going round by Sheffield or by Grantham, and coal masters along the route of the new line may rest secure that their trade shall not remain undeveloped because of the lack of facilities for carrying. The long delay in opening the line may, however, account for the fact that so little stir was caused by its opening. In other places along the line a good many people believed that the news of the opening was too good to be true; to tell the truth, Sheffield people did not seem to care much about the matter. They could get to Mansfield via Chesterfield and Pye Bridge, and took no special interest in the new line. This will account for the fact that the tickets taken for the train, which started yesterday morning at 8.55 from Sheffield to Mansfield, could have been counted on the fingers of one hand.

Your reporter meant to ride the engine over the new part of the line, but applied for a ticket by way of experiment. The clerk had to rummage for the packet and cut the string – the application was the first that had been made. "Where are the passengers!" was the question naturally put to the guard. "Oh, there are some, look at the other end," said the official, with a knowing grin. Yes, there were three passengers – a workman employed on the line, a fiddler bound for village feast, and a timekeeper taking his holiday. Certainly the number of passengers which patronised the new route from Sheffield yesterday morning was not encouraging, but no doubt that route will by-and-by be appreciated.

Passing over the old portion of the line without remark, allow your correspondent to sketch in few words about the new route to Mansfield, as seen from the locomotive speeding along from Shireoaks Station. Leaving behind the busy place, named after an oak which overshadowed or was supposed to overshadow the point where the three shires of Yorkshire, Nottinghamshire, and Derbyshire meet, we speed onwards to Whitwell, past pleasant woodland scenery. The woods of Welbeck Abbey stretch away to the right, and some the buildings stand out from among the thick foliage. Presently Whitwell Station is reached, and here is a line to Welbeck Abbey, something less than two miles long, being made at the expense of the Duke of Portland, and for that nobleman's special use. The undertaking is costly one, but money is no object to his Grace; and, besides being useful for goods traffic, which has hitherto gone by road from Worksop to the Abbey, the short line may enable his Grace to take a run by rail, without any inconvenience, on those rare occasions when he has a mind to travel. Not far from here are the famous Steetley Quarries, from which the white stone of which so many of the ornamental buildings in the Dukeries and elsewhere are constructed has been dug, and near them the Steetley Colliery, a new opening made by the Shireoaks Colliery Company. It is pleasant to note that the Company have erected under the shelter of a wood at some distance from the colliery – wood where the early spring the white and purple violets first peep forth, and the primroses "take the winds of March with beauty" – a number of substantial houses for their workmen. How different these abodes from the tenements whose beds are, tended day and night; in relays by so many of our colliers.

But now we speed on through Creswell tunnel – a cutting of some six or seven hundred yards through hard stone, which proved so full of crevices that many a charge of blasting powder was wasted during the time the work went on. On emerging from this tunnel, we pass, on the right, a branch of the colliery line to Staveley, and presently find ourselves at Creswell Station. A glimpse of the famous Crags may here be obtained, and this station will prove very convenient for the pedestrian tourist in the Dukeries. The stations follow each other very quickly, for the distance from Worksop to Mansfield is not much more than dozen miles, and speeding through fields gay with "the buttercup, the little children's flower," and past hawthorn hedges, whose scent comes to us in spite of the smoke and flames of the furnace before which stand, we reach Langwith, hamlet embowered among trees, a little distance from which is the station of the same name.

Then, through more heavy cuttings which hide the soft woodland scenery, on to Shirebrook where on the left a windmill is lazily flapping its great sails, while, stretching away in on the left; we can catch a glimpse of Budby, and the eminence which overlooks Edwinstowe. From Shirebrook Station, it may here be noted, Hardwick Hall is far more easy of access than from Chesterfield, and from here or from Langwith the antiquarian may easily reach Bolsover Castle – so intimately associated with the names of Peveril and Hardwick Bess.

The thriving village of Mansfield Woodhouse – which would soon be but a suburb of Mansfield, if the ancient Forest Town would but show something of that capacity of growing which characterises Sheffield. But both Mansfield and its Woodhouse are "slow". A nonplussed habitant rushes up the train about to leave, attired in garments which would delight Erskine Nicol or any painter with an eye at once to colour and humour! Jog, jog goes the bundle, wrapped red handkerchief, which he carries under his arm and pants as he reaches the station. After all this exertion, close the passenger door, the turmoil of catching the train, the man has forgotten where he wanted to go. The train had been slightly delayed to give, on this opening day moment of grace which we all occasionally require and we move sorrowfully off, leaving our country cousin to collect his scattered wits, the genial Inspector entreats your reporter to remember that instead of eight passengers we might have had nine – if the would-be ninth had been able to collect his ideas!

Is needful to say anything about the arrival in Mansfield – the town of the "King and the Millar?" The days of romance are past; lf the plain truth must be told our Hag-adorned train made no sensation. No fog signals exploded at Mansfield. Not a salutary cheer was raised.

A train of six coaches left Mansfield for Worksop at ten minutes to seven yesterday morning, and the other five trains during the day were fairly full our Worksop correspondent writes: The passenger service of trains commenced on the new hue on the one hand by the Midland Company, who run from Mansfield to Worksop and on the other by the Manchester, Sheffield, Company from Mansfield, Shireoaks, and into Sheffield. At present the service consists three trains each way daily by each the Companies, thereby giving the intermediate stations on the new line the advantage of six trains each. The Midland trains are first and third class all trains, and the Manchester, Sheffield, and Lincolnshire are first, second, and third. The goods traffic has been opened some weeks from Shireoaks, as also the branch line from to Staveley through Clowne. The opening of this long-talked of line created some little stir at Worksop Station, where a number of tradespeople and others collected to welcome the first train from Mansfield.

5th Duke of Portland

Notice the mention of the Duke of Portland's railway in the two excerpts. The 5th Duke had, as we have seen, objected to the railway through his estate; however, he was a very astute man and realised that he could make use of the railway under his terms. The Duke was continuously tinkering with the nearby Welbeck Estate, building underground tunnels large enough to drive a horse and carriage along, an underground ballroom and a multitude of other projects. He took a great interest in the construction of the new line and planned to build his own branch line to serve Welbeck. Failing that, he wished for his own private station at Whitwell with covered platforms and a bridge, and in January 1871 he negotiated with the MR for private access to Whitwell Station. However, although the MR built Whitwell station to suit him, which set him back £400, William John Cavendish Bentinck-Scott, the 5th Duke of Portland died on 6 December 1879 and the branch to Welbeck was never built.

More press reports

The Derbyshire Courier of Saturday 5 June 1875 described Mansfield Woodhouse as:

A model of a station, the building is entirely of wood and is relieved with some very pretty ornamentation. A kind of entrance hall, one side of which is nearly all glass, leads to the ticket office, an apartment which unlike many of its kind has not been erected with special facilities to let the wind in. The ladies waiting room is a little gem, tastefully furnished and carpeted and the whole aspect of the place is a pleasant contrast to the dreary, disheartening den built in the earlier days of railway enterprise. The company seems to have overlooked that gentlemen, as well as lady passengers, would use the train and there is a strange absence of gentlemen's waiting rooms along the line, a defect that ought to be remedied.

Published in 1888 by Frederick S. Williams, The Midland Railway, its rise and progress, had this to say about the route:

The district, too, through which the line would pass, deserved better accommodation. At Steetley, between Whitwell and Worksop, are the quarries of valuable stone from which it is believed that Southwell Minster was erected, and which the chairman of the committee remarked was probably "the most famous of all building stones." The quarries at Mansfield are of high quality, but have only a limited though lucrative trade.

The proposed railway, with the branch intended to be made to Newark, would open what one witness described as "most magnificent quarries of magnesium stone." The line would also pass in the neighbourhood of the finest timber district in England. The Duke of Newcastle's agent stated that the mere thinning's of 4,000 acres of woodland fetched from £6,000 to £10,000 a year; and that they were used chiefly for pit and manufacturing purposes. The Shireoaks Colliery, too, which the line would approach, contained several beds of valuable coal; and the engineer and manager expressed a conviction that the entire district which the line would traverse was "a mineral field" or, as another said, "Full of coal." Mr. Heming, the agent for the Duke of Newcastle, also stated his belief that the "entire length" of the line was "full of minerals."

These opinions have since been confirmed: and eventually, as the time drew on for the opening of the line, thousands of acres of coal-fields were leased to coal-owners, and it is believed that the Mansfield and Worksop line will rival, if not out vie, the mineral productiveness of the Erewash.

Mansfield station

Mansfield was originally the terminus of the earliest railway in the area; the 1819 built horse-drawn Mansfield and Pinxton Tramway, this being beyond the scope of this book other than to give a brief history of its purchase by the MR.

The MR had acquired the rights to the Erewash Valley Railway and soon began to realise that a direct Nottingham to Mansfield railway using part of the Mansfield and Pinxton Tramway would be advantageous, but were concerned about two other railways being promoted: the Boston, Newark & Sheffield Railway and the Nottingham, Mansfield & Midlands Junction Railway. The MR was right to be concerned as these two companies jointly purchased the Mansfield & Pinxton Company in 1846.

The MR continued with their decision to build a line from Nottingham to Mansfield, and as Parliament favoured their plans, an Act for the Nottingham and Mansfield railway (initially connecting with the Mansfield & Pinxton north of Kirkby in Ashfield) was passed on 16 July 1846.

On 9 July 1847 the MR got its Mansfield and Erewash Valley Extension Act which sanctioned the acquisition of the tramway, and its incorporation into a line between Codnor Park and Mansfield. Although the line from Long Eaton Junction to Codnor Park opened on 6 September 1847, ownership of the tramway still remained a problem. The Railway Commissioners resolved the matter on 15 February 1848 when they issued a certificate, by the authority of which the Mansfield & Pinxton Railway was amalgamated with the MR and immediately dissolved. The MR then used the final section of the extended Leen Valley line to a new brick-built station at Mansfield, which was opened on 10 October 1849 adjacent to the original Mansfield & Pinxton one, both later being incorporated into the goods yard.

The construction of the line forward to Worksop required a third station to be built, this one slightly to the north-west of the other two, and it was built of local stone in the Italianate Style. It had two platforms under an all-over glass roof and was more than adequate for the time.

Passenger service

Initially the services for passengers consisted of three MR trains from Mansfield to Worksop and Retford and three MS&LR trains from Mansfield to Sheffield. Trains departed Mansfield for Worksop at 7.10am, 11.45am and 6.10pm, and for Sheffield at 10.30am, 4.10pm and at 8.10pm. They left Sheffield at 8.55am, 1.55pm and 6.35pm, and Worksop at 9.10am, 1.20pm and 7.50pm. The Worksop Guardian newspaper reported that:

The first MS&LR train left Sheffield at 8.55am and arrived at Mansfield at 10.10am decorated with flags, flowers and evergreens much to the surprise of the local inhabitants as no advance announcement had been made. All stations along the line are amply well laid sidings with space for enlargement and the line passes through an entirely agricultural area.

New MR Retford branch proposed

November 1875 saw the MR submit proposals to build a 24 chain branch to a new station in East Retford. This branch was to diverge from the MS&LR line just east of the London Road Bridge, terminating in Parks Paddock. It would be accessed by utilising their running powers between Worksop and Retford; however, they didn't reckon on the GNR who objected to the company using their running powers in that way to their Retford Station. Thus for a period the MR Mansfield to Retford services changed engines at Worksop and an allowance of five minutes was put into the timetable to reflect this.

This new station would have been more central for Retford but would have meant MR passengers intending to use the GNR main line would either have to change trains in Worksop, or change stations in Retford. Perhaps fortunately the portion of the bill which included the East Retford Branch didn't survive to become part of the 1876 Act.

Mansfield expands

As passenger traffic increased at Mansfield the station became inadequate, and as such it was decided to improve capacity by adding a bay platform outside the train shed, next to Platform 2. This was brought into use on 1 September 1892; the Board of Trade report by Major Marinden was dated 4 October and read as follows:

Mansfield Station required two signal boxes to work the new platform and they were a South Signal Box with 20 levers and 8 spare, the North Signal Box with 16 levers and 4 spare. The station is to be worked as a terminal using both directions. At North Box levers 4 & 5 should be interlocked and at South Box levers 15–22 should be interlocked, fitted with locking bar, facing point bolt and gauge tie. Runaway points to be fitted on the Up line from Worksop, north of the station.

And so Mansfield Station gained its final layout.

In 1897 the Lancashire Derbyshire & East Coast Railway (LD&ECR) opened their line from Chesterfield to Lincoln, along with a branch to Beighton to connect with Sheffield (see the Author's books about this railway for further details), their main line crossing the MR line at Shirebrook. To connect the MR at Shirebrook Station with the LD&ECR at Warsop Junction, the Warsop Curve was constructed. This opened for passenger traffic on 9 January 1899 and goods on 16 January 1899. In return for running powers over the MR, the LD&ECR granted the MR running powers to Edwinstowe and it was under these powers that a passenger service commenced on 20 March 1899. Services began at 7.15am from Mansfield, with subsequent departures at 9.40am, 1.00pm and 6.30pm. Departures from Edwinstowe were at 8.55am, 10.55am, 3.10pm and 7.20pm. Journey time was 25 minutes outward and 27 minutes return, trains called at Mansfield Woodhouse and Shirebrook, followed by Warsop.

On 1 July 1903 the MR introduced a service from Mansfield to Sheffield via the LD&EC line to Beighton Junction and the Sheffield District Railway which ran from Treeton Junction to Brightside Junction, this involving the MR providing the locomotive and the LD&ECR the coaching stock. The train initially used the Warsop Curve and travelled to either Warsop or Edwinstowe, where the service reversed. However, in November 1903 the MR submitted plans for new spurs connecting Shirebrook and Langwith Junction (LD&ECR), which involved Up and Down single lines to join with a flying junction at Langwith Junction. The contracts were awarded by the Works and Ways Committee in March 1904 to Charles Baker of Sheffield for an estimated £6,293 15s 0d. The new lines were approved in the Midland Railway Additional Powers Act:

Langwith Junctions Railway No. 1 37 chains and Railway No. 2 34 chains, junction with LD&ECR in Parish of Pleasley and terminating in Parish and Urban District of Warsop.

The Down line left the MR line opposite Shirebrook Junction signal box and immediately north of the curve to Warsop Junction. It then climbed at 1 in 65 before curving round to join the LD&ECR at Langwith Junction East. The Up line left the LD&ECR east of the bridge over the MR and descended at 1 in 63 to join the MR line at Shirebrook Junction. These connections became known as "The New Foundout" and opened to passenger services on 1 October 1904, thus allowing direct running from Mansfield to Sheffield and the practice of having to run round at Warsop or Edwinstowe ceased. The MR continued to provide the engine, which was usually a Sheffield-based MR 2P Class 4-4-0, and the LD&ECR the stock.

The MR offered a service of four trains per day utilising the connections, the July 1906 timetable showing that there were departures from Mansfield at 10.27am, 2.00pm Saturdays Only (SO), 4.20pm and 7.00pm, with a journey time of 1 hour 20 mins to Sheffield. In addition a direct service to Ollerton continued to run via the Warsop Curve, with departures at 7.15am, 9.30am, 6.30pm and a SO 10.30pm working.

An agreement stated that the LD&ECR had running powers into Sheffield Midland Station, as long as the MR continued to operate the service. According to George Dow in Volume three of his trilogy:

At a GCR Board meeting on 10 November 1905, it was mentioned that negotiations were taking place with the object of transferring the LD&ECR to the Great Northern Railway (GNR), and this

Above: LMS 2P 4-4-0 No. 351 pauses in the Beighton branch platforms of Shirebrook North, with a Sheffield to Mansfield service. The rolling stock consists of five ex-Great Northern Railway six-wheel coaches and the loco carries the shed plate No. 25, the pre 1935 designation for Sheffield (Grimethorpe), thus giving a date range between 1923 and 1935 in this otherwise undated shot. ***(Vic Forster)***

sent shock waves around the Board Room. The General Manager, Sir Sam Fay, and Solicitor and Accountant Dixon Davies, were instructed to approach the LD&EC in the interests of the Great Central as a matter of urgency, and this they did, throwing the maximum terms to which the company would go at the LD&EC directors. Fortunately the GNR had rebuffed the first approaches of the LD&ECR and as such the GCR soon had the LD&ECR in its pockets. Needless to say the MR and GNR were incensed at the prospect of the take-over, the MR having good reasons to be upset, for it had invariably gone out of its way to be helpful to the LD&EC, while the GNR was smarting at the way the GCR leapt in and took the company from under their noses.

The GCR thus had the MR, GNR, Great Eastern, North Eastern, London & North Western and the Sheffield District (SDR), organised against the Parliamentary proposals for takeover. However agreements with the GNR & GER and a protective clause for the SDR somewhat appeased the situation, the GNR being happy with the offer of running powers over those parts of the LD&EC where it did not at present enjoy them. The GCR also agreed not to make use of LD&EC powers to run into the MR Sheffield station, as long as the Midland continued to operate the passenger service between Sheffield and Mansfield, still providing the motive power, but utilising GCR rolling stock. The MR, and after grouping, the LMS, thus took great care to ensure that the GCR (and the later LNER) were never given an opportunity to resurrect the powers, which would undoubtedly have happened if it had ceased to provide the service!

The GCR would thus take over the LD&ECR Company on 1 January 1907.

After opening of the line to Mansfield the MS&LR ran a service from Sheffield to Mansfield via Shireoaks and Woodend Junction, the 1877 Bradshaw's showing three trains per day, departing Sheffield Victoria at 8.55am, 1.55pm and 6.50pm, passing Shireoaks at 9.30am, 2.26pm and 7.25pm, arriving Whitwell ten minutes later, and Mansfield at 10.10am, 3.00pm and 8.05pm. In the reverse direction they left Mansfield at 10.35am, 3.30pm and 8.15pm, passing Shireoaks at 11.08am, 4.03pm and 8.53pm, with an arrival at Sheffield of 11.45am, 4.35pm and 9.30pm.

However, by the 1903 timetables the service had been diverted to run via Worksop and reverse there, passengers from Mansfield being advised to change trains for Shireoaks. After this there were no passenger trains scheduled to pass over the Shireoaks West Junction to Woodend Junction curve. The service would continue until 1 January 1906 when the MS&LR (by now renamed the Great Central Railway (GCR)) trains from Sheffield to Mansfield would cease to operate, with the MR taking then taking over the paths between Woodend Junction and Mansfield and working the three former GCR train times.

Above: Johnson 3F 0-6-0 43431 stands at Shirebrook station on 22 April 1950 with a special Whitwell to Nottingham working. Allocated to 16D Mansfield from 1 January 1948, the loco moved to 41B Sheffield Grimesthorpe during the four-week period ending 8 March 1958. The three-way gantry at the end of the platforms is visible just over the last coaches of the train. ***(R.J. Buckley/Author's collection)***

Left: A Station Hotel would be built close to the station in many towns and villages served by rail. Creswell's was on the corner of Skinner Street and Elmton Road. Although since closed as a pub, the building has been converted into self-contained flats. ***(Author's collection)***

Worksop

Top: Before we begin our journey towards Mansfield, it would be good to remind ourselves of the Midland Railway (MR) presence in Worksop. Here 2228 Class 0-4-4T No. 691 has arrived at Worksop station with a stopping train from Nottingham, sometime in 1906. This loco was renumbered 1402 in November 1907 and remained in service until September 1946, then based at 15D Bedford. ***(Courtesy of the Midland Railway Study Centre, Bernard Matthews Collection)***

Above: An unidentified Johnson 0-4-4T crosses Albion Close Bridge on the approach to Worksop, with an afternoon Retford to Mansfield train c1900. This glass plate negative was taken from the garden of a house on Sherwood Road. Notice the neat lines of cabbages, the train being viewed through the gooseberry bushes. The train is possibly the 1.00pm departure from Retford, due Worksop at 1.12pm and Mansfield 1.47pm. ***(Richard Allsopp)***

MANSFIELD, WORKSOP, and RETFORD.—Midland.

	mrn	mrn	aft
Mansfield d	7 10	1145	5 20
Mansfield W	7 15	1150	5 25
Shirebrook	7 23	1158	5 33
Langwith..	7 28	12 3	5 38
Cresswell ..	7 35	1210	5 45
Whitwell ..	7 40	1215	5 50
Worksop.. a	7 50	1225	6 0
242 d	7 55	1230	6 5
Retfrd 241	8 10	1245	6 20

Fm Hull, 242	mrn	aft	aft
Retford dp	8 50	1 0	5 35
Worksop.. a	9 5	1 15	5 52
d	9 8	1 20	6 15
Whitwell ..	9 18	1 30	6 25
Cresswell ..	9 23	1 35	6 30
Langwith..	9 30	1 42	6 37
Shirebrook	9 35	1 47	6 42
Mansfield W	9 42	1 54	6 46
Mansfield a	9 48	[illegible]	[illegible]

Left: The Bradshaw's 1877 Timetable for Great Britain & Ireland containing the times for the MR trains between Mansfield and Worksop, showing three services per day that ran as far as Retford. Notice an allowance of five minutes on the Up and three minutes on the Down at Worksop for the change of locomotives from MR to MS&LR (and vice versa), as the GNR initially refused to allow the MR locos into their station. ***(Author's collection)***

MANSFIELD AND RETFORD—Weekdays.

M. S. & L. Goods Trains stop at Mansfield Woodhouse Junction when required during the hours the Signal Box is open

Miles.	STATIONS.	1 Passenger.	2	3 M.S.&L. Goods.	4 M.S.&L. Coal.	5 Goods from Nottingham. T	6 M.S.&L. Passenger	7 M.S.&L. Coal.	8	10 Goods, &c., from Nottingham.	11 Passenger
		a.m.		a.m.	a.m.	a.m.	a.m.	a.m.		a.m.	a.m.
..	MANSFIELD ... dep	7 5	..	8 15	..	8 20	10 30	..	..	10 40	11 55
1½	Mansfield Woodhouse	7 10	..	8 19	..	..	10 34	..	..	10 50	11 59
4½	Shirebrook	7 17	..	8 25	..	8 35	10 42	..	..	11 5	12 6
6	Langwith	7 22	..	8 30	..	..	10 46	..	..	11 15	12 11
..	Langwith Col. Sidings	..	..	..	..	8 48	..	..	..	11 25	..
8¾	Elmton & Creswell	7 28	..	8 37	..	9 10	10 50	..	..	11 35	12 17
10¼	Whitwell	7 33	..	8 43	..	9 20	10 54	..	..	..	12 22
12	Steetley Coll. Sidings	..	..	..	8 45	9 30	..	11 50	..	Z	..
..	Shireoaks Colliery	..	..	..	..	See p. 180, Tr. 11	..	..	..	..	..
..	Shireoaks Junction	..	..	..	8 50		11 0	..	..	..	..
15	Workshop arr.	7 42	..	9 20	To Workshop, via Shireoaks.	9 45	..	12 0	..	See page 181 Train 26.	12 32
	dep.	7 43	..	Attaches where required.		9 55	..	..	..		12 33
19	Checker House	B	..			..	..	..	..		E
22¾	RETFORD arr.	7 57	..			10 20	..	..	..		12 47

Miles.	STATIONS.	12 Goods, &c. from Nottingham N	14 Pick-up Goods from Nottingham. O	15 Min. Empt'es from Kirkby. Junction.	16 M.S.&L. Mineral.	17 M.S.&L. Passenger	18	19 Passenger	20 M.S.&L. Goods.	21 Mineral Empties.	22 M.S.&L. Passenger
		p.m.	p.m.	p.m.	p.m.	p.m.		p.m.	p.m.	p.m.	p.m.
..	MANSFIELD ... dep	12 56	12 35	2 45	..	3 30	..	5 35	7 15	7 50	8 45
1½	Mansfield Woodhouse	..	..	Q	..	3 34	..	5 40	7 19	..	8 49
4½	Shirebrook	S	1 10		..	3 42	..	5 47	7 25	..	8 57
6	Langwith	..	1 35	..	..	3 46	..	5 52	7 30	..	9 1
..	Langwith Col. Sidings	1 35	1P55	3 15	..	..	..	..	..	8 10	..
8¾	Elmton & Creswell	1 50	2 20	3 20	..	3 50	..	5 58	7 35	..	9 5
10¼	Whitwell	2 0	..	..	..	3 54	..	6 3	7 40	..	9 9
12	Steetley Coll. Sidings	2 15	3 0	See page 182, Train 51.	4 10	..	..	..	..	..	..
..	Shireoaks Colliery	2 30	3 30		..	..	..	..	..	..	..
..	Shireoaks Junction	..	..		4 20	4 0	..	..	..	..	..
15	Workshop arr.	2 40	3 40		..	..	..	6 12	7 55	On Saturd'ys only runs when req.	9 18
	dep.	See page 181, Train 33.	3 50		..	..	..	6 13	Attaches where required.		..
19	Checker House		..		..	..	..	B			..
22¾	RETFORD arr.		4 15		..	..	..	6 27			..

Miles.	STATIONS.	25 M.S.&L. Goods.	26 M.S.&L. Engine and Break.	27 Passenger	28	29 M.S.&L. Passenger	30	32 M.S.&L. Empties	33 Passenger	35 Goods, &c., to Nottingham
		a.m.	a.m.	a.m.		a.m.		a.m.	p.m.	p.m.
..	RETFORD dep.	Detach where requir'd	..	8 38	..	..	..	10 45	1 0	Starts fm Shireoaks at 12.5 p.m. on S'dys wh req. & stops at Steetly.
3¾	Checker House		..	B	..	..	..	..	G	
7¼	Workshop arr.		..	8 51	..	..	..	..	1 12	
	dep.	7 0	..	8 52	..	..	..	..	1 13	
..	Shireoaks Junction	..	..	..	..	9 15	..	..	..	
..	Shireoaks Coll. arr.	..	..	..	..	..	..	..	..	
	dep	..	7 40	..	..	..	..	..	..	
10¾	Steetley Coll. Sidings	..	7 50	..	..	..	..	11 0	..	12 20
12½	Whitwell	7 13	..	9 2	..	9 22	..	..	1 23	12 40
14	Elmton & Creswell	7 17	..	9 7	..	9 26	..	..	1 28	To Kirkby Junction only if req'd. See p. 185 Train 41.
..	Langwith Col. Sidings	..	..	..	..	..	..	..	..	
16¾	Langwith	7 24	..	9 13	..	9 30	..	..	1 34	
18¼	Shirebrook	7 28	..	9 18	..	9 34	..	..	1 39	
21¼	Mansfield Wood- arr.	7 36	..	9 24	..	9 43	..	..	1 45	
	house dep.	..	..	9 26	..	9 44	..	..	1 47	
22¾	MANSFIELD arr.	7 40	..	9 30	..	9 50	..	..	1 51	1 5

Miles.	STATIONS.	36 Goods, &c., to Nottingham.	37 M.S.&L. Passenger	38 M.S.&L. Empties.	39 Mineral to Nottingham.	40 Goods, &c., to Nottingham.	41 M.S.&L. Goods.	42 Passenger	43 Goods, &c., to Nottingham.	44 Goods and Passenger to Nottingham	46 M.S.&L. Passenger	47 Mineral to Dunston and Barlow.
		a.m.	p.m.	p.m.	p.m.		p.m.	p.m.	p.m.	p.m.	p.m.	
..	RETFORD dep.	10 50	..	..	Q	S	Detaches Traffic where req.	7 0	V 6 15	6 15	..	On Sat. runs wh req'd. only betw'n Langw'th & Mansf'd See page 172, Train 133.
3¾	Checker House	U	..	..	See page 186 Train 72.	See p'ge 187, Tr. 82.		B	S	X	..	
7¼	Workshop arr.	11 15	..	..				7 13	6 35	6 35	..	
	dep.	11 25	2 37	..		4 0	5 35	7 14	6 50	8 10	7 52	
..	Shireoaks Junction	11 30	..	3 10		..	..	..	See p. 187, Tr. 90	Sats. only. See p. 187, Train 97.	..	
..	Shireoaks Coll. arr.	..	..	..		..	..	..			..	
	dep	..	..	..		4 20	..	..	..		..	
10¾	Steetley Coll. Sidings	11 50	..	3 20		4 35	..	..	..		..	
12½	Whitwell	12 15	2 47	..	..	4 50	5 48	7 24	7 5	8 20	8 2	
14	Elmton & Creswell	12 40	2 51	..	3 40	5 10	5 52	7 29	7 45	8 26	8 6	
..	Langwith Col. Sidings	1 5	..	..	4 20	5 30	..	..	..	..	..	8 40
16¾	Langwith	1 40	2 55	..	..	..	5 59	7 35	7 53	8 35	8 10	..
18¼	Shirebrook	2 0	2 59	..	..	..	6 3	7 40	7 57	8 41	8 14	..
21¼	Mansfield Wood- arr.	2 10	3 8	..	..	..	6 11	7 46	8 5	8 48	8 21	..
	house dep.	2 25	3 9	..	..	..	..	7 48	..	8 50	8 24	..
22¾	MANSFIELD arr.	2 30	3 15	..	4*40	5W50	6 15	7 52	8 10	8 55	8 30	9W 0

Trains having on Coal for Mansfield Loco. must detach it at the Loco. Sidings.

B Stops at Checker House when required to take up or set down Passengers. **E** Stops at Checker House when required to set down Passengers from Whitwell and Stations East thereof. **G** Stops at Checker House when required to take up Passengers for Whitwell and Stations beyond. **N** Makes an extra trip between Elmton and Creswell and Worksop when req'd. **O** Shunts as req'd. for through Tr'ns. Stops at Mansfi'd Woodhouse and Whitwell for tariff purposes, and to attach important traffic when req'd. Arrive. Shireoaks 3 10 p.m. Stops at Whisker Hill Sidings for No. taking. See page 181, Train 34. **T** Detaches only at Mansfield Woodhouse, Whitwell, and Worksop. Attaches at Pleasley Junction when required. Shunts Burkitt's Sidings, Langwith, when required. Stops at Whisker Hill Sidings for No. taking. On Thursdays runs 10 minutes later Worksop to Retford. **U** Stops at Rushey Siding whe . required. Detaches traffic for Staveley at Elmton & Creswell and detaches at Pleasley Junction when required. Shunts at Langwith for 33 Train. Stops at Norwood Sidings. See page 186, Train 62. **V** Makes up load when required at Langwith Col. Stops at Shirebrook if req. Takes Mansfield Woodhouse traffic through to Mansfield. London Goods on this Train are transferred to No. 42 Train at Worksop. **X** Conveys Passengers between Worksop and Mansfield and intermediate Stations. **Z** On Saturdays runs to Shireoaks if required.

Left: Midland Railway Working Timetable Section F (Erewash Valley & Branches) dated May 1886, showing goods and passenger traffic between Mansfield and Retford. ***(Dave Phillips collection)***

Below: Tickets from Mansfield to Worksop: By MR train dated 15 July 1919; MR & MS&LR train dated 6 May 1894; and, just to prove that the MR services did go to Retford, a Mansfield to Retford ticket dated 28 May 1914. Note that it states "By Midland train to Worksop". ***(All courtesy Midland Railway Study Centre)***

Left: The Nottingham to Worksop service became a victim of the Beeching Axe and ceased on 12 October 1964. The route then became freight-only between Shireoaks Junctions and Radford Junction, leaving Mansfield with the dubious reputation of being the largest town in the country without a station. That all changed with the advent of the Robin Hood Line project, and 150012 stands at Worksop with the 11.13 arrival from Nottingham during the Robin Hood Line Phase 3 opening Fun Day on 24 May 1998.

Left: Nottingham-based Driver Martin Bromley is seen being met by Town Crier Harry Bodkin and Bassetlaw District Council Chairman Janet Pimperton, with her grandson Richard Mellor. The Robin Hood Line turned into a real success story, with passenger numbers climbing up until the Coronavirus Pandemic in 2020.

Left: In 2003 Central Trains, the then operator of the franchise, rebranded 170513 as a mobile advert for the Robin Hood Line. Here it is at Worksop on 16 May waiting to form 2D14 13.40 Worksop to Nottingham, its first run in the new Robin Hood livery.

Below: Detail of the centre of 170513. *(All Author)*

Above: We begin our journey to Mansfield, passing Worksop West and crossing Gateford Road. Here 2-6-2T 40094 heads the five-coach 5.30pm Worksop to Nottingham train on 5 May 1961.

Right: 41H Staveley allocated Robinson Class O1 2-8-0 63646 blows off steam as it waits to access Worksop Yards at Shireoaks East Junction, with a train of Esso tank wagons and box vans on 6 June 1963. The line towards Woodend curves off left here.

Below: Class O4 2-8-0 63824 heads along the main line towards Shireoaks West Junction at Shireoaks East Junction on 5 May 1961. ***(All Alan Smalley)***

Above: While the tank train seen on the previous page waits on the main line, Gresley Class O2 2-8-0 63926 comes tender first along the east curve from Woodend Junction with a loaded coal train at 12.55 on 6 June 1963. This loco was allocated to 36E Retford Thrumpton (GC) from the four-week period ending 23 February 1952; just three months after the photo was taken, it was withdrawn on 22 September 1963. It was sent for scrapping at Rigleys (Bulwell Forest) during February 1964.

Below: 16B Kirkby-in-Ashfield-allocated Stanier 3P 2-6-2T 40089 rounds the curve towards Woodend Junction at Shireoaks East Junction with the 3.31pm Worksop to Nottingham on 7 September 1961. Introduced to service on 17 April 1935, the loco worked around the Manchester area until it was transferred to 16B around 29 April 1961. It succumbed to withdrawal in the week ending 4 August 1962 and was sent for scrapping at Cashmore's (Great Bridge) in early 1963. ***(Both Alan Smalley)***

Woodend

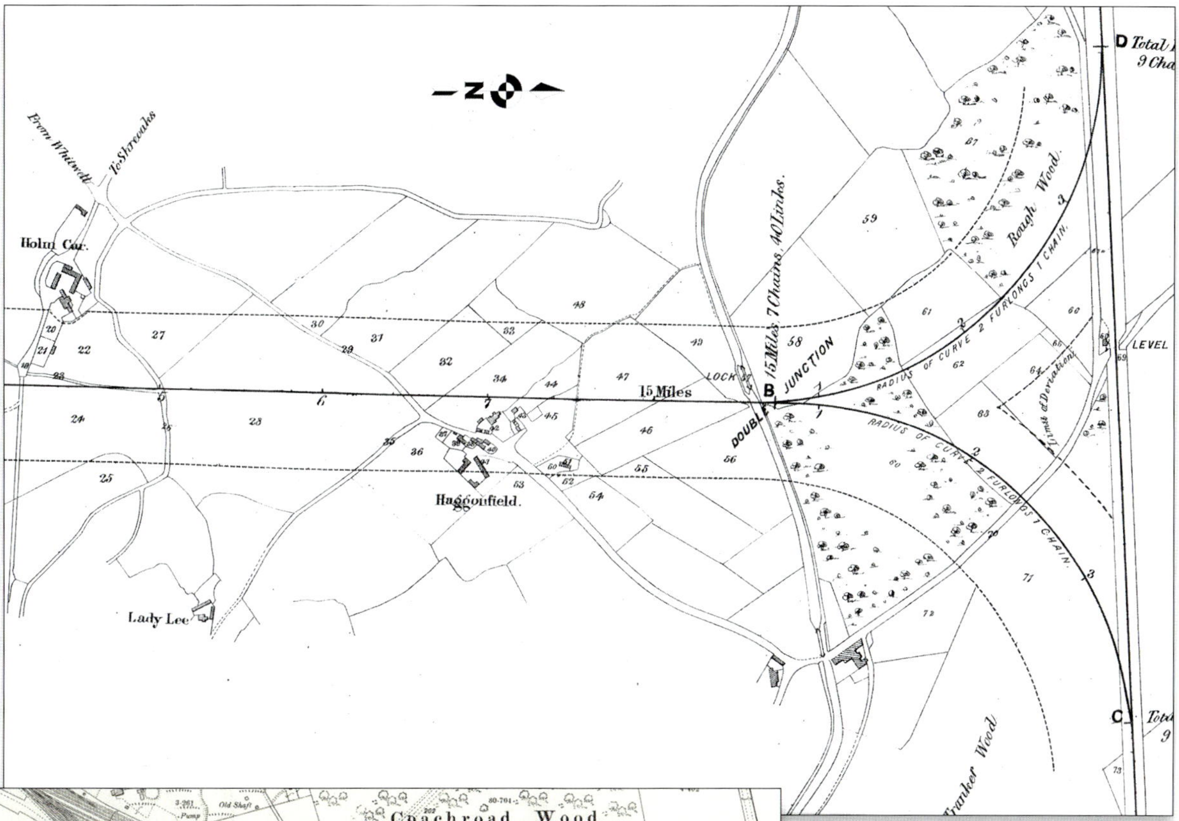

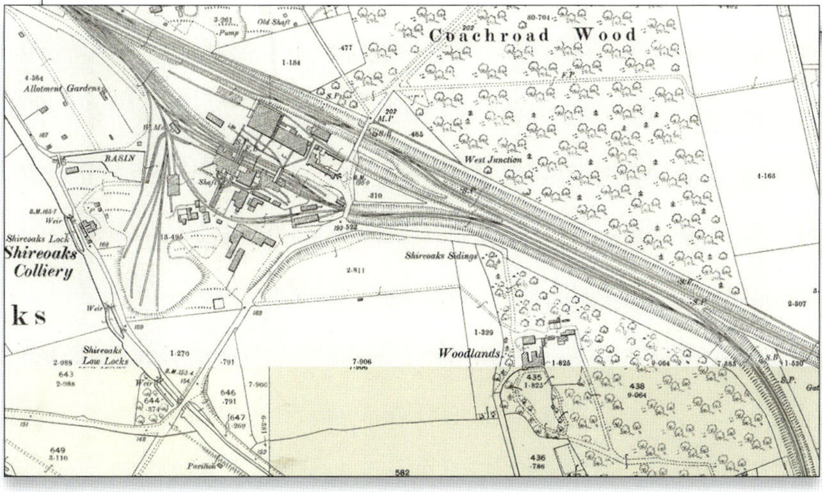

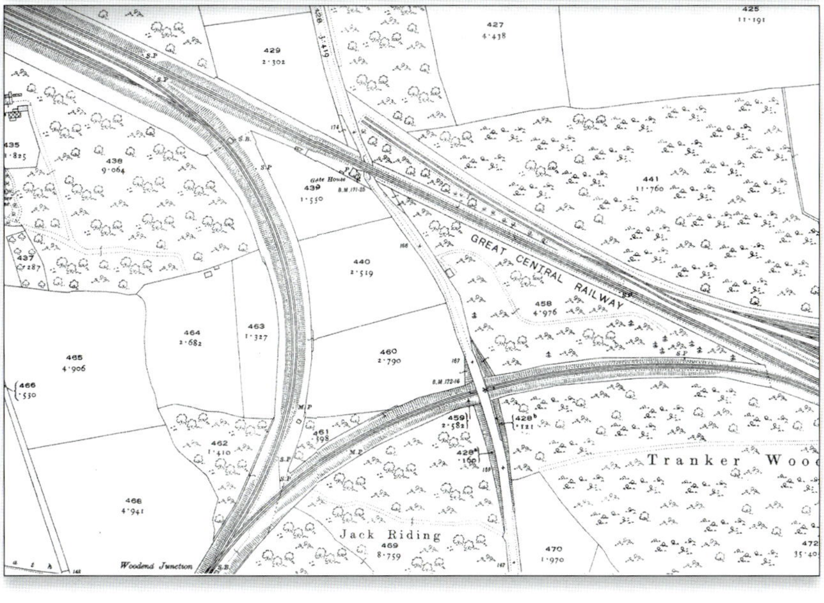

Above: Original surveyor's plans for the triangular connections from Woodend Junction, showing the extent of the railway boundary line. The line from Mansfield would come in from the south (left) and split at Woodend Junction a distance of 15 Miles, 7 Chains, 40 Links. The east curve would turn to connect with the MS&LR line towards Worksop (towards the bottom) and the west curve to Shireoaks Colliery, later Shireoaks West Junction (to the top). The construction of the railway would wipe away the original Haggonfield Farm, which was rebuilt slightly further west of the line. ***(Author's collection)***

Above left: 1920 map of Shireoaks Colliery area with the curve towards Woodend Junction heading off bottom right.

Left: The connections at Woodend and Shireoaks, Shireoaks Colliery Sidings was to the top left, a signal box being provided to control access into the sidings. To the right of the map, at Shireoaks East Junction, is the commencement of Worksop Up Yard. ***(Both Courtesy National Library of Scotland)***

Above: Ex-Midland Railway 1798 Class 0-6-0 No. 3320 rounds the west curve down the 1-in-72 gradient from Shireoaks West Junction to Woodend Junction whilst working Trip 24. Originally 2043 it received the number 3320 after 1907. The train originated from Dinnington Colliery Junction on the South Yorkshire Joint Railway, and conveyed private owner wagons of coal from Hickleton and Firbeck Collieries (amongst others) to Kirkby Yard. The South Yorkshire Joint Railway will be covered in Volume 3. ***(P. Ransome Wallis/Author's collection)***

Left: Shireoaks Colliery in 1905. Notice the brand new wagons built by the Shireoaks Coal Company (SCC). ***(Phil Whitehead collection)***

Below: The Midland Railway opened the first Shireoaks Colliery Sidings signal box to control the colliery sidings before 1 November 1875, but this was superseded by this Type 3 style 'box on 9 February 1904. It closed on 25 September 1966. ***(Mike King)***

Above: Stanier 8F 2-8-0 No. 48272 has just passed Shireoaks West Junction and is taking the curve towards Woodend Junction on 21 January 1964. The train had originated at Dinnington Colliery and was heading to Kirkby Yards. On the left is the former MR connection to Shireoaks Colliery which, at that time, was disused. It was later reinstated to allow locos to run round MGR trains when the colliery changed to that method of operation in the 1980s. The train is passing Shireoaks Colliery Siding's Up Home signal, beneath which is Woodend Junction's No. 13 Distant signal. In 1920 the SCC built the village of Rhodesia near the small established settlement of Haggonfield, to provide housing for coal miners. It was named after long-time Chairman Mr G Preston Rhodes, the chairman of Shireoaks Colliery. At the 1939 AGM of the SCC, Rhodes announced plans for the construction of pit-head baths at Shireoaks. Work was still progressing during 1943, but it is assumed that they were completed before the end of the war, and they can be seen on the embankment top behind the train.

Below: Having just passed Woodend Junction 'box, Class 8F No. 48701 takes the west curve as it heads to Shireoaks West Junction and the South Yorkshire Joint Line at 3.53pm on 26 April 1962. This is bound either for Dinnington or Harworth Collieries, and would be a driven by a Kirkby-in-Ashfield crew. ***(Both Alan Smalley)***

Above: A typically filthy, and thus unidentifiable, WD 2-8-0 crosses the Chesterfield Canal and Shireoaks Road en route to Worksop Yard in the very early 1960s. At this time the vast majority of the canal was in a derelict condition with rotten lock gates, and in parts totally un-navigable. Just beyond the bridge is Lock No. 45 Doefield Dun; here, the gates look to be in good order, but in fact the lock was out of commission and blocked to access from the other side. Today the lock has been restored to working order. The low bridge headroom of 10ft 3ins has caused accidents over the years, where drivers of large vehicles have ignored the sign and tried to pass through, with the inevitable results! Another problem has been flooding due to the proximity of the canal to the road dipping beneath the bridge. ***(Peter Hawkins, courtesy Chesterfield Canal Trust)***

Below: Another unidentified loco, this time a MR Class 4F 0-6-0, standing in front of Woodend Junction 'box with an engineer's train on Sunday 15 October 1961. A red flag can be seen on the track between the two telegraph poles, indicating the line is under possession. Woodend Junction No. 15 signal can be seen to the extreme left and, as mentioned, Doefield Dun lock has been blocked off with stop planks to prevent access, which can be seen in the foreground. The photographer's trusty cycle is propped up against the fence, awaiting his return! ***(Geoff Warnes, courtesy Chesterfield Canal Trust)***

Right: Gresley O2 2-8-0 No. 63979 rounds the curve from Shireoaks East Junction to Woodend Junction at 3.00pm on 5 May 1961. The loco was allocated to 36E Retford Thrumpton (GC) at the time of the photo, but was withdrawn for scrap on 10 September 1962. It was reduced to a pile of metal at Doncaster Works the same year.

Below right: As viewed from Tranker Lane overbridge, Ivatt "Mickey Mouse" Class 2F / 2P 2-6-0 No. 46499 rounds the east curve from Woodend Junction with a three-coach train at 6.37pm on 29 April 1964. This would have been the 5.11pm departure from Nottingham, due at Worksop at 6.44pm. A 16D Nottingham engine since November 1963, it was transferred to 8F Springs Branch (Wigan) during the week ending 23 May 1964, shortly after the image was taken. Later moving to 12C Barrow in Furness and thence 10A Carnforth, it was withdrawn from there during the week ending 6 May 1967.

Left: Stanier 3P 2-6-2T No. 40094 passes Woodend Junction on 5 May 1961. The west curve round to Shireoaks West can be seen. A former north-west engine, this loco was recorded as being transferred to 16B Kirkby-in-Ashfield during the five weeks ending 6 May 1961, it would be withdrawn during the week ending 7 October 1961. ***(All Alan Smalley)***

Right: Taken from Woodend Junction 'box, 47307 passes with a train of MCVs for Tinsley on 1 November 1979. Resignalling is underway; notice the colour light signal just beyond No. 12 Up Home signal awaiting commissioning. This would become Shireoaks Station SS798, and after the advent of Worksop PSB in 1997, WP798. ***(Richard Paget)***

Left: On 25 August 1989, while on duty at Worksop West, the author was talking on the circuit phone to the signalmen at Shireoaks Station, Shireoaks East Junction and Worksop East as 56013 was working a diverted Markham Colliery to Didcot Power Station MGR service. As it was heading along the west curve single line to SS798 signal (which was at red) to wait for a passing train heading from Woodend Junction towards Shireoaks East, the driver of the Class 56 lost control and couldn't stop. He slipped past the signal and derailed on the trap points. Part of his train hit the train passing on the east curve and knocked 14 wagons over! As we were talking, all the track circuits at Woodend lit up and the Shireoaks Station signalman's words were "Oh Sh*t summat's happened at Woodend!" Here 56013 waits for the recovery team to move the derailed wagons out of the way. ***(Author)***

Above: Network Rail liveried Class 31 No. 31285 comes round the east curve from Shireoaks East Junction to Woodend Junction. The train is 3Q18 08.51 Derby–Worksop–High Marnham–Worksop–Derby and was measuring the track geometry along the route. It is just passing the Banner Repeater for WP796 signal on 23 April 2013. ***(Author)***

Below: 58019 "Shirebrook Colliery" waiting to remove the derailed wagons as the crane lifts them back onto the track. ***(Author)***

Above: The Robin Hood Line passenger services through to Worksop were initiated in 1998 and originally worked by Central Trains. Here 153383 and an unidentified sister, working 2D20 16.42 Worksop to Nottingham on 25 September 2008, cross the restored Chesterfield Canal Doefield Dun lock just to the south of Woodend Junction. ***(Author)***

Right: Robin Hood Line logos. Left: Original design. Right: New design introduced in 2022. ***(Author/Courtesy Bolsover District Council)***

Whitwell

Above: An early view of Whitwell Station, looking towards Worksop. Notice the height of the Up Home signal to allow a view over Station Road bridge. Also notice the horse box in the dock platform behind the wall on the left. Could this have been for use by the Duke of Portland? ***(Author's collection)***

Right: An Edwardian period view southwards from Station Road bridge. A MR Johnson 1P tank loco is in the platform with a good number of passengers in attendance. Lower quadrant No. 36 Down Starting signal is prominent in the foreground; this carries the older style white with black dot on the rear of the arm. When W.C. Ackfield was appointed Signal Superintendent for the MR in 1906, the use of dots on signal arms was discontinued in favour of vertical bands. ***(Author's collection)***

Below: A comparison view from 1980, just before the station was dismantled stone-by-stone and transported to the Midland Railway-Butterley, for re-erection as Butterley Station. Very little else has changed over the years but No. 36 signal is now an upper quadrant signal. ***(Roger Wainwright)***

Right: On 18 July 1992 the station has now gone but No. 36 Starting signal still clings on – but not for much longer. The 'box has been closed and disused for some time, but the signals were removed and the 'box demolished in the late 1990s as part of Project EROS (Early Reduction of Signalling), a Railtrack initiative to reduce the number of mechanical signal boxes in local areas. ***(Author's collection)***

Above: Welbeck Abbey began as a monastery, founded in 1154, and stood for 384 years until the dissolution of the monasteries under King Henry VIII. The church was demolished, and the land and buildings passed into private hands, being bought by Bess of Hardwick's youngest son, Sir Charles Cavendish in 1607. Since then, Welbeck has continued to be handed down through the family and the extensive estate still covers 15,000 acres across Nottinghamshire and Derbyshire. The 5th Duke of Portland is famous for being the "burrowing Duke" who spent his time and wealth at Welbeck, commissioning an impressive range of buildings that included a maze of underground tunnels.

Right: William John Cavendish-Scott-Bentinck, 5th Duke of Portland (17 September 1800–6 December 1879).

Far right: The Duke's most extraordinary and famous construction is a network of underground tunnels and structures beneath Welbeck Village. He employed up to 1000 Irish workmen experienced in railway building and, with their expertise, constructed 2.5 miles of tunnels – some of which were large enough for two horse drawn carriages to pass side by side. However, this is the closest Welbeck Abbey got to being served by a railway – narrow gauge tracks in some of the underground tunnels; this one is near the kitchens. ***(All Author's collection)***

Above: Whitwell Colliery was one of five collieries originally owned by the Shireoaks Colliery Company Limited, hence the wagons with Shireoaks branding. His Grace the 6th Duke of Portland cut the first sod on Saturday 24 May 1890, and the sinkers reached the Top Hard seam at a depth of 311 yards on Friday 23 October 1891. Here a youth forms the foreground of the photo. The embankment in the distance is still in existence today, albeit heavily overgrown. ***(Author's collection)***

Left: Class O2 2-8-0 63986 sets back from the Arrival/Departure Road into the Duke of Portland's Sidings on 1 June 1963. The sidings were so called because they were built on the route that the 5th Duke of Portland had planned to build his railway to the Welbeck Estate, as mentioned in the main text. ***(R.J. Buckley)***

Right: A Permanent Way Gang work on 8, 10 and 11 points at Whitwell Colliery on 26 March 1991. The gate is across the Duke of Portland's Siding, the track beyond having been lifted. ***(Robin Stewart Smith)***

Right: Retford Thrumpton (36E)-based B1 4-6-0 61212 passes Whitwell Station signal box on an Up Excursion train. This loco spent its entire life allocated to Retford, and was withdrawn from 36E on 1 November 1964. According to the 1956 Handbook of Stations, the goods yard on the left had a 1.5-ton crane to handle goods while the signal box dated from 14 February 1893, replacing an earlier example. ***(Steve Godman collection)***

Left: A busy scene at Whitwell in 1973; a Class 37 stands alongside the 'box on the Down Main with a train of HEA wagons; No. 36 signal is at "Danger" against it. A pair of Class 20s are about to pass on the Up Main, possibly heading to Shirebrook depot for service or fuel. Meanwhile, a Class 56 is having a rake of HAAs loaded in the colliery sidings, carried out with the aid of mechanical shovels. ***(Author's collection)***

Right: During 1973 Class 31 5563 departs from Whitwell with an engineer's train of rails, running as 9X93 to Doncaster Wood Yard. Although the station has been closed nine years it is still intact, and would remain so until 1980. The loco was allocated to 40B Immingham at the time of the photo. It moved to Stratford in May 1977, by then numbered 31145, and returned north to Tinsley in 1987. It was withdrawn in 1997 and cut up in 1999. ***(Author's collection)***

Left: A similar scene on 25 October 1985 sees a loaded MGR train depart from Whitwell behind 56091. The station buildings and platforms have now gone. At the time of writing, this loco was operated by DC Rail, a national freight operator and a member of the Cappagh Group of Companies. It is in DC Rail grey Livery and named "Driver Wayne Gaskell". ***(Author's collection)***

Above: Whitwell Station 'box, by origin a Midland Railway box, was heavily "Easternised" in 1953 with a replacement 38-lever McKenzie & Holland frame. It also received Tyer & Co "Black Box" instruments. Here an unidentified Class 47 passes No. 3 signal with a HAA set for one of the area's collieries. The eagle-eyed will spot a brake van to the right of the loco; this was attached to at least one "Conflat L" wagon with Type "A" containers for Whitwell Quarry. ***(Author's collection)***

Right: The former goods shed was utilised by Walvin's waste paper recycling company for a few years in the 1970/80s, but after they departed it remained in a derelict condition until it was demolished and the goods yard cleared for housing, construction of which commenced in 2022. Here Midland Mainline-liveried 170109 works 2W22 17.26 Nottingham to Worksop on 30 May 2003. This was a fill-in turn from Nottingham to Worksop for a Midland Mainline unit, and was the only time these units worked along the Robin Hood Line. ***(Author)***

Left: After storage in Worksop Yard, Class 37 No. 37800 "Cassiopeia" hauls Elizabeth Line unit 345060 past Whitwell as 5Q58 11.02 Worksop to Old Oak Common on 5 March 2020. The cleared goods yard still awaits any development. ***(Author)***

Above: Typical Robin Hood Line style nameboard at Whitwell. ***(Author)***

Above: 1960s Edmondson style 2nd Class Single ticket from Langwith to Whitwell. ***(Author's collection)***

Above: The Stage 3 extension of Robin Hood Line services from Mansfield to Worksop required all intermediate stations to be rebuilt. The new Whitwell station is seen under construction on 6 December 1997.

Right: Almost complete, Whitwell undergoes transformation into a new Robin Hood Line station on 20 March 1998.

Below: 58046 "Asfordby Mine" passes the then unopened station at Whitwell with 7B63 from Thoresby to West Burton on 16 April 1998. ***(All Author)***

Left: Whitwell Tunnel seen from rail level just after completion of the works in 1875. Notice the neat cutting sides, and the ballast almost to the rail head, which is not conducive to good drainage. ***(Inspire Picture Archive)***

Below: 147 years later, a pair of Colas operated Class 56s Nos. 56090+56094 head towards Whitwell Tunnel on 3 November 2018 with 3J89 05.05 Toton to Toton Railhead Treatment Train via Shirebrook and Worksop. The branch to Whitwell quarry is still there beneath the undergrowth, although the access pointwork has long been removed. ***(Author)***

Right: "Peak" 45022 "Lytham St. Annes" emerges from the south portal of Whitwell Tunnel with the diverted 09.50 Edinburgh to Penzance on 30 March 1975. All Midland Main Line trains were diverted via Shireoaks, Creswell and Shirebrook due to Tapton Junction (north of Chesterfield) being re-laid that Easter Sunday. ***(J.S. Gilkes)***

Whitwell Quarry

Below: Planning permission was granted on 5 March 1957 for the extraction of limestone from land south of the Worksop to Mansfield railway line, and in 1960 a rail connection was provided at Milepost 150½ between Whitwell Tunnel and Whitwell Station. The signalling was controlled by Whitwell Station signal box, and the single-track branch was 743 yards long from the main line connection to the sidings. The branch had two level crossings; the first was a farmers' crossing at 606 yards, and the second was at 719 yards for an internal roadway in the Whitwell Quarry complex. There were three double-ended sidings on the approach to the loading bunker, where the empty wagons were delivered. An internal shunter propelled the wagons beneath the bunker to the three loaded sidings beyond. There was a by-pass line from the empty sidings to the loaded sidings, from which was a short cripple spur. This 1964 image shows the rail sidings at the bottom; a Class 04 2-8-0 can be seen to the lower left, having brought a brakevan into the sidings. ***(Adrian Wynne collection)***

Left: A 12-ton lime wagon built by the Gloucester Railway Carriage & Wagon Co. Ltd for the Steetley Lime & Basic Co. Ltd in March 1936, lettered "Return to Steetley Sidings Whitwell LMS". The owner's plate attached to one such wagon shows it was based at Worksop, ***(Wagon photo HMRS, other Author's collection)***

Right: British Railways introduced the "L-type" container with a capacity of 4 tons, top hatches for loading and bottom doors for discharge. The cube-shaped containers rode on dedicated four-wheeled, vacuum-braked wagon known as a "Conflat L", which were specially designed with holes in the floors to allow the containers to be discharged without removal from the wagon. Here are 08263 & 08255 with Trip 9T63 to Worksop in the quarry sidings. ***(Phil Sangwell / Creative Commons Attribution 4.0 International License)***

Centre right: Railfreight Construction Sector Class 56 No. 56065 propels 6Z61 Toton to Whitwell Quarry empties onto the quarry branch on 19 April 1990. Prior to the removal of the facing crossover just beyond the occupation bridge this train would have come straight into the arrival road on the left. However, now it would pass through the former station site before setting back into the arrival road. The quarry branch is now long disused and although the trackwork is still in place, all pointwork has been removed. According to Lafarge; "There are significant level differences between the main line and the disused spur to the Lime Works, as well as the spur crossing the main quarry/ Lime Works HGV access and exit routes. The loading facilities are only suitable for loading HGVs and would require significant modifications for the loading of railway rolling stock. The use of rail depends entirely on customer demand, the location of those customers and whether they have suitable unloading facilities. At present there is no customer requirement for the quarry to be rail connected and the costs of making a connection would be significant."

Right: A moment in time as the crew enjoy a joke as a mechanical shovel loads the train. Robin Breddy is in the doorway of the loco, with Bob Hill on the ground, unfortunately the Driver has not been identified as he is looking the other way.....maybe he is a shy man! Robin retired from the railway in 2004 and has helped the author source photos. ***(Both Robin Stewart Smith)***

Elmton & Creswell Junction

Right: A look at some of Creswell's signal boxes. Creswell Station 'box had opened before 1 November 1875, and is seen here shortly after opening with a moustached signalman on the steps. It was renamed Elmton & Creswell Station in 1886 but was replaced on 6 November 1887, the new 'box retaining the same name.

Above: With the houses of Welbeck Street in the background, Creswell Colliery Sidings North was situated on the Up side. It opened on 18 May 1896 with a 16-lever frame. The notice issued for opening read: "The connection between the Bolsover Colliery Co's siding and the Down Main Line, now worked by Guards and Shunters from a stage, and the signals also worked by Guards and Shunters from the stage will be removed and dispensed with, except the Distant signal for the Down Main Line, which will remain in use as the Creswell Colliery Sidings North Box Down Main Line Distant signal". It basically replaced a stage Ground Frame and was open for traffic only during weekdays, being closed at night and Sundays. On Monday 17 August 1896 Creswell Colliery Sidings South was opened, situated about half a mile on the Langwith side from Elmton & Creswell Station, on the Langwith side. The notice for this read: "The Starting signal for Creswell Colliery Sidings North 'box will be moved a short distance nearer to the signal box, the Distant signal for the Down Main Line dispensed with and the Distant signal for the Down Main line previously worked by Elmton & Creswell box will be controlled from the Creswell Colliery Sidings North box".

Above: South 'box closed on 14 March 1942, and on 28 April 1946 a new box was opened at the junction of the Clowne Branch to supersede both Elmton & Creswell Station and Creswell Colliery Sidings North 'boxes. Above right: The 48-lever frame was a LMS Type 11c, a 1938 experimental development of the LNWR frame with "stirrup" catch handles, 4½ inch centres and sloping locking trays. The unique frame was kept in store at Crewe during World War II until it was fitted into the signal box in 1946. Seen here in the 1970s, the branch to Seymour Junction was worked by tablet initially to Oxcroft Colliery No. 3, then Seymour Junction. Right: The tablet machine for the Clowne Branch in Elmton & Creswell 'box. ***(All Author's collection)***

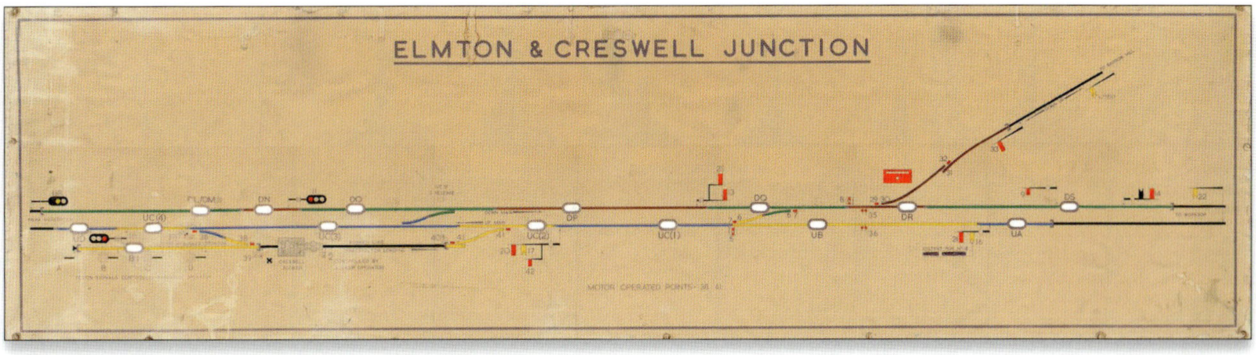

◊ **Top**: Elmton & Creswell 'box diagram. ***(Neil Baker)***

Middle: 58016 sweeps round the curve from Whitwell with 6G56 West Burton Power Station to Bilsthorpe on a very warm and sunny 28 June 1993. The signalman's 1796cc 1983 Vauxhall Carlton, registration number A378 CAP, waits for his shift to end.

Above: Ten months later and much wetter, 28 April 1994 sees 58039 "Rugeley Power Station" passing with 6C15 Worksop to Thoresby Colliery. This time the car is a MkII Ford Escort, B770 OPY, first registered in March 1985.

Left: 58035 is at the head of 7G34 Rufford to West Burton passing No. 13 signal. The lower signal is No. 25 for the Clowne Branch, while the "Dolly" is No. 5. ***(All Author)***

Creswell Station

Cresswell station opened to passengers on 1 June 1875. It was renamed Elmton & Cresswell on 10 April 1886, and the second "s" was dropped from 1 May 1887. Looking north towards Whitwell we see the station goods yard, with a train of coaches being readied to return to Nottingham. On the left, a further rake of coaches is in the bay platform. These would probably have formed a train for Chesterfield via Clowne and Staveley. Notice, above those coaches, the junction signals for the branch to Clowne with Creswell Station 'box just beyond.

Right: The 1905 Ambulance class pose on the Up platform at Creswell. Notice Creswell Colliery Sidings North signal box in the background.

Below: The advent of the Great War on 28 July 1914 led to an initial call for 100,000 volunteers. This saw almost half a million men enlisting in two months, Creswell being no exception. It is understood that around 700 men enlisted; sadly, almost 100 were killed, of which 22 were in the Battle of the Somme. Here, some of the volunteers are waiting transportation from the station, with their wives and children seeing them off. One has to wonder how many in this photo never returned home. ***(All Author's collection)***

Left: The LMS introduced a Sunday railmotor service from Mansfield to Whitwell in the 1930s. Here is the train ready to depart Elmton & Creswell for Mansfield with 1875-built Class 1P 0-4-4T No. 1249 in charge. This loco was numbered 58033 in BR days and would last until September 1950. ***(Geoff Hurst collection)***

Below: A section of 1882 Bradshaw's timetable, showing Mansfield, Worksop and Retford. Checker House station featured in Volume 1.

MANSFIELD, WORKSOP, and RETFORD.—Midland

Mls		mrn	mrn	aft	Frm Hull, 272	mrn	aft	aft	Sats. only.
—	Mansfield ..dep	7 5	1153	5 35	Retford ..dep	8 38	1255	7 0	
1½	Mansfield Wood-	7 10	1157	5 40	Checkr House	a	a	a	
4½	Shirebrk [house	7 17	12 5	5 47	Worksop	8 52	1 11	7 14	8 10
6	Langwith......	7 22	12 9	5 52	Whitwell....	9 2	1 21	7 24	8 20
8¾	Cresswell	7 28	1214	5 58	Cresswell	9 7	1 26	7 29	8 26
10¼	Whitwell	7 33	1218	6 3	Langwith....	9 13	1 32	7 35	8 35
15	Worksop 272..	7 42	1227	6 13	Shirebrk [hse	9 18	1 37	7 40	8 41
19	Checker House	a	a	a	Mnsfld Wood-	9 24	1 43	7 46	8 48
22¾	Retford 271 arr	7 57	1242	6 27	Mansfld 237a	9 30	1 49	7 52	8 55

a Stop when required.

Below: September 1892 Bradshaw's for trains over the Clowne Branch.

MANSFIELD, AND CLOWNE BRANCH.

		Wednesdays only.	A	B	A	B
London (St. Pancras)	12 ·	..	..	9 0	10 35	3 0
Nottingham	6 0	..	10 30	12 40	1 30	5 45
Mansfield ......dep.	7 0	8 50	1 10	1 10	3 40	7 25
Mansfield Woodhouse	7 4	8 55	1 14	1 14	3 44	7 31
Shirebrook..........	7 11	9 2	1 21	1 21	3 51	7 39
Langwith	7 15	9 6	1 26	1 26	3 56	7 46
Elmton and Creswell	7 20	9 12	1 32	1 32	4 2	7 56
Clowne	7 32	9 19	1 39	1 39	4 9	8 3
Netherthorpe	7 43	9 30	1 50	1 56	4 20	8 14
Staveley	7 48	9 35	1 55	2 3	4 26	8 20
Whittington	7 54	10 9	2 3	2 8	4 29	8 27
Chesterfield ....arr.	8 0	10 15	2 8	2 14	4 35	8 32
Derby ....arr.	9 55	11 25	3 30	3 30	5 40	..
London (St. Pancras)	12 55	2 35	5 55	5 55	9 45	..

		Wednesdays only.	A	B	A	B
London ......dep.	..	..	..	..	10 35	..
Derby .... „	..	10 30	12 45	12 47	2 55	7 5
Chesterfield ..dep.	8 30	11 25	2 5	2 25	5 0	9 15
Whittington	8 35	11 32	2 10	2 31	5 5	9 21
Staveley	8 37	11 45	2 20	2 36	5 8	9 24
Netherthorpe	8 44	11 51	2 26	2 42	5 13	9 31
Clowne	8 55	12 2	2 37	2 53	5 23	9 43
Elmton & Creswell	9 1	12 9	2 44	3 0	5 28	9 48
Langwith	9 14	12 15	2 50	3 6	5 37	9 57
Shirebrook	9 18	12 19	2 54	3 10	5 41	10 1
Mansfield Woodhse	9 24	12 25	3 0	3 16	5 47	10 7
Mansfield......arr.	9 30	12 30	3 5	3 22	5 52	10 12
Nottingham .. arr.	10 5	2 50	4 0	4 0	7 1	
London (St. Pncrs)	12 55	6 0	8 0	8 0	10 15	

A Saturdays excepted. B Saturdays only.

On Saturdays only a Train leaves Chesterfield at 6.25 p.m. arriving at Creswell at 6.55, and Mansfield at 7.52.

Table 243 MANSFIELD, STAVELEY TOWN, and CHESTERFIELD–Week Days only

Miles		a.m T X		p.m	
	Mansfield .... dep		..	..	..
1½	Mansfield Woodhouse...	..	..	..	..
4½	Shirebrook	..	..	..	..
6	Langwith	..	..	..	..
8¾	Elmton and Creswell....	7 56	..	4 27	..
11¼	Clown and Barlborough.	8 3	..	4 35	..
15½	Staveley Town..........	8 21	..	4 48	..
17¾	Barrow Hill and Staveley	..	..	4 57	..
19¾	Whittington ....[Works	..	..	5 0	..
21	Chesterfield......... arr	..	..	5 5	..

Miles		a.m		p.m T V
	Chesterfield......... dep	8 14	..	
2¼	Whittington	8 20	..	..
3¼	Barrow Hill and Staveley	8 26	..	..
5½	Staveley Town...[Works	8 32	..	6 32
9¾	Clown and Barlborough.	8 44	..	6 50
12¼	Elmton and Creswell....	8 50	..	6 56
15	Langwith	..	..	..
16½	Shirebrook	..	..	..
19½	Mansfield Woodhouse...	..	..	..
21	Mansfield .... arr	..	..	..

T Saturdays only. Runs until 13th September inclusive.
V Through Carriages Blackpool (North) dep. 2 15 p.m to Hucknall arr 8 0 p.m (Tables 160, 241 and 236.)
X Through Carriages Hucknall dep. 6 55 a.m to Blackpool (N.) arr. 12 52 p.m (Tables 236, 244 and 160.)

For OTHER TRAINS between Mansfield and Elmton and Creswell, see Table 236—Barrow Hill and Staveley Works and Chesterfield, Table 241.

Above: LMS June 1947 timetable for Mansfield to Chesterfield, via the Clowne Branch. Notice that by now the two remaining services only ran between Elmton & Creswell and Staveley or Chesterfield. ***(All Author's collection)***

Table 236 NOTTINGHAM, SUTTON JUNCTION, MANSFIELD, and WORKSOP

Week Days / Sundays (Runs until 13th September inclusive: second column)

Miles		a.m	a.m S	a.m	a.m	a.m		a.m S	p.m S	a.m	p.m	p.m	p.m	p.m	p.m	p.m		Sun a.m 🅐		Sun a.m 🅐	Sun p.m 🅐	Sun p.m 🅐
	208 London (St. Pan.) dep	9N30	D	..	..	4 20	..	8 55	..	1150	1255	..	3 15	..	4 50	5 32	..	12s0	..	1015	2 50	4 55
—	**Nottingham** dep	5 47	..	7 30	8 25	9 45	..	1211	..	3 7	4 33	5 12	6 3	6 35	7 40	9 26	..	1010	..	1 25	6 45	9 10
2¼	Radford	5 53	..	7 36	8 31	..	..	1217	..	3 13	..	5 19	6 10	6 41	7 46	..	..	..	..	..	..	..
4	Basford	5 58	..	7 41	8 36	..	..	1222	..	3 18	4 42	5 24	6 16	6 46	7 51	9 35	..	..	..	..	..	9 19
5½	Bulwell	6 5	..	7 50	8 41	9 56	..	1227	..	3 23	4 47	5 29	6 21	6 51	..	9 40	..	1021	..	..	..	9 24
8½	**Hucknall**	6 15	6 55	7 58	8 49	10 4	..	1235	..	3 31	4 55	5 37	6 29	6 59	8 0	9 48	..	1029	..	1 41	7 1	9 32
9¼	Linby	6 18	6 59	8 2	8 52	..	..	1239	..	..	4 58	5 41	6 32	7 3	8 5	9 51	..	..	..	..	..	..
10½	Newstead	6 22	7 6	8 8	8 56	1011	..	1245	..	3 40	5 2	5 47	6 36	7 9	8 11	9 55	..	..	..	1 47	..	9 38
11¼	Annesley	6 25	7 11	8 12	8 59	..	..	1249	..	3 44	5 5	5 51	6 39	7 13	..	9 58	..	..	..	..	..	..
13¼	Kirkby-in-Ashfield	6 32	7 19	8 18	9 6	1019	..	1255	..	3 50	5 11	5 57	6 45	7 19	8 19	10 5	..	1041	..	1 55	7 12	9 47
14¼	Sutton Junc. arr	6 35	7 24	8 21	9 9	1022	..	1258	..	3 53	5 14	6 0	6 48	7 22	8 22	10 8	..	1044	..	1 58	7 15	9 50
	Sutton Junc. dep	6 39	7 26	8 22	9 10	1023	..	1259	..	3 54	5 15	6 1	6 49	7 23	8 23	1010	..	1046	..	1 59	7 16	9 51
17	**Mansfield** arr	6 43	7 30	8 26	9 14	1027	..	1 3	..	3 58	5 19	6 5	6 53	7 27	8 27	1013	..	1050	..	2 3	7 20	9 55
	Mansfield dep	6 49	7 35	..	..	1036	..	..	1 52	4 3	..	6 10	6 58	..	8 32	..	..	..	..	..	..	..
18½	Mansfield Woodhouse	6 56	7 39	..	..	1040	..	..	1 56	4 7	..	6 14	7 2	..	3 36	..	..	..	..	..	..	..
21½	Shirebrook	7 3	7 45	..	..	1046	..	..	2 2	4 13	..	6 20	7 8	..	8 42	..	..	..	..	..	..	..
23	Langwith	7 9	7 50	..	..	1051	..	..	2 7	4 18	..	6 25	7 13	..	8 47	..	..	..	..	..	..	..
25¾	Elmton & Creswell	7 16	7 56	..	..	1057	..	..	2 12	4 24	..	6 31	7 19	..	8 53	..	..	..	..	..	..	..
27¾	Whitwell	7 21	..	..	..	11 2	..	..	..	4 29	..	6 36	7 24	..	8 58	..	..	..	..	..	..	..
32	**Worksop** arr	7 30	..	..	..	1111	..	..	..	4 40	..	6 45	7 33	..	9 7	..	..	..	..	..	..	..

Week Days / Sundays (Runs until 13th September inclusive: S C column)

Miles		a.m	a.m	a.m	a.m	a.m	a.m	a.m	p.m S	p.m E	p.m S	p.m	p.m	S C	p.m	p.m	p.m	Sun a.m 🅐		Sun p.m 🅐	Sun p.m 🅐	Sun p.m 🅐
—	**Worksop** dep	..	..	6 35	..	8 44	..	1124	..	..	..	..	5 33	..	6 57	8 10	9 55	..	..	..	..	..
4¾	Whitwell	..	..	6 49	..	8 55	..	1135	..	..	..	..	5 46	..	7 11	8 21	10 6	..	..	..	..	..
6¾	Elmton & Creswell	..	..	6 54	7 32	9 0	..	1140	1237	..	2 28	..	5 51	6 56	7 15	8 26	1012	..	..	..	..	..
9	Langwith	..	..	7 0	7 38	9 6	..	1146	1243	..	2 34	..	5 57	7 3	7 21	8 32	1018	..	..	..	..	..
10½	Shirebrook	..	..	7 5	7 43	9 11	..	1151	1248	..	2 39	..	6 2	7 9	7 26	8 37	1023	..	..	..	..	..
13½	Mansfield Woodhouse	..	..	7 11	7 49	9 17	..	1157	1254	..	2 45	..	6 8	7 17	7 32	8 43	1029	..	..	..	..	..
15	**Mansfield** arr	..	..	7 15	7 53	9 21	..	12 1	1258	..	2 49	..	6 12	7 21	7 36	8 47	1033	..	..	..	..	..
	Mansfield dep	5 40	6 38	7 20	7 58	..	10 0	12 7	1 3	1 16	..	5 10	6 19	7 26	..	8 55	..	8 30	..	1235	5 42	7 36
17½	Sutton Junc. arr	5 45	6 43	7 25	8 3	..	10 5	1212	1 8	1 21	..	5 15	6 24	7 32	..	9 0	..	8 35	..	1240	5 47	7 41
	Sutton Junc. dep	5 46	6 44	7 26	8 4	..	10 6	1213	1 9	1 22	..	5 16	6 25	7 34	..	9 1	..	8 36	..	1241	5 48	7 42
18¾	Kirkby-in-Ashfield	5 50	6 48	7 30	8 8	..	1010	1217	1 13	1 26	..	5 20	6 29	7 40	..	9 5	..	8 40	..	1245	5 52	7 47
20¾	Annesley	5 55	6 53	7 35	8 13	..	1015	1222	1 18	..	..	..	6 34	7 46	..	9 11	..	..	..	..	..	..
21¾	Newstead	5 58	6 56	7 38	8 16	..	1018	1225	1 21	1 32	..	5 26	6 37	7 51	..	9 14	..	..	..	..	5 58	7 53
22¾	Linby	6 1	6 59	7 41	8 19	..	1021	..	1 24	1 35	..	5 29	6 40	7 56	..	9 17	..	..	..	..	..	..
23½	**Hucknall**	6 4	7 2	7 44	8 22	..	1024	1229	1 27	1 38	..	5 33	6 43	8 0	..	9 20	..	8 49	..	1254	6 3	7 58
26½	Bulwell	6 10	7 8	7 50	8 28	..	1030	1235	1 33	1 44	..	5 39	6 50	..	..	9 26	..	8 55	..	..	..	8 4
28	Basford	6 14	7 12	7 54	8 32	..	1034	..	1 37	1 48	..	5 43	6 54	..	..	..	..	..	..	..	..	8 8
29¾	Radford	6 19	7 17	7 59	8 37	..	1039	..	1 42	1 53	..	5 48	6 59	..	..	..	..	..	..	..	..	..
32	**Nottingham** arr	6 24	7 22	8 4	8 42	..	1046	1244	1 49	1 58	..	5 56	7 4	..	..	9 36	..	9 4	..	1 7	6 16	8 15
133½	208 London (St. Pan.) arr	10 5	..	1110	1225	..	1 55	4 0	5 55	5 55	..	1045	..	..	..	5U30	..	2 35	..	5 35	11 0	4a40

a a.m. C Through Carriages from Blackpool (North) dep. 2 15 p.m (Tables 160, 244 and 243).
D Through Carriages to Blackpool (North) arr 12 52 p.m (Tables 243, 244 and 160) E or E Except Saturdays
N Night time. Dep. 11 50 p.m. on Sundays. S or S Saturdays only. s Saturday night. U Arr. 5 15 a.m on Sundays.
🅐 Third class only.

For **OTHER TRAINS** between Kirkby-in-Ashfield and Mansfield, see Table 239—
Mansfield and Elmton and Creswell, Table 243.

Above: LMS June 1947 timetable for Nottingham to Worksop. Notice there is no Sunday service between Mansfield and Worksop.

Above: A selection of tickets issued to and from Elmton & Creswell and a MR luggage label. ***(All Author's collection)***

Right: As Creswell Colliery Rapid Loader Bunker looms in the background, Brush Type 4 47368 powers through the remains of Creswell station's platforms on 17 May 1977, before Classes 56 and 58 took over these duties. The loco was new to 40B Immingham on 17 August 1965 as D1887. During the week ending 9 September 1967 it moved to 41A Tinsley before returning to Immingham. There followed periods at Tinsley, Crewe, Tinsley again and back to Crewe, from where it was withdrawn in 1996. ***(Richard Paget)***

Left: We are now firmly in the Class 58 period, and the class would hold sway on coal traffic along this line until the advent of the Class 66 after privatisation. 58045 heads towards Worksop on 9 April 1990 with 7G60 Welbeck Colliery to West Burton Power Station. The platform remains have been further pared back and there is little sign of them, although hidden by the bushes on the left is the still-extant Up side station building. Like 58039 seen earlier at Whitwell, this loco was refurbished in black and orange livery, given the number 5812 and shipped to the Netherlands to work for ACTS on container traffic. After the contract expired, it was returned to the UK but was subsequently sent to work in France in July 2009. It was withdrawn again due to a cracked wheel, and in July 2010 was purchased by the Class 58 Loco Group to provide spares for their preserved 58016. Following stripping, it was cut up at EMR Kingsbury in October 2010. ***(Robin Stewart Smith)***

Left: 58023 passes the Down signals with 6G15 Worksop to Thoresby Colliery on 28 April 1994. This loco is still with us in preservation and, at the time of writing, was based at Leicester Loco depot, where it had been used as a shunter, but was being prepared for main line running again. The building on the right is not railway related but was built for a local vehicle spares company, who also own the derelict remains of the station buildings. The remains of the Up platform can be discerned just in front of the concrete fence. ***(Author)***

Left: Looking from the signal box, 58026 passes Creswell station on 17 August 1994 with 7F10 Welbeck to Cottam Power Station. The Station Master's house can be seen on the left, whilst poking up above the train, beyond the car parts warehouse, are the remains of the station building. This loco was one of many sent abroad for the construction of new railways in France. After cessation of the contract the loco was stored at Alizay, France, but has since been cut up for scrap. ***(Author)***

Left: A photo of the station taken after nationalisation. Notice the goods shed at the far end of the station and the Station Masters house on the extreme right. The smaller Down side station building, also in view, was demolished after the station closed. ***(Author's collection)***

Right: A 1970s photo of the platform remains, with the edging stones removed. While the goods shed is just a pile of rubble, the former Station Master's house is still visible on the right. ***(Author's collection)***

Left: Creswell station reopened with Stage 3 of the Robin Hood Line project. Here local schoolchildren wave off 150016 after speeches had been made during the Robin Hood Line Stage 3 Opening Fun Day event, held on 25 May 1998.

Right: The speeches were made by dignitaries including Transport Minister Gavin Strang (front), Bolsover Council Chairman Pamela Richardson (right front), Derbyshire County Council Leader Councillor Martin Doughty (next to cab) and Nottinghamshire County Council Leader Sir Dennis Pettitt (behind, with glasses). The day was well patronised and goodies were given out on the train. ***(Both Author)***

Norwood

Right: Norwood Siding signal box, seen in 1875 just after opening, controlled the level crossing on Mags Lane along with a small siding on the Up side just beyond the 'box. Hanging out of the window is Joseph Vale, who took the post on 20 July 1875. On 5 March 1885 the 'box was reduced in status to Gatebox and the Gate Keeper position was taken by Benjamin Hardy. The 'box was replaced by a 5-lever Ground Frame (GF) on 14 December 1886, although the crossing keeper's house remained after closure of the 'box. ***(Author's collection)***

Left: The GF hut as seen on 16 June 1961, with the crossing keeper's dog overseeing operations! ***(Mike King)***

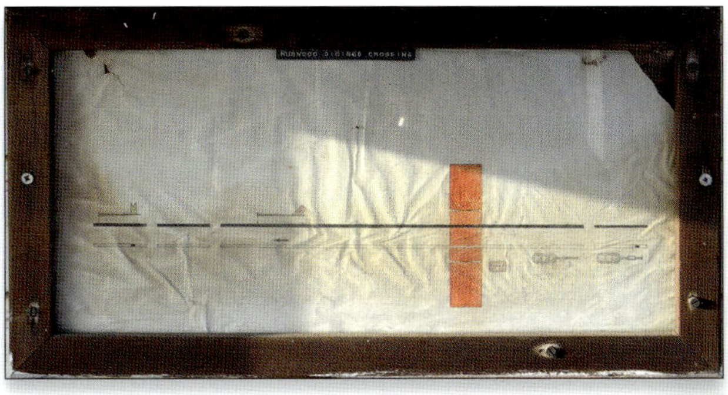

Above, left & below right: Although the hut was renewed, the frame and diagram remained the same. Here 66067+ 67029 pass the crossing as 0F54 12.00 Doncaster to Toton. ***(Author)***

Left & above: The GF was replaced on 2 July 2017 by a Henry Williams IFS panel situated in a location cabinet. Here 156410 passes the crossing with 2W06 09.26 Nottingham to Worksop on 3 November 2018. ***(Author/Andrew K Overton)***

Langwith

Above left: When the Robin Hood service was being planned it was decided that, rather than rebuilding the original station in Langwith Maltings, the community would be better served by building the new station about half a mile further north in the larger communities of Nether Langwith and Whaley Thorns – hence "Langwith-Whaley Thorns". The new station is seen on 6 December 1997 during construction on a new site just to the north of the Langwith Colliery site. ***(Author)***

Left: Access to the platforms is gained via long sloping ramps from an existing overbridge; Langwith Colliery was once to the right of the bridge. The station opened in May 1998 and is seen here on 24 August 2011 from the cab of a loco. ***(Author)***

Right: On 9 February 2005 66720 "Metronet Pathfinder", in Metronet GBRf livery, passes a snowy Langwith-Whaley Thorns with 6B55 Welbeck Colliery to West Burton Power Station. The weather was causing chaos to the timetable at the time, with cancellations and delays inevitable. ***(Derek Wilson)***

Left: East Midlands Trains Class 158 158847 arrives at Langwith-Whaley Thorns in much better weather on 8 April 2019 with the 15.38 Worksop to Nottingham Robin Hood Line service. Notice the railings and lamps have been repainted. ***(Robin Stewart-Smith)***

Above: Langwith Station looking north on opening in 1875; it would see its first passenger train on 1 June that year. Three staff members are watching the photographer, one nonchalantly leaning on a platform barrow. It is entirely possible that they were the first three staff employed here: Station Master George Hull, Porter James Pembleton and Signalman George Hurle. Notice the early Midland Railway signals, with the lamps further down the post; they were worked by Langwith Station 'box. ***(Author's collection)***

Below: Shoppers alight from the 14.25 Mansfield to Worksop service on Saturday 24 March 1962, with Fairburn 2-6-4T 42222 in charge. Until the closure of Langwith Colliery Sidings South in March 1942, the post also supported South 'box's No. 1 Down Distant Signal. Allocated to 16B Kirkby in Ashfield at the time, the engine was transferred to 1A Willesden from the week ending 25 May 1963. It was withdrawn from there almost two years later on 8 May 1965. The two shoppers (of which the one on the right is Mrs Liz Bennett) will wait for the train to pass before using the boardwalk to cross the line – Langwith, in line with most of the stations, had no footbridge. ***(H.B. Priestley/Neil Baker collection)***

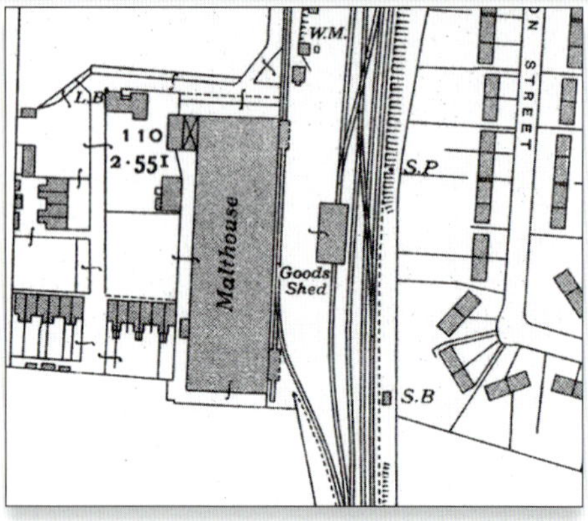

Top: On Easter Sunday 1975 Sheffield to London trains were diverted due to engineering works at Tapton Junction. Two "Peak" locos pass in this wonderful image overlooking Langwith. 45055 approaches the camera at the head of the southbound 1V86, while the now-preserved 45133 takes 1S68 north. The armless former Langwith Station Up Starting signal post remains in situ, which also carried Shirebrook Junction's No. 34 Up Distant signal. This was removed when the new Shirebrook East Junction opened in 1974, and No. 34 was moved further north and converted to a colour light signal. Langwith Colliery is prominent on the skyline. Notice the red-painted door of both the goods shed and that of part of the maltings. ***(John S. Gilks)***

Above: William Burkitt, a maltster from Chesterfield, had been waiting for the railway line to be built through Langwith, and in 1874 bought land from the Duke of Devonshire to erect a maltings. By 1876 a building 201 feet long by 88 feet wide, designed by S. Rollinson of Chesterfield, was erected near the station. It had three floors – two for growing and one at the top for storage of malt – and had a capacity of about 42 tons. There were three malt-making kilns and a coal-fired barley-drying kiln; the coal brought into their own railway sidings via a connection from the goods yard. Converted to gas in 1927, the company also made a request to the colliery for electricity, but was refused although mains power was gained in 1946 from the Notts and Derby Power Company. R. Peach & Co. of Burton upon Trent leased the maltings from 1923 to 1928 for an annual rent of £725, but bought them in 1935 for £4,382. Rail connections were in use until at least the bad winter of 1962/63. In a tale told by PWay Ganger Frank Lloyd, they were called to free some wagons from the maltings. A pool of ice had formed on the points adjacent to where the box van is stood in the photo, due to steam produced in the malting process condensing and running down from the nearest of the three condensing stacks. As quick as they were working, the ice was refreezing and they had to resort to pneumatic drills to fully remove it! Malting continued up to 1986, ceasing due to a glut of malt but recommenced from 1989 to 1991.

Left: With the Maltings behind, this machine is working on installing a new drainage system to alleviate the flooding which had occurred in the cutting between Langwith and Shirebrook, in 1977. ***(All Neil Baker collection)***

Chapter 2

The collieries along the main line

Coal, the "Black Gold" as it was sometimes known, was to become the lifeblood of the railway and along the route from Nottingham to Worksop there would eventually be collieries at Annesley, Bestwood, Hucknall, Kirkby, Linby, Newstead, Radford, Sutton, Sherwood, Shirebrook, Warsop, Langwith, Creswell, Whitwell, Steetley and Shireoaks. Only the nine collieries relevant to the section of line between Shireoaks and Mansfield will be considered here.

Shireoaks

The only colliery to be in production when the line was opened was located at the northern end of the line at Shireoaks. This Colliery was Worksop's first coal mine and was the first colliery to access the "concealed coalfield" paving the way for all collieries west of this point. At the time of shaft sinking on 9 April 1854 it was deepest colliery in the UK. The 5th Duke of Newcastle cut the first sod and it took almost 5 years to sink 515 yards – the prized Top Hard seam being reached on 1 February 1859. Coal production commenced in June 1859, development being funded by the Duke until the Shireoaks Colliery Company (SCC) was formed on 1 April 1864.

By 1871 the colliery was producing 180,000 tons annually from a workforce of 600. Struggling to meet its order for coal the SCC opened up four further collieries at Steetley, Whitwell, Clowne Southgate and Harrycrofts. Shireoaks Colliery was connected to the MS&LR line and also had a basin on the adjacent Chesterfield Canal, then when the MR line was built at Woodend a connection into the colliery was made from the south to west curve, between Woodend Junction and Shireoaks West Junction.

The colliery developed its own foundries, wagon works, gas works and electricity generators, with wagons being manufactured at a rate of one per week. Whilst most were used by the company, in a distinctive livery of bright red, bearing the legend "Shireoaks" in white and black lettering, a surplus was also produced for sale to other companies. More photographs of Shireoaks can be found in Volume 1.

Steetley

Although Southgate Colliery, Clowne, had been the next new pit planned by the SCC, its start was delayed whilst waiting for a railway connection to be developed, and so the next to be sunk was actually Steetley. This was a single shaft mine sunk in 1873, the Top Hard coal seam being reached at 579 yards from the surface in December 1875, and at the time this was the deepest shaft in the midland counties. Situated at Darfoulds about a mile away from Shireoaks, it was originally called Manor Pits, Darfoulds. An underground connection with Shireoaks Colliery provided the ventilation system and a second means of egress via Steetley's single downcast shaft and Shireoaks No. 2 (upcast) shaft. The colliery was only served by the MR line and there were no other branches to it.

Whitwell Colliery

There were no further collieries sunk alongside the route of the line for a period of 10 years, the sinking of Whitwell in 1890 breaking the hiatus. This colliery was situated on Belph Moor near Whitwell and the Top Hard seam was reached at a depth of 311 yards on 23 October 1891. An underground connection was made with Steetley to complete ventilation, allowing coal production to start in 1894, before the completion of Whitwell No. 2 shaft in 1898. Whitwell was an excellent producer and of the SCC's pits it worked the most seams, extracting coal from the Top Hard, High Hazel, Clowne, Sough and (briefly) Thorncliffe seams. Again the MR had the monopoly of the colliery traffic as it was only connected to their line.

Creswell

The Bolsover Colliery Co. Ltd was formed in 1889 and secured a lease on land at Creswell from the Duke of Portland. Shaft sinking commenced at Creswell in 1894; 2 shafts were sunk and the High Hazel seam was reached at 329 yards, the shaft continuing down to the Top Hard Seam at 440 yards. Coal production commenced in 1897. This colliery was also connected to the MR line and to the LD&ECR line between Langwith Junction and Beighton.

Langwith

By the 1870s, The Sheepbridge Coal and Iron Company of Chesterfield already had four collieries in operation, and an upturn in the demand for local coal led the Company to sink Langwith and Glapwell Collieries between 1877 and 1880. Referred to as the "jewel in the crown" for the Sheepbridge Company, rights to work coal were purchased to the west of Whaley village, from the Earl of Bathurst. Costing £46,000 to develop it was capable of producing 500 tons of coal per week initially. The colliery was connected to the MR line and to the LD&ECR line between Langwith Junction and Beighton, which ran parallel to the MR in the Creswell area.

Sinking commenced of the 14-foot diameter No. 1 shaft in March 1876 and reached the 5-foot 10-inch thick Top Hard seam at 565 yards on 9 February 1878. No. 2 shaft reached the Top Hard on 1 June 1878 at a depth of 538 yards. By 1896 under the management of John Bennett, 1,044 men were employed underground working the Top Hard seam, with 240 on the surface. Tuesday 18 December 1921 saw 2,476 tons of coal turned in two seven-hour shifts, a record output for the colliery at the time and possibly a record for the Nottinghamshire/Derbyshire Coalfield.

Modernisation started in the 1950s, with coal faces mechanised and Langwith became the first colliery in the country to operate a Rapid Loading Bunker (RLB). Erected in 1967 by J. G. Jenkins Ltd of Retford, a train of MGR wagons could be loaded in 20 minutes.

Welbeck Colliery branch

Welbeck Colliery was sunk in 1915 and was accessed via a branch from the LD&ECR (by then GCR) at Welbeck Colliery Junction;

the Midland Railway never proposing to build a branch to the colliery. This was rectified in 1925 when the LMS proposed to build a branch which was authorised as part of the LMS Act of 30 June 1926. The act authorised the following work:

Welbeck Colliery Branch 3 miles 22 chains commencing in Urban District of Warsop, junction with Mansfield and Worksop railway, 1 chain north of the Chesterfield and Lincoln railway bridge of LNER, terminating in Parish of Cuckney in Welbeck Colliery Yard, junction with end of Colliery empty wagon siding.

The contract was awarded to Messrs Mitchell for a cost of £63,000 to be completed by December 1928, the trackwork was indeed laid by December 1928 and the branch was opened for traffic on 3 January 1929.

Warsop Main

In 1893 the Staveley Coal & Iron Co. leased land from the Fitzherbert's Estate some two miles south of Langwith for a 99-year period, to sink a coal mine. The success of the Langwith mine working of the prolific Top Hard Seam led them to begin sinking Warsop Main Colliery which began producing coal in 1895 and proved to be a very successful enterprise by also exploiting the Top Hard Seam. Warsop Main was accessed via a branch which ran from a connection just south of Shirebrook Station, controlled by Shirebrook Station signal box, skirting the east side of the goods shed and then curving round to the colliery. Empty sidings were arranged alongside the branch, which also had a connection from the LD&ECR line at Warsop Junction.

Shirebrook

The Shirebrook Colliery Company began sinking twin 19-foot diameter shafts for their colliery in 1895–6, and the Top Hard Seam was reached a year later at a depth of about 600 yards. By 1909 the Shirebrook Colliery Company was exporting coal to France, Russia, Italy, Spain, Germany, Norway and Sweden, the coal leaving via one of two rail connections. The colliery had connections to the MR line to the south of Shirebrook Station, and also the Great Northern Railway Leen Valley extension line at the other side of the town.

Pithead baths made the miners lives easier when they opened in 1932, and new steel lattice headgear replaced the wooden ones in 1933. Coal seams worked at Shirebrook were the Top Hard, Main Hard, Main Bright, Deep Soft, Piper, Blackshale and Tupton.

Sherwood Colliery

In 1901 a tender for the sinking of two shafts for the Sherwood Colliery Company was submitted by mining contractors Charles Walker and John F. Eaton, with operations at the new site commencing on Whit Tuesday 1901. Sinking operations began with a formal opening ceremony performed on Monday 10 February 1902 with the first coal being reached in September of 1902. The 20-foot diameter shafts would have to sink much further to reach the main coal seams and it would not be until 1903, one year after operations had begun, that the Top Hard coal seam measuring more than five feet in depth was found 430 yards down. An area of land adjacent to the MR line was cleared for sidings, with signal boxes and connections at both ends to allow traffic to travel north or south.

Sherwood Colliery Sidings South signal box had a 28-lever MR Tumbler frame and opened on 25 October 1903 in connection with the new colliery and at the same time shortening the absolute block section between Mansfield Station North and Mansfield Woodhouse signal boxes. Sherwood Colliery Sidings North opened slightly later on 28 August 1904.

Colliery workers' platforms

Two colliery platforms were erected along the main line, the first was at Langwith Colliery when on 8 August 1894 the Works and Ways Committee approved the building of the station, with the Sheepbridge Coal Company contributing £200 of the £400 it would cost to build, the Company giving free access to the site. The first mention of the station was in the WTT dated 1 January 1895. The second platform to be built was Shirebrook Colliery Platform, a single platform located on the Up line just north of the colliery branch junction, this making its first appearance in the WTT of 1 July 1911.

Above: A contemporary postcard showing the collieries at Langwith, Norwood and Glapwell, all of which had Midland Railway connections. ***(Author's collection)***

Steetley Colliery

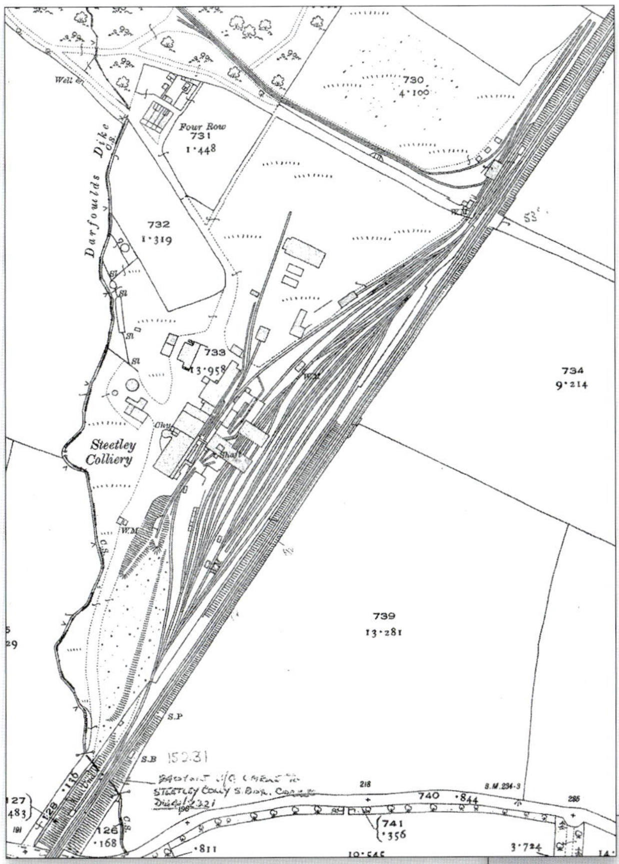

Above: To allow egress from the colliery and quarry towards Woodend Junction, this small Ground Frame was provided, released from Steetley Colliery Sidings 'box. This view is from the brakevan of a train after departing the colliery and heading towards Worksop. The Shunter has just replaced the points back to normal and is about to walk back to the colliery. ***(Author's collection)***

Left: Map of Steetley Colliery and connections dated 1922; Steetley Colliery Sidings signal box is at the south end of the colliery complex. The line diverging top left to top right is the access to the Steetley Quarry complex; the colliery and quarry shared the sidings to the north of the colliery. ***(Author's collection)***

Right: The view from Steetley Colliery Sidings 'box on 28 August 1981 as an unidentified Class 47 passes with an empty wagon set for one of the North Notts collieries. Steetley Colliery has a mix of HAA and 16-ton mineral wagons on view; the colliery was one of a number never set up for MGR operation – instead the internal diesel loco shunted wagons into trains ready for the main line loco to collect. Main line engines would either bring in a new set of wagons for loading, or run "light" from Worksop or Shirebrook, then take out a loaded set. ***(Richard Paget)***

Above: A view of the colliery across the wheat fields from Darfoulds. Steetley Colliery Sidings 'box is just out of view to the left. After the colliery amalgamated with Shireoaks it was closed in 1983, and soon demolished. ***(Author's collection)***

Above: Peckett 0-4-0ST Works No. 2043 of 1943, No. 9 "Steetley", seen performing shunting duties amongst HAA wagons during 1974. ***(Richard Paget)***

Above: D2607 arrived at Steetley in February 1974, it was out of use by August 1983, and was scrapped on site by Coopers Metals on 12 June 1984. ***(Author)***

Above & right: During the wars, in many industries women commonly took on roles left by men sent away fighting – and the railways were no different. Signalwoman Edna Molesworth (nee Gardner) stands on the 'box steps and on the verandah. She commenced duties at the signal box on 4 May 1944 and worked 9am to 5pm, 6 days a week. ***(Both Edna Molesworth/Frankie Spowart collection)***

Left: Steetley Colliery Sidings on 25 October 1969. ***(M.A.King)***

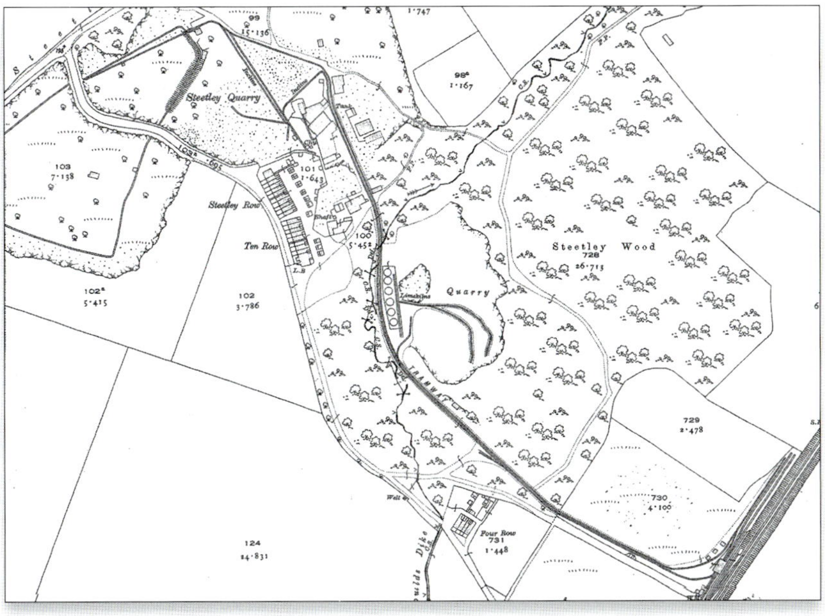

Steetley Quarry

Left: Map of the Steetley Quarry complex, dated 1922; the main line is at bottom right. Dolomite was quarried here long before the railway era, but in 1885 the quarry was bought by Mr Isaac Sharples to form the "Steetley Lime and Building Stone Company". In 1888, plant was installed to produce Doloma used for furnace linings, and the rail connection dated from between 1884 and 1899. By the latter date a standard gauge track ran north-west from the main line immediately north of Steetley Colliery to lime kilns in Steetley Wood and onto the quarry plant, where short narrow gauge lines ran north-east into the quarry. By 1914 a new quarry opened east of the lime kilns, also with narrow gauge track. Experimental work started in 1915 to produce stabilised dolomite bricks (known as dolofer suitable for the steel industry), leading in 1937 to the setting up of the "Refactory Brick Company of England". By 1951 the whole of the wood had been quarried and standard gauge track was in place around the perimeter of the works, with shunting carried out by a steam loco. Rail traffic ceased at the brickworks around 1957, and the loco was transferred to the quarries division until rail traffic ceased there too. The quarry was closed in 1960 and the raw materials were subsequently supplied from the nearby Whitwell Quarry and works. The workings were known as Steetley Lime & Basic until 1944, and then became Steetley Co. Ltd until 1958, after which it became Oughtibridge Silica Firebrick Co. Ltd. Notice the rows of houses for the workers, which were known as Steetley Row and Ten Row. ***(Ray Richardson/ Author's collection)***

Below: The Steetley complex from the air. The main line is top right, with the quarry railway curving around behind the tower building. Steetley Row and Ten Row are at the bottom of the image. ***(Author's collection)***

Below left: Hawthorne Leslie 0-4-0ST "Hebe", Works No. 3368 of 1919, came straight from the builders to the quarry in that year. It served there until its demise in 1960.

Above right: Yorkshire Engine Co. 0-4-0ST "June", Works No. 2407 of 1942, was also new to the quarry. Both locos were scrapped in June 1960. ***(Both Ray Richardson/Author's collection)***

Creswell Colliery

Above: Creswell Colliery empty sidings area with a selection of Private Owner wagons in evidence. These include from the left, Co-operative Wholesale Society London Branch, H. Bolden Forest Gate London, M Hannon & Co. Stratford London and an LD&ECR wagon. The LD&ECR had their own connection into the colliery from their Langwith Junction to Beighton line.

Left: As viewed from Colliery Road overbridge, looking south-west on 16 August 1961, Creswell Colliery is seen with a rake of 16-ton wagons in what was then the Up lay-by siding, with access via a ground frame at the south end. In 1969 a new coal preparation plant was built at the colliery and on 13 February 1977 a Rapid Loading Bunker (RLB) was commissioned to improve the speed of loading coal into wagons. This siding then became part of the Bunker Line. ***(Both Author's collection)***

Left: With Creswell Colliery in the distance, 58002 passes the site of Creswell Sidings (on the right), on 25 January 1987. The RLB stands out on the extreme left. ***(Richard Paget)***

Below: A selection of wagon labels from Creswell Colliery, the one on the right being pre-nationalisation for Fairford via Bordesley, the consignee being Paul & Co. and the commodity 6 tons of cobbles. ***(Author's collection)***

Date 26 OCT
Sender - NATIONAL COAL BOARD
East Midlands Division - No. 1 Area
FROM
CRESWELL COLLIERY
A/c of
TO P/S FLETTON
L N E Railway G N Section
Via Tuxford
T C
Weight
Owner and No. of Wagon 5696
Description
Hazel Washed Singles
Consignee:
British Sugar Corporation
1

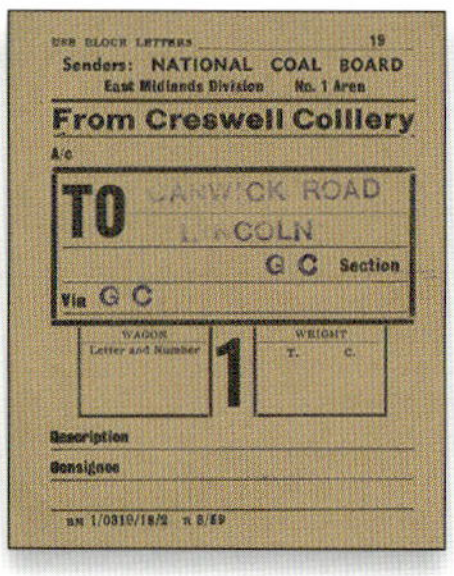
USE BLOCK LETTERS 19
Senders: NATIONAL COAL BOARD
East Midlands Division No. 1 Area
From Creswell Colliery
A/c
TO CANWICK ROAD LINCOLN
G C Section
Via G C
WAGON Letter and Number
1
WEIGHT T. C.
Description
Consignee
RM 1/0810/18/2 R 8/59

Date
Sender: NATIONAL COAL BOARD
East Midlands Division No. 1 Area
FROM
CRESWELL COLLIERY
A/c
TO Chelmsford
G E Sec'n
Via Lincoln & March
T C
Weight
Owner and No. of Wagon
Description
Consignee
RM 1/0672/4 R 6/55
1

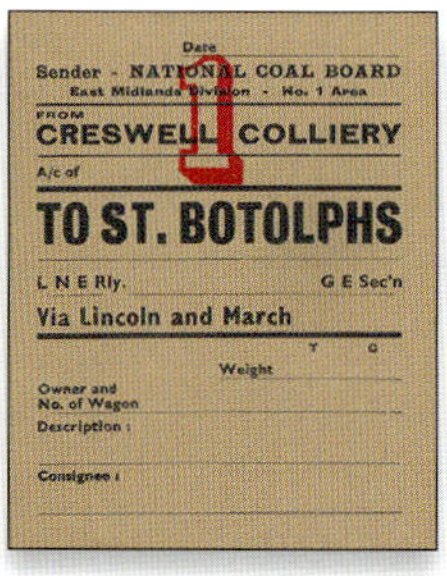
Date
Sender - NATIONAL COAL BOARD
East Midlands Division - No. 1 Area
FROM
CRESWELL COLLIERY
A/c of
TO ST. BOTOLPHS
L N E Rly. G E Sec'n
Via Lincoln and March
T C
Weight
Owner and No. of Wagon
Description:
Consignee:
1

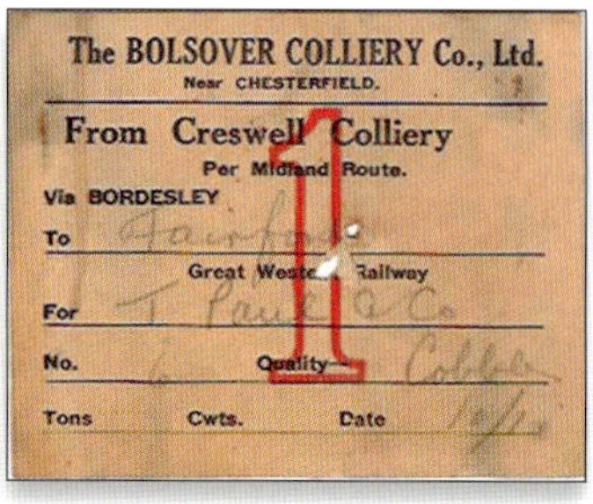
The BOLSOVER COLLIERY Co., Ltd.
Near CHESTERFIELD.
From Creswell Colliery
Per Midland Route.
Via BORDESLEY
To Fairford
Great Western Railway
For T Paul & Co
No. 6 Quality Cobbles
Tons Cwts. Date
1

Right: The former Up Lay-By siding on the left is now the Bunker Line and here is 58002 passing Creswell Colliery with a train of black gold from one of the Notts collieries, to West Burton or Cottam Power Station. ***(Author's collection)***

Right: A great view of the bunker and colliery from the colliery spoil heap. Here 56020 is setting back beneath the RLB as it is loaded on 18 June 1980. The method of working here was the train would be drawn through the RLB on to the head shunt, to take the tare weight of the wagons. It was then propelled back to load and once complete, if the train was to head north the engine would detach, then run round to the other end via the Up Main. If it was heading south it would depart the bunker line via No. 38 points. (See the Elmton & Creswell 'box diagram) ***(John Vaughan/Author's collection)***

Left: Creswell Colliery ceased production in 1992 and by spring the coal preparation plant and RLB had already been demolished. Passing the part demolished bunker on Sunday 28 June 1992, are 20057+20154 at the rear (with 20059 + 20168 leading). "The Worksop Whistler", which was run by the Worksop Open Day Committee, ran from Derby to Derby via coal mines in the Derbyshire/Nottinghamshire area, including Bolsover, Welbeck, Bilsthorpe and Bevercotes Collieries, and High Marnham Power Station. ***(Author's collection)***

Right: After the closure of Worksop Yard, as discussed in Volume 1, it began to be used for the storage of new and off-lease rolling stock. Here 47727 "Edinburgh Castle/Caisteal Dhun Eideann" and 47749 "City Of Truro" top and tail new 720519 past the site of the RLB as 5Q11 09.49 Derby Adtranz Litchurch Lane to Worksop Down Yard on 18 February 2020. Creswell Colliery has gone and coal trains along the route are now a thing of the past. ***(Author)***

Langwith Colliery

Right: A postcard of Langwith Colliery. ***(Author's collection)***

Right & below: Langwith Colliery's Coking By-Products Works would be built on land opposite the colliery, and this would also become the site of His Majesty's Explosive Factory–Langwith during World War I. In 1915 the government decided that the nation needed to produce its own supplies of the explosives accelerant ammonium perchlorate, relying up to that time on imported chemicals from either France or Sweden. France no longer had surplus production, given its own war efforts, and importation from Sweden ran additional risks from Germany's U-Boat fleet. Britain thus agreed with the Swedish suppliers to produce the chemical under licence in a new factory in the UK. As the process of manufacture was energy hungry an economic supply was necessary. This lead to the siting of the new factory on a plot of 27 acres of land, immediately north of Langwith Colliery's Coking By-Products Works. The By-Products Works generated a waste stream of producer gas that could be used to fire steam-driven electrical generating turbines, and also made ammonium sulphate, which could be used in the production of ammonium perchlorate. Construction commenced in November 1915, part opening in 1916, the remainder in 1917. The site was operated by the adjacent Langwith By-Product Company Limited and apart from several sidings had its own dedicated halt on the main line. After the Armistice production at Langwith was rapidly wound down, ceasing totally in 1919. Most of the site's staff had left by 1920 and from 1921 to 1927 the site remained empty. It was finally purchased by auction in 1927 by the Sheepbridge Company, who demolished the works in 1928. (Source: https://war-work.com/his-majestys-explosive-factory-langwith/) ***(Both Neil Baker collection)***

Left: Wagon No. 8343, a 7-Plank Sheepbridge Coal & Iron Co. private owner wagon, built by Charles Roberts of Wakefield. Its livery was red, with black strapping and white shaded lettering. ***(HMRS)***

Left: Langwith Colliery Sidings as seen looking north on 24 January 1971. The MR had provided a 'box here entitled Langwith Colliery Sidings before October 1876, but it was renamed Langwith Colliery Sidings North c1880. They replaced it with this one on 31 January 1897, the name reverting to Langwith Colliery Sidings on 22 March 1942. The bridge in the distance carries the former LD&ECR line from their Langwith to Beighton route, into Langwith Colliery. The 'box had a 14-lever frame, numbered 1-12 and "A" & "B". ***(Mike King)***

Right: Langwith Colliery Sidings diagram. The 1-in-80 and 1-in-100 gradients of the LD&ECR route from Langwith Junction to the summit at Clowne ensured engines had to work hard, and loaded trains would often struggle. The subsequent increase in MGR train weights made things no better, but with the construction of the M1 Motorway proceeding northwards in the mid-1960s, progress got to a point where it would have crossed the Beighton Branch at Barlborough thus necessitating a bridge. To avoid the expense of this the Ministry of Transport paid for the construction of a new double track chord from the LD&ECR Beighton Branch to the former MR lines just to the north of Langwith Colliery Junction, where the lines ran parallel in the vicinity of Norwood Crossings. Controlled by Langwith Colliery Sidings and Langwith Colliery Junction, its counterpart on the LD&ECR side, this new route opened as of 9 January 1967 and allowed trains to travel along the easily graded couple of miles of the Beighton Branch then cross to the ex-MR line and head for Worksop. ***(Mike King)***

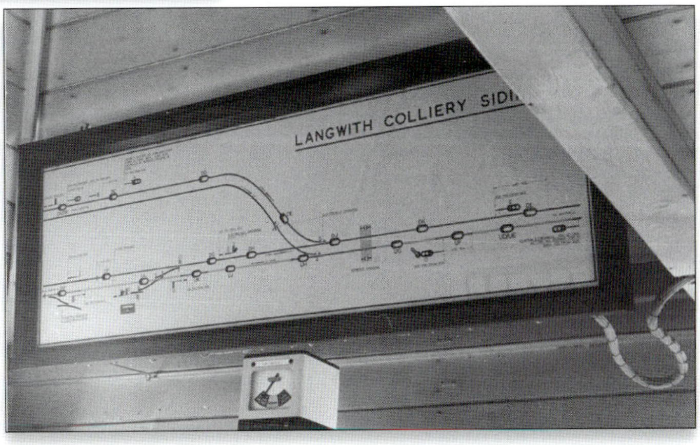

Right: The chord can be seen on the diagram, and in the photo, Norwood Crossing is in the distance. ***(Derek Talbot)***

Below right: Langwith Colliery Sidings South, although it doesn't state such on the name board. The first 'box here was opened between 1880 and 1881, but was superseded by this one, which opened on 16 December 1894. This 'box closed on 22 March 1942, Langwith Colliery Sidings North 'box then losing its North suffix. The object on the post is an elevated ground disc, one of the type which turned through 90 degrees between "On" and "Off". The 'box was situated adjacent to the colliery station, the footbridge giving access to the Down platform. A report in the Mansfield Courier on Saturday 17 November 1894 stated: Railway Improvements. - A new station has been erected by the Midland Railway Company adjacent to the Langwith Colliery, and was formally opened on Wednesday. The station, for the present, will be for the accommodation of workmen who travel by train between Mansfield and Langwith. The new station will be a great convenience to the men. ***(Author's collection)***

Warsop Colliery

Right: In 1893 the Staveley Coal & Iron Co. leased land from the Fitzherbert's Estate to sink Warsop Main coal mine. Production began in 1895 and proved to be very successful by exploiting the Top Hard Seam. In 1935 it was one of the most proficient mines in the country, employing some 2,500 and producing a weekly output of around 21,000 tons of saleable coal. 1953 saw the mine reorganised, including tower-mounted, electrically-powered winding systems; this was completed by 1960. In 1985, following a cost-cutting exercise which resulted in 200 job losses, the then-manager Mr P. Goodwin announced that the pit's future was secure. By 1989, however, the colliery was reportedly losing £200,000 a week and faced closure. The last shifts were worked around 25 August 1989; demolition started on 25 September and the second headgear was toppled on 28 November 1989. ***(Author's collection)***

Right: Photo of a shipment of coal departing Warsop Main sometime between 1915 and 1918, possibly bound for Admiral Jellico's fleet at Scapa Flow to help in the war effort. The loco looks like a Deeley 2736 Class 0-6-0 built in 1905/6. The lettering on the Staveley wagons is clean and new-looking on every wagon, so it is probable they have been painted specifically for this publicity shot. The top line of lettering most likely says STAVELEY Coal & Iron Co. Ltd, with the wagon fleet number in the bottom left hand corner. There looks to be about thirty visible wagons, each carrying ten tons of coal with the tare of each wagon being around the six ton mark. ***(Author's collection)***

Train of Staveley coal ready for dispatch from Warsop Main Colliery.

Right: The new order at Warsop Main as 47314 departs with a loaded MGR train for one of the power stations in 1978. These wagons hold 32 tons of the black stuff. ***(Anthony Guppy collection)***

Below: 56075 brings a rake of loaded HEAs from Warsop Main Colliery beneath the LD&ECR line; Warsop Junction signal box is just above the loco. The former LD&ECR sidings and colliery connection was on the right at a higher level, with a connection to the former MR line just in front of the loco. The LD&ECR connection closed in 1976, all traffic then departing via this MR connection which ran behind Shirebrook Diesel depot to connect with the main line at Shirebrook. ***(Ivan Stewart collection)***

Shirebrook Colliery

Above: Sinking of the twin shafts for Shirebrook Colliery took place in 1895-96 by the Shirebrook Colliery Company. In this view c1908, the twin headstocks are prominent. By this time the manager was Mr. L.O. Roberts who oversaw the 1,345 men employed underground and 282 on the surface.

Right: A 1930s view, taken from Wood Lane Bridge of the "Full" sidings at the colliery with a mixture of LMS and Shirebrook Colliery Ltd wagons. Notice the aerial ropeway taking spoil to the tip.

Left: Shirebrook Colliery No. 271, a 5-plank wagon built by Hurst Nelson of Motherwell, is seen when new.

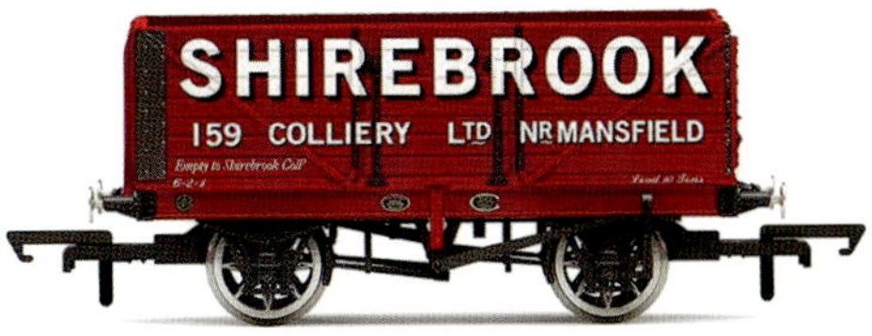

Above right: This 00 gauge model illustrates the wagons' bright red with white (shaded black) lettering. ***(All Author's collection)***

Above: After arriving from the north and running round in Shirebrook Sidings on 14 February 1991, 58034 "Bassetlaw" is now entering the colliery. ***(Dave Peachey)***

Left: Looking north from near the Down Main connection on 25 July 1992, the colliery approach tracks are seen with the tall Rapid Loading Bunker (RLB) structure to the right. The colliery had closed on 25 May 1991, and all connections to the former bunker line removed by 22 May 1994. The bridge was known locally as "Red Bridge", and the legend "SHIREBROOK COLLIERY • BEST COAL • STEAM • FURNACE • HOUSE" in large letters was once emblazoned across it. ***(Andrew K. Overton)***

Left: On 26 August 1988, 7G64 for West Burton Power Station is being loaded beneath the RLB. Having run to the far end of the line, it now propels back during loading. The 2,500 ton capacity bunker was built by Babcock Engineering, and the signalling commissioned in May 1968. The yellow internal shunting loco is DL15, a Hudswell Clark 0-4-0 Diesel Hydraulic Works No. D1344 built in 1965. ***(Robin Stewart-Smith)***

Above: The Institute of Mining Engineers ran several tours and here is the one they ran on 26 November 1989, entitled the "North Midland Railtour". This took in collieries and branch lines in the area, the collieries visited on this occasion being Bentinck, Shirebrook, Thoresby, Rufford, Mansfield, Clipstone, Bolsover and Avenue Carbonisation Plant. It is seen here at Shirebrook Colliery, where it was booked to arrive at 10.37 and depart at 10.42; however, actual times were 11.00½ to 11.11½ ***(Info www.sixbellsjunction.co.uk, photo Robin Stewart-Smith)***

Left: As viewed from the colliery spoil heap on 12 March 1993, Trainload Coal livery 56114 "Maltby Colliery" has just come beneath the bunker and is heading towards the buffer stops. The train will form the 10.41 to Cottam Power Station. Back in the 1990s it was not unusual for photographers to gain access to collieries to take photographs, a set of steel toecap boots, a high visibility vest and a hard hat were all that was required, free reign then usually being granted, something that today's Health & Safety would frown upon. On this day the photographer gained height by scrambling up the spoil heap without incident, and in doing so allowed us a glimpse into the inner workings of the colliery. ***(Antony Guppy)***

Sherwood Colliery

Above: Sherwood Colliery c1930. Coal was first mined here from the Top Hard seam at in 1903, followed by the Dunsil seam in 1916. Between them, these two seams kept the pit working until the mid-1950s. A drift from the Top Hard gained access to the reserves of the Deep Soft, being completed just as the Dunsil seam was worked out in 1957. By 1959 the Top Hard was exhausted, and it would be ten years before the Deep Hard was reached in 1969; this and the Piper seams were worked as one when possible. The Deep Soft was exhausted by 1977, and production switched to the Yard seam and the Blackshale reserves in 1984.

Above: Sherwood was the last pit in the old North Nottinghamshire Area to use steam winding gear, the boiler house and chimney being prominent here in this colourised postcard. ***(Both Author's collection)***

Right: A similar viewpoint in the 1970s, when the colliery was part of the NCB North Nottinghamshire Area. *(Ash Edwards)*

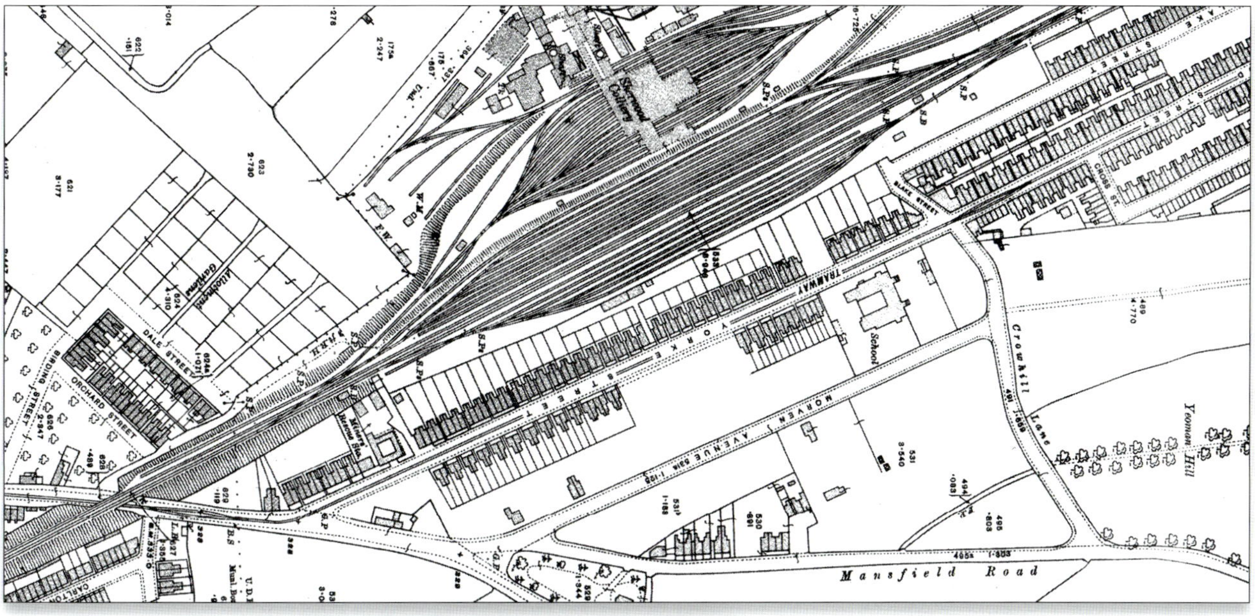

Above: A 1914 map of the colliery complex, which also shows the location of two of the signal boxes. Starting from the top, Sherwood Colliery Sidings North is annotated S.B. and is just to the left of Blake Street. Sherwood Colliery Sidings South is adjacent to the Miners Rescue Station at the end of Yorke Street. Sherwood Colliery Sidings were brought into use in 1903 and new Down Sidings added in June 1938. The Empty Wagon Sidings and Down Lie-by were taken out of use on 12 February 1987. Between Sherwood Colliery Sidings South and North, the colliery running line and three running round sidings were brought into use on 31 October 1904. See later for details of the 'box that controlled these. ***(Author's collection)***

Above left: The map also shows a tramway running along Yorke Street, one of the routes of the Mansfield & District Light Railway which operated an electric tramway in Mansfield from 16 July 1905 to 9 October 1932. Top-covered Car No. 13, built by Brush Electrical Engineering Co. of Loughborough, is seen at the High Street Mansfield Woodhouse Terminus in 1907.

Above: Tram No. 3 is seen about 100 yards short of the Nottingham Road/Berry Hill Lane Terminus. The houses in the background are on High Oakham Road. ***(Both John Law collection)***

Right: Peckett 0-6-0ST Works No. 1678, Sherwood No. 4. Purchased new for Sherwood Colliery Ltd in 1927 and seen at the colliery on 19 May 1959. It was withdrawn in August 1969 and scrapped in April 1970. ***(RCTS FA14162 Collection Jack Faithfull)***

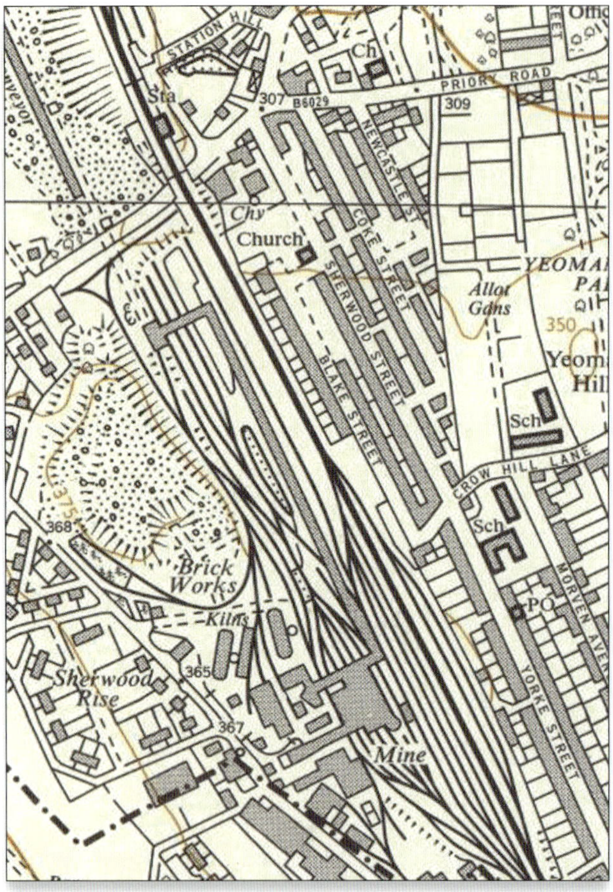

Left: A later map of the colliery complex, showing details further north. The road coming in almost centre left and passing beneath the railway is Debdale Road. Adjacent to this is a turning triangle in the track layout; north of this, crossing Debdale Road, is a conveyor system for moving spoil onto the colliery tip. Adjacent to the conveyor was an aerial ropeway; both systems can be seen in the image below. ***(Reproduced courtesy of the National Library of Scotland)***

Above: The ropeway and conveyor system can be seen here. The wagons are on the right-hand curve of the turning triangle; the newly-built wall beyond borders Debdale Road. Once a common feature of colliery spoil heaps, aerial ropeways have all but disappeared. Indeed, the sole remaining working example in England is the Claughton Aerial Ropeway, built in 1924 to bring shale from a quarry on Claughton Moor, approximately 1¼ mile distant from – and 750ft above – Hanson Brick Works. ***(Author's collection)***

USE BLOCK LETTERS 19 MAY 1960 19
Sender: NATIONAL COAL BOARD
East Midlands Division No. 3 Area
From SHERWOOD COLLIERY
A/c
TO P/S EASTCROFT LONDON RD GN
MID.
Via KIRKBY BEESTON
WAGON Letter and Number 60757
1
WEIGHT T. C. 10 8
Description WASHED DEEP SOFT DOUBLES
Consignee NOTTM GAS WKS
RM 5/3/RC961 R 10/58

Right: Wagon label for coal from Sherwood Colliery for Nottingham Gas Works, ***(Author's collection)***

Above left & left: In photographic grey livery with black shaded lettering, here is Motherwell-based, Hurst-Nelson & Company built wagon No. 1044 dating from 1907. The model version of the wagons shows the bright red livery. ***(HMRS Collection/Author's collection)***

Left: Sherwood 7-plank wagon No. 575 painted in red with black (shaded white) lettering, with a capacity of 10 tons. Poor coal load distribution is evident in this 1943 photograph in Charles Roberts yard in Wakefield. The lettering bottom right says: Return empty/Repairs advise} Sherwood Colliery. Just above the number 575 is a spring-loaded wagon label holder, where labels of the sort shown above were attached to the wagons to show the coal destination and consignee. ***(HMRS collection)***

Above: The 28-lever Sherwood Colliery Sidings North 'box opened on 28 August 1904, and is seen on 2 July 1966. Because of its position between the main line and the Up Sidings and the resulting limited space, the base is narrower than the operating floor. The 'box closed on 17 November 1968 and was replaced by a Ground Frame (GF). The houses behind are on Blake Street, Mansfield Woodhouse. ***(Malcolm Rush)***

Above: Sherwood Colliery Sidings South also had a 28-lever frame but was of conventional Type 3a design, opened almost a year earlier on 25 October 1903, and is seen on 3 January 1986. Between North and South 'boxes there was another box entitled Sherwood Colliery Sidings, which opened in 1904. It was renamed Sherwood Sidings on 12 October 1929, and was replaced by Sherwood Sidings No. 1 GF on 14 June 1938. ***(Robin Stewart-Smith)***

Below: Looking south from the colliery access towards the signal box. The signals showing "Off" are (top) Sherwood Colliery Sidings South Home and (bottom) Sherwood Colliery Sidings North Distant. ***(Author's collection)***

Right: The 28-lever frame inside Sherwood Colliery Sidings South on 11 February 1979. Closure came on 24 January 1988, with replacement by a 3-lever London and North Western Railway SK.446 ground frame entitled "Sherwood Colly GF (South)". It was released by Sutton Junction signal box which, by then, was the next box south. According to one source the GF was never a success and was prone to failure, resulting in numerous callouts for the Area Movements Inspector. ***(Malcolm Rush)***

Left: Two views on 28 September 1979 from Sherwood Colliery Sidings South signal box. 56028 arrives as 6F66 with empty wagons from Cottam Power Station. The train is passing No. 27 signal, to the right of which are the former Up Carriage Sidings which clearly have not been used in some time.

Right: Having passed the 'box, the train has set back through No. 7 and No. 9 points and is propelling the wagons along the Running Line. It looks like the steam winder is still in operation? ***(Both Malcolm Rush)***

Below: Monday 11 April 1983 saw a revised method of working brought into use, from a new concrete pad for loading adjacent to the former running line. Here 58034 "Bassetlaw" takes the signal for the shunting neck during loading in the summer of 1986. Notice that the colliery chimney has gone. ***(Phil Sangwell)***

Right: Trainman Roland Lennox operates the 3-lever London and North Western Railway Sherwood Colliery GF (South), which replaced Sherwood Colliery Sidings South 'box. Once the train had departed for Toton the GF was thus redundant. That footboard looks particularly slippery with the frost – Roland would have had to watch his footing!

Left: The colliery despatched its final train destined for Ratcliffe Power Station on Saturday 1 February 1992, behind 58050. It was given a suitable send-off with the loco carrying a homemade headboard to commemorate 90 years of the colliery, made and supplied by Sherwood colliery employee Mel Smith who is seen on the far right. Others identified in the photo are the Shirebrook-based crew Driver Dave Connolly and Trainman Roland Lennox (both centre with hi-vis bib vests), ex-Sherwood Colliery Surveyor Robert Quincey who had just transferred to Calverton Colliery (far left), and both of his sons at the front in matching jackets. ***(Both Diminsdale Freight collection)***

Chapter 3

Branch lines Seymour to Creswell via Clowne

The 5¾ mile single line between Seymour Junction, Clowne and Creswell was completed by late 1871. However, it would not be opened throughout until 1 June 1875 when the Worksop line opened. Initially the only traffic to use it was coal from Barlborough Colliery, but the branch would also serve Oxcroft and Southgate Collieries. Steeply graded from both ends to its summit at Clowne the route was cut through limestone which required deep cuttings, but there were no tunnels.

The Derbyshire Times and Chesterfield Herald for Saturday 7 October 1871 made the following comment:

The Staveley Branch of the Mansfield and Worksop Railway (Midland) was completed last week. It is not expected to be opened before the completion of the whole line of rails, about two years hence. There has been one sale of wood, &c, and another is expected shortly. 4,000 or 5,000 men have been employed in all, and about 400 at one time. No fatal injuries have taken place in connection with its construction. There are about 20 bridges, 4 under and 1 over the line. Viaducts are erected over the Wood Croft Valley, near Clowne, 70 feet high and 10 chains long. There is large culvert near Seymour Colliery, and numerous other smaller ones at different parts of the line. About 40 horses, 100 waggons, two locomotives, and two portable engines have been employed in the construction of the line. The branch is about five miles long, and was commenced about two years since. The contractor is Joseph Firbanks, Esq., Peckham.

Passenger traffic along the Clowne Branch

It was to be a long 13 years before passenger traffic commenced between Mansfield and Chesterfield via Elmton & Creswell, on 1 November 1888. There would be one station at Clown, the town having adopted many names over its 1000 year history. It all began with "Clun", which is thought to be a Celtic word meaning "spring", relating to the abundance of life-giving natural springs located in and around the town. It has also been known through the years as Clune, Clon, Clouen, Clown and latterly Clowne, with added "e". The station would be renamed Clowne and Barlborough by British Railways in 1951.

The Derbyshire Times and Chesterfield Herald of Saturday 3 November 1888 reporting on the opening to passengers:

THE CHESTERFIELD AND CLOWNE BRANCH OF THE MIDLAND RAILWAY. TRIP BY THE FIRST PASSENGER TRAIN.

As previously chronicled by us, the branch of the Midland Railway has recently been finished. Although it has been used for mineral traffic for several months, the Board of Trade inspection was not completed until few weeks ago. Last Friday several of the officials of the Railway went over the line, but the first passenger train over the new line left Chesterfield at 8.40 on Thursday morning, being accompanied by Mr. Loveday, Chief traffic inspector, and number of subordinate officials. The engine was bedecked with a garland and at various points along the route large numbers of persons had congregated. The train, which consisted of 14 carriages left Chesterfield platform a few minutes late, with a large number of persons aboard. It proceeded along the old Chesterfield line passing the station of Whittington, Staveley station, has been enlarged to suit the requirements of the new line which by the way is a single one. Just after leaving this station, and close to Staveley Iron Works the new line branches away from the old, and continues its single course through a somewhat deep cutting for some distance until it reaches a descent of 1-in-66.

*Having passed under a bridge, over which the road is carried, the line begins to rise. Staveley Church is passed on the left, and the Staveley Co.'s Hartington Colliery on the right. (*either this reporter was sat with his back to travel, or got his left and right mixed up, as the colliery was on the left – author*) Under another bridge, over which a road goes, and then the line crosses the Chesterfield and Stockwith Canal. Up another incline and the station of Netherthorpe is reached. This is single line station, and is placed on the right hand side of the rails. The buildings are commodious and look more than adequate to serve the population of the place.*

*Having passed the fan of sidings for the Seymour pit on the right hand side, the line leaves the Ireland Colliery Branch on the left (Right), and crosses a stream by means massive girder bridge (*here he has misquoted as the line passes Ireland Colliery first, then the fan of sidings for Seymour*). Leaving the Seymour Colliery branch on the left hand line proceeds on shortly afterwards diverting from the unfinished line to Glapwell, etc, which branches off to the left (Right) hand side at right angle, then a gradual ascent until Seymour Colliery is passed the left, and then a steep incline follows.*

The road leading from Woodthorpe to Bolsover is crossed on the level and Bank House Farm is next on the right. Soon afterwards a deep wide gorge is crossed by means of steep embankment. The Staveley Company's Barlborough Pit is passed at an incline of 1-in-60. After going through deep rock cutting a descent is apparent until the station of Clown, where a great number of persons had assembled.

Leaving Clowne, the descent continued. A deep rock cutting is passed through, and a stream traversed, after which away to the left are the sidings leading up to the Shireoaks Company Pit (Southgate Colliery). Immediately afterwards the station of Elmton and Creswell is ran into, which is on the old line. Here three carriages are added to the train, and it proceeds through a flat Country for some time, with few houses, until the Langwith Colliery is reached on the left, followed by the station of Langwith, where on the right hand side of the line are Mr. Samuel Barkitt's extensive malthouses.

A very deep cutting through the characteristic red sandstone is passed through, and the pretty station of Shirebrook is reached. The Station Master here has evidently a taste for horticulture as his late flowers testify to the mild climate hereabouts.

The line passes over a steep embankment and through another cutting and then joins the Teversall branch and Mansfield Woodhouse is reached and soon afterwards Mansfield, the destination of the train.

The journey has been accomplished without hitch, although the train is a few minutes late. The train as stated before was filled with passengers but this may be partly accounted for by it being market day at Mansfield and also no doubt some persons went out of curiosity. There is little doubt however that the line will be extensively used both ways and will be found very convenient to persons wishing to attend either Chesterfield or Mansfield markets.

A correspondent says: – The line cuts through a populous district, which has for many years suffered from inadequate railway accommodation. Besides giving a more direct route to Nottingham via Mansfield, easy access will thus be given to pleasure-seekers to Creswell Crags, the Dukeries and other places of interest in the vicinity. For the present there will be three trains in each direction daily. There will be an immense amount of goods traffic on the line, more particularly of minerals, the railway passes through the centre of coalfields belonging to the Duke of Portland, the Duke of Devonshire, Mr. W. P. Arkwright (Sutton Scarsdale), the executors of the late Mr. W. H. de Rhodes, &c, which are leased and worked chiefly by the Staveley Coal and Iron Company, the Shireoaks Colliery Company, &c. Seymour Junction extensions are being carried forward towards Bolsover, Sutton, Glapwell, &c, which will give a very direct route to Mansfield and Nottingham, it will be some time before this portion of the line is completed for passenger service, although a great amount of mineral and other traffic is at present being worked from Glapwell (which belongs to the Sheepbridge Coal and Iron Company) and the Company's Markham Collieries, to Staveley Station.

The collieries served along the branch

The Staveley Company sank Barlborough No. 1 Colliery in 1871, to a depth of 1,603 feet to get to the 64-inch-thick Deep Hard seam, which was used mainly for iron production at the company's works. By 1878, the complex was complete with railway sidings, washery and brick works. The colliery was purchased in 1930 by the Oxcroft Coal Company Ltd (formed in 1901 and a part of the Staveley Company "Empire") to develop the High Hazel seam. The MR's branch to Oxcroft Colliery No. 1 left the Clowne Branch near Woodthorpe, at Oxcroft Junction, and opened in September 1902. Barlborough No. 1 became known as Oxcroft No. 3 and continued working until 1946, when severe geological conditions and water problems severely affected production. Fortunately a new face was developed, which allowed the colliery to work until closure in 1949.

Southgate (or Clowne) Colliery was close by Clowne station and situated on the Southgate estate. Sinking by the Shireoaks Colliery Company began in 1877, the Top Hard seam was reached at 321 yards in March 1877 with the initial capacity for 120,000 tons annually. The LD&ECR Beighton Branch line was adjacent and their colliery sidings were brought into use on 10 May 1896, but as the colliery was also served by the MR line a connection between the two lines was brought into use on 16 November 1896.

On 17 January 1929 a massive in-rush of water from the temporarily abandoned Oxcroft Colliery finally forced the closure of Southgate. The LD&ECR/MR connecting line was closed on 25 April 1937 and in 1955 a scheme to reopen Southgate and connect with Creswell Colliery's workings was started, but never completed, the shafts being filled in 1961. Today the site is the Station Road Industrial Estate where a brick-built power house still remains in use by an engineering firm, albeit clad in pressed steel.

There were plans to sink drifts from the surface at the Oxcroft workings down to the Oxcroft No. 3 workings in order to extend its working life, although work commenced in 1938, it was suspended at the outbreak of the war. The drifts were completed by 1944, linking the Oxcroft No. 1 and No. 3 Collieries together. Winding of coal out of the Oxcroft No. 3 (formerly Barlborough No. 1) ceased in 1949, the production being brought to the surface via Oxcroft No. 5 drift and washed on the reconditioned plant of Oxcroft No. 1. So, while surface plants and shafts had closed at the former Barlborough No. 1, its coal take (i.e. the allocated area of coal allowed to be worked by individual collieries) was still being worked there well beyond 1949. Oxcroft No. 1 Colliery closed in 1974 with the line from Oxcroft Junction closing in February 1976; however, it reopened to serve the Oxcroft Opencast Disposal Point in 1980. The men were transferred to Markham and other local collieries.

End of the line

Passenger traffic was never heavy and would decline over the years, WW2 seeing the services over the Clowne line reduced to one train per day each way on weekdays. This had been timed to leave Chesterfield at 8.47am and run as far as Elmton & Creswell; however, during the school term it would then run as an unadvertised school service to Shirebrook. In that period, at the end of the school day on the return journey it left Shirebrook at 4.10pm, unadvertised as far as Elmton & Creswell, where it then formed the 4.30pm departure to Chesterfield. The normal Saturday trains were suspended in the late 1940s; however, a summer Saturdays only train ran from Elmton & Creswell to Blackpool; after the war this service then commenced from Radford near Nottingham. The weekdays only service between Chesterfield and Elmton & Creswell finally ended on 5 July 1954; however, it continued as a parcels only service until at least 19 September 1955.

Wikipedia claims that "the last train was operated, remarkably, by a brand new DMU" and gives a link to the source, which was the book Lost Railways of Derbyshire by Geoffrey Kingscott. In this there is a photo which purportedly shows the final scheduled train to call at the station, and is credited to David Chaplin whose family lived in the Station House. A sentence in the book states:

Regular passenger services were withdrawn in 1954 (David remembers the last train) but again excursions and football specials continued for a few more years.

The photo does indeed depict a new looking Cravens Class 105 DMU; however, these units did not enter service until 1956 so that photo couldn't be the final scheduled train. The author would surmise that the author of the book has miscomprehended the photo supplied by David, and this actually shows some sort of special service that traversed the line in the late 50s. This would make more sense, as the DMU is painted in original green with cream lining, sans "Speed whiskers", which had been applied by 1958.

The final steam hauled 7.50am Radford to Blackpool excursion over the branch was on 18 August 1962, it returned from Blackpool North to Radford, hauled by "Black 5" 4-6-0 45270.

The branch continued to be used for coal trains to Bolsover Coalite from Clipstone and Rufford Collieries until 1987, loaded MGR trains from the Seymour direction did not use the branch very often as they required banking due to the steep 1-in-66 up-hill gradient to Clowne. The final loaded train to be assisted over the branch was on Friday 20 January 1989, and light engine movements between Barrow Hill and Shirebrook Depot for fuel continued until 1991 when these depots closed.

The final special train from the Creswell direction to Seymour ran on Saturday 27 June 1992, this being the "Dukeries Collier" railtour top-and-tailed by 56024 & 20168+20059, and the final train to traverse the route did so on 22 April 1994 when 47676 "Northamptonshire" worked 2Z01 inspection special from Doncaster, via Seymour Junction and Elmton & Creswell to Clipstone. The line was officially severed on the Creswell side of Oxcroft Junction on 4 September 1996; however, traffic into Oxcroft Opencast Disposal Point (DP) continued until 2006.

The main function of the DP was the processing of coal during opencast mining of the immediate area; it began sending out trains of opencast coal in January 1980. Originally accessed via a GF on the Clowne line, following closure of this line onwards to Creswell the one-mile line between Seymour Junction and Oxcroft Junction remained open to serve the disposal point, a staff being collected from Seymour Junction box by each train into the plant.

In 1993 it was reported that the fall in coal traffic and the move to road had reduced the DP workings from about 40 trains each week to less than 15; however, even with this reduction trains did continue for another 13 years. It was announced locally that the last train of coal would run on 24 January 2006, running as 6K33 10.46 Worksop to Oxcroft, to form a train for West Burton. After coal traffic had ceased, the Branch Line Society's "Peterborough Re-Re-Avoider" railtour, which visited the site on 4 March 2006 behind 66061 and 66175, was thought by many to be the final train, but this was not to be the case.

There was a brief respite in the working life of Oxcroft DP when UK Coal commenced a coal recovery operation to sift through nearby pit tips, with the aim of recovering around 14,000 tonnes of coal (the National Coal Board having worked in metric tonnes from the 1970s onwards). However, in the almost two-year period that the line had been mothballed, Seymour Junction box had been heavily vandalised and fire damaged, and due to the theft and vandalism of almost all the signalling between Foxlow Junction (on the Old Road near Barrow Hill), Hall Lane Junction and Seymour Junction, a new method of train working had to be introduced. This took the form of Working by Pilotman from Barrow Hill to Oxcroft via Seymour. All the points were clamped and the signalling suspended. Trains ran from Barrow Hill via the Staveley Goods single line to Summit Junction, then on to the Down Seymour Goods line to Hall Lane Junction, crossing over via Sheffield PSB No. 4157 points at Hall Lane to run facing road on the Up Seymour Goods line all the way to Seymour Junction, then crossing over again via the former Seymour Junction No. 12 points on to the Oxcroft line. Return trains took the same route back to Barrow Hill.

Most of the recovered coal was removed by road but a very short term flow of trains began from the site on 20 November 2007 when 66186 arrived at Oxcroft with 6K06 07.03 from Worksop; this would form 7F92 11.30 for Cottam Power Station. The 21 November 2007 loaded train was hauled by 66115 as 7F92 11.30 to Cottam, and the very last train of all to leave the site would only be partially loaded. This ran on Thursday 6 December 2007, being hauled by 66126, again as 7F92 for Cottam Power Station. Once trains ceased running again, over a short period of time Seymour Junction box was reduced to a pile of bricks and had gone by 2011.

Permission for working the coal stocking expired in 2009 and Derbyshire County Council refused planning permission to extend the licence for the site in 2010, and in that year track was stolen by professional thieves between Seymour Junction and Oxcroft Disposal Point, with the whole of the Disposal Point trackwork being removed, along with sections of the Bolsover branch. The whole complex has since been demolished and Network Rail issued Network Change documents for the lines in the area which read:

Barrow Hill North (Goods Line) Junction to Seymour Junction (BAC2) & Elmton and Creswell Junction to Seymour Junction (BAC3)

Former single track section for just over a mile before it became double track leading from Barrow Hill North Junction to a number of former East Midlands collieries in the Bolsover/Seymour/Oxcroft area. Closed under Short Term Network Change. There is a Third Party proposal to develop a freight terminal at Markham Vale which will see part of the route between Barrow Hill North Junction / Foxlow Junction and Bolsover returned to an operational status. The route between Seymour Junction and Oxcroft Junction is closed under Short Term Network Change and is permanently closed between Oxcroft Junction and Elmton and Creswell.

The Reopening Question?

There has been talk in the past of a potential reopening of the Clowne Branch, the Robin Hood Line success spurring others to want the same for their line. In 1997 it was said that Derbyshire County Council was tentatively examining the possibility of a Creswell to Sheffield via Clowne and Staveley passenger service, and, Bolsover District Council's 2000 Local Plan had stated:

"There is the possibility of re-opening the line through Clowne which would link the Robin Hood Line with Sheffield via Staveley, Beighton and Woodhouse. It has already been agreed that a feasibility study of this route should be carried out, using funds from the Single Regeneration Budget."

Moving into the new millennium, in 2002 W.S. Atkins Ltd, (as they put it: "one of the world's most respected design, engineering and project management consultancies"), carried out a multi-modal study for the government, with a suggestion that Clowne and Staveley stations could be reopened on a new "Creswell to Staveley and Chesterfield line". In this scheme a new parkway station would be built to serve the M1 Motorway at the Markham Employment Growth Zone (now known as Markham Vale), on the site of the long closed Markham Colliery, the parkway being served by a new Birmingham–Castle Donington–Nottingham–Mansfield–Chesterfield service. Costings for the reopening of the Clowne branch and ancillary works came in at £29m, with a projected opening date of 2011.

June 2006 saw proposals put forward by Chesterfield Borough Council to create a new park and ride facility at Seymour Junction, with reopening to passenger trains on the branch from Seymour, via Clowne to Elmton & Creswell. They also agreed with the Atkins plans for a new rail freight terminal on the former Bolsover branch at Markham Vale, with road access to the freight terminal from a new junction 29A of the M1. The road link was built, and plans for the terminal showed rail access off the Seymour Junction to Bolsover line. It was said that there would be:

"A dedicated rail head with 20m deep loading yard designed for a reach stacker operation, able to serve 750m long trains with 375m long siding and availability to split trains, with the ability to use unlicensed shunter vehicles between the unit and rail head".

Nothing yet has come of the ideas for passenger trains and as with a lot of plans, although the construction of the Markham Vale freight terminal went ahead, it has not at present been rail connected.

In 2011 a contract was let for the lifting of the remaining track along the branch from Oxcroft Junction to Elmton & Creswell, the work being undertaken by Tees Rail Ltd, using railed and off track machines to lift some 5 miles and 2 chains of track. Work began on 25 January 2012 and was projected to last for three weeks; however, it took longer than envisaged, with some time spent clearing the track and cutting rails into sections, before lifting commenced. This was particularly difficult on the Clowne Branch which was very overgrown, some sections being impassable due to bramble and tree growth.

On lifting of the track panels it was evident that the ballast on the Clowne Branch was in poor condition, being mainly ash based, with worn track and rotten sleepers. Any reopening plans would thus have required deep digging, reballasting and complete track renewal along the route. The condition of the track and ballast along the line from Seymour Junction to Bolsover and Oxcroft Junction was much better with deep ballasting and mostly modern track; however, much of it had already been stolen.

Today the route of the Clowne Branch has been surfaced and is known as the Clowne Greenway cycle/walkway which links the communities of Clowne, Creswell and Woodthorpe and according to Derbyshire Council, is a great off-road commuter route to Markham Vale Enterprise Park.

Pleasley to Teversall

Just to the north of Mansfield Woodhouse a branch connected with the Mansfield–Worksop line at Pleasley Junction. On 18 April 1886 Pleasley Junction signal box was commissioned and on 11 May 1886 the Teversall & Pleasley Branch opened to passenger traffic, this line connected to the MR's Erewash Valley Line and eventually the Doe Lea Valley Line to Bolsover at Pleasley Colliery West Junction. The Sheffield Daily Telegraph for Thursday 29 April 1886 reported the opening of the Teversall Line:

THE NEW TEVERSALL AND EREWASH VALLEY RAILWAY.

On Saturday next the new Teversall and Erewash Valley line of the Midland Railway will be opened for passenger traffic, and the railway accommodation of the districts affected will be materially increased. The line runs from Mansfield, through the important colliery districts of Pleasley, Tibshelf, Blackwell, and joins the Erewash Valley line at Alfreton Station, which will be the changing place. With the opening the new line the directors of the railway company have decided to stop a morning and evening express at Alfreton to and from Nottingham.

The Sheffield Independent for Friday 30 April 1886 elaborated:

The New Line between Mansfield and Alfreton — This line will be opened on Saturday for passenger traffic, and will open out a colliery district of much importance, namely, Pleasley, Teversall, and Tibshelf. Arrangements have been made for stopping a fast train every day at Alfreton — the 7.30am going south, and the 7.25pm going north.

There were stations along the route at Pleasley, Teversall, Whiteborough, and Tibshelf & Newton, all opened without ceremony on 11 May 1886. Notice that in railway terms Teversall is spelt with two LLs; however, the town name is spelt with just one, as in Teversal.

Although passenger trains began to run, they were not convenient for those wishing to frequent Chesterfield Market on Saturdays. As such a campaign was run to get the MR to provide Saturday market trains, and this was reported in several of the local newspapers. Reporting on the monthly meeting held by Chesterfield Town Council, the Derbyshire Times for Saturday 12 June 1886 had the following paragraph:

THE NEW RAILWAY LINE TO PLEASLEY. Councillor Moffat said the council will no doubt be aware of the new railway line that has been opened between Chesterfield and Pleasley, but found the train fare was 2s. 7d., of which the Pleasley people complained bitterly, as they wished to attend the Chesterfield market, and he would move that the Town Clerk be instructed to communicate with the Railway Company asking them to meet the wants of the people of the neighbourhood, by providing a market train on Saturdays at a reduced rate. Councillor Glossop seconded the motion which was carried and the council meeting then terminated.

The Nottinghamshire Guardian for Friday 13 August 1886 ran:

Midland Railway Company and Chesterfield Corporation – At a meeting of the Chesterfield Town Council, held on Wednesday, the Mayor (Ald. T. P. Wood) presiding, the Clerk read a letter he had received from the general manager of the Midland Railway Company, in reply to a communication from the Council, asking that the Clown and Doe [Lea] line of railway might be opened as speedily as possible for passenger traffic. The letter stated that the line was in the hands of the company's engineer, and he was making preparations for the opening of the line for passenger traffic. He (the general manager) could not tell the Council how long it would be before passenger trains could be run. (Some laughter.) The Clerk also read another letter from the Midland Railway Company with reference to the running of market trains on the Pleasley and Teversall branch every Saturday. The communication stated that the request of the Corporation with regard to running market trains had been very carefully considered, but the company ware not convinced of the necessity for running such trains. Seeing that market trains were already running to Mansfield, any attempt to divide the traffic would, in their opinion, make both services unremunerated, especially in view of the fact that the Chesterfield and Mansfield markets were both held on the same day. – An opinion was expressed in the discussion which followed that the Midland Railway Company were not very desirous of considering the interests of the town, and some members urged that steps should be taken to induce the Great Northern Company to enter Chesterfield.— Mr. Moffat said that numbers of people at Pleasley and other places affected were anxious to come to the Chesterfield market — The Mayor suggested that Mr. Moffat should get up a memorial from the inhabitants to the Midland Railway Company to induce them to alter their decision, and Mr. Moffat said that he would do so.

The Nottinghamshire Guardian of Friday 15 October 1886 stated:

THE PLEASLEY AND TEVERSALL RAILWAY— At a meeting of the Chesterfield Town Council on Wednesday, the Mayor (Aid. T. P. Wood) presiding, Councillor Moffat stated that he had got up a petition signed by persons residing in the neighbourhood of Pleasley, in favour of running market trains on Saturdays on the Pleasley branch of the Midland Railway to Chesterfield. There were 632 signatures. He suggested that a deputation from the Council wait upon the directors of the company, and in accordance with his suggestion the Mayor, Aid. Gee, and Councillor Moffat were appointed a deputation. The company some time ago declined to run the market train to Chesterfield as Mansfield market was on the same day.

A month later the Sheffield Independent for Wednesday 10 November 1886 declared:

Railway Accommodation in this District. The Mayor reported that he and Alderman Higginbottom had presented the petition got up by Mr. Moffat, asking the Midland Railway Company to run market trains on the Pleasley and Teversall Railway, to the Midland Railway Company, and they had promised to let it have their careful consideration.

And the Friday 19 November 1886 edition of the Mansfield Reporter said:

Most energetic efforts are being made by gentleman at Chesterfield to induce the Midland Railway Company to run cheap market trains from Pleasley on the new line to that town. So far the Company has not acceded to the request made to them from this quarter but a memorial in favour of the cheap trains to Chesterfield has been taken around Teversal, Stanton Hill and Pleasley for signature by the colliers and another workmen, the promoters are leaving no stone unturned to accomplish the object.

The campaigning and letter writing eventually bore fruit as the Derbyshire Courier for Tuesday 28 December 1886 announced:

THE TIBSHELF & TEVERSALL RAILWAY – MARKET TICKETS TO BE ISSUED TO CHESTERFIELD.

We are glad to be able to announce that the Mayor of Chesterfield (Ald. T. P. Wood) has received communication from the Manager

Above: In a scene that could have been in the Teversall area in July 1935, but is actually in Wales, an LMS Motor Lorry delivers a carpet to the Halfway Bridge Post Office near Bangor in North Wales. This is how parcels and miscellaneous items dropped off at the stations along the branch would have been forwarded. ***(Author's collection)***

of the Midland Railway Company intimating that the directors have favourably considered the petition asking them to issue market tickets to Chesterfield, from places on the new Tibshelf and Teversall Railway. On and after January 1st, 1887, market tickets will be issued at the following third-class fares for the double journey: From Pleasley 1s. 7d., Teversall 1s. 4d. Woodend 1s. 2d. and Tibshelf and Newton 1s. The tickets will be available for the outward journey by a train leaving Mansfield at 1.55 p.m., and reaching Chesterfield at 3.2 p.m.; and for the return journey by the train leaving Chesterfield at 7.15 p.m.

The services would be worked by Mansfield-based locos and crews, invariably a Kirtley or Johnson 0-4-4T would suffice to haul a train of four non-corridor coaches on a 37-minute schedule, for the 12½ mile run.

Passenger service ends

Although certain trains connected with a St Pancras service at Alfreton, thus providing a convenient route from Mansfield to London, it was insufficient to make the trains profitable. The peak years of passenger services over the line had been reached by 1914 and after the end of the Great War, with the advent of motor buses spurred on by army surplus vehicles, they were able to offer a better and more convenient service for the villages along the route. Whiteborough Station would close in October 1926, and by 1930 the service was so poor the LMS announced its withdrawal, passenger trains over the line thus lasted for just 44 years.

As with other branches revenue from coal traffic was more important, and the closure of Tibshelf Collieries on 18 August 1939 dealt the next blow.

After nationalisation British Railways had a policy of renaming stations where confusion over names could occur, typically in towns and villages where two or more stations existed. Even though it had closed to regular passenger traffic, Pleasley became Pleasley West, the nearby GNR station becoming "East", while the ex-MR Teversal station became "Teversall Manor" with the ex-GNR station becoming "East". Even though the GNR station had never provided any passenger services, as the station also provided other services such as goods and excursions, they were therefore renamed.

Passenger excursion trains continued to use the line until at least 3 March 1964, when the section of line between Pleasley Junction and Pleasley Vale Sidings closed, thence all traffic would enter and return from the Westhouses end of the line. Hollins Siding to Pleasley Colliery closed on 4 January 1965, and Pleasley Colliery began sending coal out via Shirebrook utilising an underground conveyor. Teversall Colliery closed in 1980 and the line from Butcherwood Sidings and Pleasley Colliery closed from 7 January 1981, being lifted by November 1982.

Pleasley anecdote

It is always good to hear tales about railway locations, so here is one about Pleasley Junction sent to the author by Andrew Weekday, who used to know a relief signalman named Tom who covered as far as Pleasley Junction.

Tom had many tales from his lifelong career on the railway and one of them concerned the driver of the rail mounted steam crane that worked in Sills Quarry adjacent to the railway at Pleasley Junction. Tom first got to know George the steam crane driver when the timber trestle across Butterley Reservoir was being infilled in the 1920s, Sills must have had a hand in the job. The work was done one road at a time with single line working over the other road. George and his supervisors were obviously in close contact with signalmen at Butterley Station and Butterley

Junction signal boxes (the boxes at either end of the single line) to avoid any conflict with traffic. (This was done over several months so tablet instruments were installed in both boxes which remained open continuously as a result. This was the last fling for Butterley Junction which was closed and abolished once the work was complete, access to the Ripley Town branch being via a ground frame thereafter.... but back to Pleasley Junction and George.) Tom knew that George liked a bottle of beer (or two) with his lunch. Whilst relieving at Pleasley Junction he noticed that George had taken to having a nap in the crane cab after his lunchtime "stiffeners". By coincidence, at the same time someone discovered a large stock of out of date detonators at Mansfield Woodhouse; I'm not sure if this was the traffic side or the Permanent Way (or possibly both) but someone arrived at Pleasley Junction 'box with several packets of old detonators and a request to Tom to "run them off" in the sidings when the tripper arrived to shunt. Never one to miss the chance for a practical joke, and it being just after lunchtime, Tom enlisted the help of the chap who'd come to the box to help him. He made sure he had a few minutes between trains and set off with his assistant into the quarry. Apparently the track in the quarry was on something of a gradient so, making sure George was asleep in the cab, the old detonators were laid out along both rails on the low side of the crane, starting several yards beyond it. Task accomplished they set off back out of the quarry, releasing the handbrake on the crane before quickening their pace to be out of sight before the crane reached the first of the detonators. Apparently the sudden and unexpected detonation of explosives caused quite a stir in the quarry, but nowhere less than in the cab of the crane! I've no idea how Tom squared that one up but he avoided a trip to Derby to explain himself!

Doe Lea Valley Line

In 1838 George Hodgkinson Barrow, the owner of the Staveley Forge and collieries, began negotiations with the Duke of Devonshire for a new lease at Staveley. He also proposed that his younger brother Richard Barrow, himself wealthy, could be persuaded to invest in the business. In June 1840 George Barrow signed a new lease and gained control of all the mines, beds of coal and ironstone in the manor of Staveley. Richard Barrow did indeed become involved with the management of the works, and on 28 February 1843 signed his own lease, thus taking total control of the business.

The North Midland Railway had opened their section of line from Derby to Rotherham on 11 May 1840, the whole route, from Derby to Leeds, opening on 30 June 1840. This passed through Staveley and by early 1841 traffic on the line was increasing; however, the amount of minerals conveyed was almost outstripping the accommodation at the disposal of the company. It was in anticipation of this significantly increasing traffic that Richard Barrow inaugurated a major programme of expansion of the business, and naturally Barrow sought to utilise the railway to transport commodities.

As we know, the Midland Railway was formed by the amalgamation of the Midland Counties Railway, the Birmingham and Derby Junction Railway and the North Midland Railway, the MR being incorporated on 10 May 1844.

A new colliery had opened at Speedwell in 1854 and a branch was constructed from Staveley to serve it (Speedwell was superseded by Ireland Colliery on the same site), but this also served Seymour Colliery which opened in 1855, and it was here that two of the routes we will be looking at would connect.

As Richard Barrow's business expanded, coal from his collieries was sent by railway to all parts of England, besides supplying the iron works, and being a close friend of James Allport the General Manager of the MR, he had won contracts to supply the MR with 80,000 tons of coal, becoming one of their leading suppliers.

The Staveley Coal and Iron Company was registered in 1863 and first appeared in provincial stock exchange reports from 1864, and by that time there were some 60 miles of rails owned by the company, not to mention a large amount of wagons and some locomotives.

Sanctioned by the MR Additional Powers Act of 21 July 1863, the MR planned to build a line into the Doe Lea Valley from Seymour, which would also serve Markham No. 1 Colliery. An Act of 1865 (New Lines and Additional Powers) saw the MR acquire the Staveley railways from 1 May 1866. Although there is some evidence to say the MR were running workmen's trains before acquisition, there are, however, none in the timetables until August 1875. The MR began mineral traffic working officially from 1 August 1866 to the original terminus of the branch which was 1 mile 28 chains from Seymour.

Ten years later the MR Additional Powers Act of 28 July 1873 authorised the company to build the "Doe Lea Extension" 4m 16ch southwards to the parish of Ault Hucknall; however, in a change of plan authorised by another Additional Powers Act of 29 June 1875, this extension would be slightly longer and to the east of the Doe Lea River. Due to the lengthy process of land acquisition the MR had to seek an extension of time, which was granted by the MR Additional Powers Act of 17 July 1878. The line eventually opened to Glapwell Colliery on 1 September 1886 for goods traffic and workmen's trains, initially a service of workmen's trains from Staveley to Glapwell consisted of a 6.00am departure from Staveley calling at Seymour and Markham collieries, returning at 12.45pm (Saturdays only) calling at Markham, Seymour, Ireland and Hartington collieries, or 4.10pm (Saturdays excepted) calling at all collieries to Staveley.

Still not finished with the area the MR Additional Powers Act of 16 July 1883 authorised the company to build the "Doe Lea and Teversall Junction Railway" from the Doe Lea Extension Deviation (which was still in construction) to a junction which became known as Pleasley Colliery West Junction, a short distance south of the future Pleasley (West) station. The Mansfield Reporter for Friday 19 March 1886 announced the commencement of work for the Doe Lea Valley Line such:

PLEASLEY – THE NEW BRANCH RAILWAY – The new branch line of rails from Pleasley to Glapwell, which has been contracted for by Mr. Tomlinson, of Derby, has been commenced. Already a number of men are at work, and, in the event of the weather taking up, a further set of workmen are to be employed.

Glapwell to Pleasley Colliery West Junction opened to passengers on 1 September 1890, and to goods on 29 September the same year. The Derbyshire Times and Railway News for Saturday 6 September 1890 both ran the same story which announced:

DOE LEA EXTENSION – THE MIDLAND RAILWAY. The Midland Railway Company have extended their system by the opening on Monday morning of the Doe Lea Extension for passenger traffic. Two miles of the line from the Seymour Junction, which runs by the side of the river Doe Lea (from which it receives its name) was made about 25 years ago; the eight miles of line just completed which connects this with the Teversal branch line between Teversal and Pleasley Stations, which will form another route between Chesterfield and Mansfield, was commenced by Messrs, Tomlinson, contractors, of Derby, in 1884, but several difficulties have caused unusual delay in completing line. There is tunnel of some length beyond Glapwell, and near the Teversal end, the embankment has given way from time to time. The railway passes along a very beautiful valley, and will give increased facilities for tourists and others to visit Bolsover Castle, with its picturesque ruins (belonging to the Duke of Portland); and

Hardwick Hall, the ancient seat of the Duke of Devonshire; The halls of Glapwell and Sutton Scarsdale (the seat of the Arkwright's) are also near. Three neat brick stations have been erected, viz., Bolsover, Palterton and Sutton, and Rowthorn and Hardwick. The district is rich in minerals, the following collieries being near the line – The Staveley Company's Extensive Pits (known as Markham No. 1 and No. 2, working the coal under the Sutton estate), also Glapwell Colliery (belonging to the Sheepbridge Coal and Iron Company), and the new colliery sinking at Bolsover. Bathurst Firestone and Brick Works are also near, and a large number houses are shortly be put up by the Staveley and Bolsover Colliery Companies, for the accommodation of their workmen. The first train from Mansfield brought a large number of passengers, and much interest was taken in the event by the villagers along the route. At present three trains are to run each way daily, and the locality bids fair with the prospect of the new Manchester, Sheffield, and Lincolnshire Railway in the near future of having ample railway accommodation. The branch is only a single line of rail, and worked on the tablet system, and passengers change at Staveley.

Signal boxes were initially provided along the line at the following locations:

Name	Working levers	Spare levers	Opened
Clowne Branch Junction*	28	5	16 August 1877
Markham Colliery Sidings	8	2	July 1890
Glapwell Colliery Sidings	20	3	14 July 1890
Pleasley Colliery West Jn.	16	4	27 July 1890
Pleasley Colliery East Jn.	16	5	27 July 1890
*Renamed Seymour Junction			

With the sinking of Bolsover Colliery in 1890, eventually a new goods loop was installed on the line just south of Bolsover Station, along with a signal box to control it. Entitled Bolsover Station, this 'box opened on 11 June 1893 and contained a 21-lever frame with three spares.

Ramcroft Colliery

Ramcroft was the final colliery to open alongside the line, this opening in 1916, the MR Works & Ways Committee approving a request for a workers' platform on 18 April 1918. This was at a cost of £970, which the colliery company was expected to pay in full. The colliery platform was first featured in Working Time Tables (WTT) from May 1919, but on 12 September 1916 a Special Trains Notice was issued, this can be seen elsewhere. Workers' trains would continue to Ramcroft until at least July 1929 before being discontinued.

Glapwell

Having opened the line through to Pleasley and provided workmen's trains to a platform in Glapwell colliery, pressure from the residents of Bramley Vale was placed on the MR to provide a station for the general public. This led to the Ways and Works Committee obtaining estimates of £950 for the construction of one, the costs being reduced initially to £600, and then on 14 December 1891 the Committee approved the bid of £690 17s 0d from Messrs Chadwick. Construction commenced and the station at Glapwell was opened on 1 September 1892.

As the crow flies Mansfield and Chesterfield are but 11 miles apart; however, the twisting route of the railway saw the distance increase to 20 miles, and the journey took an average of 55 minutes to complete. The timetable made it frequently necessary to change trains at Staveley, thus increasing the journey time.

The passenger timetable began to dwindle as the years progressed, by 1920 Glapwell had departures for Staveley or Chesterfield at 7.49am, 1.28pm, 2.11pm and 5.16pm, with trains for Mansfield at 8.55am, 2.29pm (SX), 3.56 (SO) and 6.58, hardly a busy service. The General Strike of 1926 didn't help the cause for the line, services being reduced to three per day towards Mansfield, and by mid-1930 it was all over, the LMS Traffic Committee deciding on 25 June 1930 that the passenger traffic was unremunerative and announced:

Withdrawal of passenger Train Service between Chesterfield and Mansfield via Bolsover:-

On and from Monday, July 28th 1930, the passenger train service between Chesterfield and Mansfield via Bolsover, will be withdrawn, and the following stations closed for passenger traffic:-

Bolsover, Palterton & Sutton, Glapwell, and Rowthorn & Hardwick for all purposes.

Bolsover, Palterton & Sutton and, Glapwell stations will continue to deal with parcels and miscellaneous traffic as at present, which traffics will be conveyed by freight train and motor lorry, and should continue to be booked through to destination station. At Bolsover and Palterton & Sutton facilities will still be available for dealing with livestock etc., traffic by special arrangement. Parcels and miscellaneous traffics formerly dealt with at Rowthorn & Hardwick will be dealt with at Glapwell station. ***(C.G.P. 3872)***

Rail replacement services

An alternative service to rail could be provided by the East Midland Motor Services, itself a London Midland & Scottish Railway joint operation, it being deemed that savings of £1,028 per annum could be made by switching to road transport.

The 1921 Railways Act had consolidated over 100 operators into the "Big Four", London Midland & Scottish Railway (LMS), London & North Eastern Railway (LNER), Great Western Railway (GWR) and Southern Railway (SR), and they inherited and developed networks of feeder bus services. After 1928 they began to acquire majority shareholdings in local bus companies, such as United Automobile Services (UAS). The railway involvement in bus operations was transformed in the period 1928–30. The companies' legal powers to run bus services were unclear and each promoted private legislation (the Road Powers Acts of 1928) to obtain clarity. Concessions were demanded in return, including the key one that the railways would refrain from taking a controlling interest in bus undertakings. This led the companies to enter into partnerships with the bus combines: British Electric Traction, Scottish Motor Traction, National Omnibus & Transport Company and Thomas Tilling. The railways relinquished the majority stakes they had already acquired but also bought substantial minority shareholdings in other companies in the combined groups and eventually there were investments in 33 bus and coach companies. Where there was a local monopoly of rail services, the agreements were bilateral, but where inter-penetrating lines were common, there were two railway companies with minority shareholdings, for example, Devon General and Thames Valley Traction (both GWR/SR), Crosville and Midland Red (both GWR/LMS), and Eastern Counties, Eastern National, East Midland Motor Services (EMMS), Hebble Motor Services, Lincolnshire Road Car, Trent Motor Traction, West Yorkshire

General Superintendent's Office.

MIDLAND RAILWAY, DERBY. S.T.N.830

September 12th, 1916

TRAIN ALTERATION NOTICE.

Commencing on Monday, September 16th, a service of Workmen's Trains will run to and from Ramcroft Colliery, and additional trains will be run, and alterations made, as shown below:-

5 30am (Workmen) Chesterfield to Markham Colliery will arrive Markham at 5 53, and be extended to Ramcroft:-

Markham Colliery	dep	5 54am	Bolsover	dep	5 59am
Bolsover	arr	5 58	Palterton & S	arr	6 2
			do	dep	6 5
			Ramcroft	arr	6 10

6 15am (Workmen) Markham Colliery to Chesterfield will start from Ramcroft at 6 18, and run as follows:-

		a.m.			
Ramcroft	dep	6 18	Seymour Junc.	Dep	6 34
Palterton & S.	arr	6.22	Staveley Town		6 37
do	dep	6 23	Hall Lane Junc		6 39
Bolsover	arr	6 26	Barrow Hill	arr	6 41
do	dep	6 27	do	dep	6 42
Markham Colliery	arr	6 30	Whittington		6 45
do	dep	6 31	Chesterfield	arr	6 52
Seymour Junc.	Arr	6 33			

Staveley engine of No. 2 turn.
Chesterfield G. No.4 third class turn.

2 58pm (E.C.) Barrow Hill to Markham (S) will be discontinued, and Workmen's train run from Barrow Hill to Ramcroft as follows:-

		S p.m.			S p.m.
Barrow Hill	dep	1 25	Bolsover	arr	1 47
Hall Lane Junc.		1 28	do	dep	1 48
Staveley Town		1 31	Palterton & S.	arr	1 51
Seymour Junc.	arr	1 33	do	dep	1 52
do	dep	1 42	Ramcroft	arr	1 57
Markham Colliery		1 44			

3 22pm (Workmen) Markham Colliery to Chesterfield (S) will start from Ramcroft at 3 5pm, and run as under:-

		S p.m.			p.m.
			Seymour Junction	dep	3 30
Ramcroft	dep	3 5	Staveley Town		3 33
Palterton & S.	arr	3 9	Hall Lane Junc.		3 36
do	dep	3 10	Barrow Hill	arr	3 39
Bolsover	arr	3 15	do	dep	3 40
do	dep	3 21	Whittington		3 43
Markham Colliery	arr	3 24	Chesterfield	arr	3 49
do	dep	3 25			
Seymour Junction	arr	3 27			

Run on Goods Loop at Bolsover, and cross 2 52pm Chesterfield to Mansfield

Hasland engine of No. 5 turn
Chesterfield G No. 4 Third Class turn, and assist 1.8pm (Workmen) Chesterfield to Barrow Hill.

A train will run from Palterton and Ramcroft at 9 5pm (S) in connection with the 8 30pm Chesterfield to Glapwell arriving at Ramcroft at 9 10. A light engine to work same will leave Seymour Junct. At 8.30pm, due Palterton at 8 40.

A train will run from Ramcroft to Palterton at 10 50pm (S) in connection with the 11 2 Glapwell to Chesterfield, arriving at Palterton at 10.55. The engine working this train to return from Palterton to Seymour Junc. Coupled in front of 11 2 from Glapwell.

Staveley engine of No. 38 freight turn. Seymour Jnc. Head Shunter to act as Guard

11 15pm (FC) Chesterfield to Glapwell (SO) will convey two sets of coaches from Barrow Hill, with an engine at each end and be divided at Palterton & S. The Ramcroft portion to be propelled from Palterton & S.

1 0pm. (Workmen) Markham Colliery to Chesterfield (S.O.) will start from Ramcroft. The timings will be as follows:-

		S.O. p.m.				S.O. p.m.
Markham Colliery		12 21 as booked		Ramcroft	dep	12 45
Palterton & S	arr	12 30		Palterton & S.	arr	12 49
do	dep	12 32	12 34	do	dep	12 50
Ramcroft	arr	-	12 39	Bolsover	arr	12 53
Glapwell C.S.	arr	12 37		do	dep	12 54
				Markham Colliery	arr	12 56
				Do	dep	1 0 as booked

Staveley engs. Of No. 1 7 12 10pm (SO) turns
Chesterfield Porter Guard.

Road Car, Yorkshire Traction and Yorkshire Woollen District Transport (all LMS/LNER). The LMS and LNER also sat with the local authority on Joint Omnibus Committees in Halifax and Sheffield. (Source-Wikipedia)

EMMS came about when W. T. Underwood who worked for UAS of Lowestoft, was sent to Clowne in 1920 to establish bus services in the area. The vehicles he took with him were liveried in the United livery of chrome yellow and brown (later separated

Right: A line up of East Midland Motor Services buses are ready to take excursions from Chesterfield in the 1930s.

Above: Another facet of omnibus operation in competition with the railways, was the transportation of Parcels. This sign would be attached to a property to advertise the fact.

Right: East Midland Leyland TS7 35-seat single deck bus No. B9, registration number BAL 609 on an Edwinstowe–Worksop–Doncaster service in the late 1930s. This bus was registered new in June 1935 so could have been used on the services around Glapwell, it would pass to Southdown in June 1950. ***(All Author's collection)***

Right: Mansfield & District Tramways Ltd, Tillings-Stevens Petrol-Electric bus, registration No. AL 6613. Seen around 1924 the crew pose in front of the bus on a Mansfield to Rainworth service, this would have been a colourful image with the Red & Cream livery. ***(Val Fowler collection)***

with a cream band), the United fleet name being covered by the name of Underwood, which was how the company traded. In 1927 the company was renamed EMMS Limited and retained the yellow brown and cream livery until 1955, before changing to red and cream.

Competition was also had from the Mansfield & District Light Railways, an electric tramway network operating in Mansfield from 16 July 1905 to 9 October 1932, and consisted of five routes covering just over 12 miles. These routes began in Mansfield's Market Place and went to Berry Hill, Crown Farm, Mansfield Woodhouse, Pleasley and via Sutton-in-Ashfield to Hucknall-under-Huthwaite. The livery was red and cream, later light green and cream. The tramway was largely rural in nature but during the 1920s, the improved performance of motor transport gave significant competition to the trams from the many early omnibus companies, which expanded into other areas.

Section of line closed

Glapwell Colliery and the others in the Doe Lea Valley were still producing plenty of coal at this time; however, all their production was sent out northwards towards Seymour Junction. The condition of Rowthorn Tunnel due to mining subsidence did not help the cause of this section, as it had been receiving repairs to its northern end for some time, including the provision of ring beams to support it. As such little traffic continued on to Pleasley and the section between Glapwell and Pleasley Colliery West Junction would close to all traffic from 28 July 1930. The closure of the section also had the benefit of removing the 1 in 50 gradient through Rowthorn Tunnel, of which it was said:

Up this steep ascent only 13 wagons of coal can be brought at one time, and sometimes not even that number.

The track would be lifted by 17 October 1932, although a section at the Pleasley end would remain in situ for a short period for empty wagon storage. After closure, from January 1935 Rowthorn Tunnel found use as a mushroom farm, and at the breakout of World War II it was commandeered by the RAF, who utilised the subsidence-free southern end as an ammunition store.

Local goods traffic would continue along the remaining line until the closure of Palterton & Sutton to goods in December 1939; however, Glapwell's parcels traffic would continue for the war period and eventually ceased from 23 September 1946. The line between Glapwell Colliery and Glapwell station was used for the stabling of wagons, but was lifted in April 1959. Bolsover would cling on to goods traffic until 1 November 1962 and Glapwell Colliery Sidings signal box would be closed sometime between 1969 and 1972.

Ramcroft Colliery would be the first to close along the line in October 1966, Glapwell following in June 1974, with the line between Bolsover and Glapwell then closing; however, most of the track would remain in situ until October 1978, finally being severed at Bolsover on 18 March 1979. Today the section of route from Bolsover to Pleasley forms part of the Stockley and Rowthorn Trails.

At Bolsover occasional specials continued to call, one such being in connection with the Queen's Jubilee celebrations on 28 July 1977, and August Miners' Welfare seaside excursions ran from 1978 until 1981.

Bolsover Colliery closed on 7 May 1993, followed by Markham on 2 July, but traffic continued to the adjacent Coalite works until 2002 when Bolsover Coalite Chemicals Ltd went into administration and then receivership, and closed down finally in 2004. As with the Clowne Branch a Network Change document was issued which read:

Bolsover Colliery (Seymour Junction to Bolsover) (BOC1)

Former single track route leading from the former Seymour Junction area to former East Midlands collieries. This route is closed under Short Term Network Change up to 7 miles 220 yards. There is a Third Party proposal to develop a freight terminal at Markham Vale which will see part of this route as far as 7 miles 220 yards returned to an operational status. The route beyond 7 miles 220 yards has recently been permanently closed.

Apart from sections stolen, the track between Bolsover and Seymour was lifted by contractors in 2011, and although the site continues to be developed and grow, now covering the whole of the site of Markham Colliery, nothing has at the time of writing come of the plans to use rail to the new Markham Vale.

Mansfield to Rolleston Junction

In July 1846 the MR obtained an Act of Parliament to construct a line from Clay Cross to join their Newark to Lincoln line, with the first section being built from Rolleston the 2½ miles to Southwell. As construction was relatively easy, this section opened on 1 July 1847, the Leicestershire Mercury for Saturday 3 July 1847 stated:

NOTTINGHAM AND LINCOLN RAILWAY-The branch line between the Fiskerton station of the Nottingham and Lincoln Railway and Southwell was opened on Thursday last. It will be a very great accommodation.

On Saturday 10 July 1847 the Derbyshire Courier reported:

CLAY CROSS AND NEWARK RAILWAY – That part of the line which is completed up to Southwell from the Nottingham and Lincoln line at Rolleston, was opened for passengers and traffic on the 1st instant, and many parties from Southwell availed themselves of a ride by steam on that day.

However, the poor service of four trains per day was withdrawn just two years later at the beginning of August 1849. They would be reinstated from April 1852, removed in March 1853 and reinstated, this time on a permanent basis, on 1 September 1860.

The Midland Railway liked to hang on to their territory with the idea of being sole carrier of goods etc.; however, as was seen in other areas the proprietors of coal mines etc. wanted the cheapest way of moving their goods and were happy to encourage competition. As the GNR completed their lines in the Newark area, the MR began to get nervous about possible expansion of GNR lines towards the Erewash Valley, and its lucrative coal business. There had been discussions about a Mansfield to Southwell line when the MR were planning the extension to Worksop, it being known that there were coal reserves beneath the sandstone of the area. However, the directors decided against building the line for various reasons, until a wealthy Southwell resident threatened to build the line himself and the MR then changed their minds as there was a possibility the GNR would get involved with all the repercussions that would entail.

There was a hindrance, though, in that the line would pass through Sherwood Forest and valuable agricultural land, and there was likely to be objections from the farmers and foresters along the route chosen. To try and alleviate any such issues, rather than delve into the advantages of coal traffic, the MR pushed the fact that the line would be beneficial to the rural economy. This worked as Parliament duly sanctioned the new railway as part of the Mansfield Railways Act of 5 July 1865, although as the MR was in the process of building the Bedford to St. Pancras line they pursued an extension of time for the line to Southwell.

The Nottinghamshire Guardian of Friday 3 March 1871 reported on the inspection of the line thus:

MANSFIELD AND SOUTHWELL RAILWAY.

This line which has just been completed by the eminent contractors, Messrs Eckersley and Baylis, was inspected on the 22nd instance by Colonel C.S. Hutchinson one of the government inspectors. The Colonel was accompanied by Mr Needham, superintendent of the Midland company; Mr Barlow, consulting engineer Mr Baylis, of the firm of Eckersley and Baylis; Mr A. Terry, engineer for the contractors; Mr Carr, resident engineer; Mr Warwick, chief of the telegraphic department; Mr Prince (signals) and other gentlemen. The Mansfield and Southwell Railway is a little more than twelve miles long, passing in its course through a beautiful agricultural district and supplies an important link of railway communication, uniting the London, Erewash Valley, Nottingham and Mansfield Railways with the railway from Derby and Trent to Southwell, near to which town the new line forms its junction with the one named, and which was the starting point of Colonel Hutchinson's inspection. Two powerful locomotives, weighing about 70 tons each, were provided by the Midland Company to test the amount of deflection in the bridges, but as the safety of railway travelling depends in a great measure upon the proper arrangement of points, signals, telegraphic and otherwise, as well as the stability of bridges and permanent way, Colonel Hutchinson first commenced his work by carefully examining the points and signals at the junction of the whole of which were thoroughly tested. From the junction the line runs to Kirklington and Farnsfield, between which villages there are several shallow cuttings and small embankments.

At the latter place a goods warehouse coal sidings have been provided, and will prove a great boom to the district which abounds with small villages. The Inspector having walked over the whole of the line to this point examine in his course the bridges, culverts, signals et cetera a rest was made for refreshment, which proved most acceptable after a long and somewhat tedious walk of upwards of five miles. After a short time the inspection was resumed, and the work of particular interest, between Farnsfield and Rainworth the next station, was passed under review, the distance being four miles and the line being very similar in its formation on the whole distance gone over- about 10 miles-viz, cuttings, embankment and bridges, many of the latter being splendid specimens of workmanship, reflecting great credit upon the contractors. Before reaching Rainworth the line enters Sherwood Forest of Robin Hood celebrity. The forest, and indeed the whole district, which is of great beauty, abounds with game, which the navvies say have had a hard time of it during the winter; and it has not been an uncommon occurrence for some of the winged sorts to commit suicide against the telegraphic wires of the railway, to which the navvies had of course no objection. The work of the line from Rainworth to Mansfield has been very considerable, requiring great engineering skill in its execution. Leaving Rainworth the line is on an embankment; it then passes through a cutting 32 feet deep and 54 chains in length, then over another embankment and through a cutting 25 feet deep and 25 chains long, and forward to Southwell Road which is passed by a girder bridge having a span of 66 feet, and which was put to the severest possible test, the engines running backwards and forwards over it together at full and slow speed, and also by both engines standing upon it. The deflection caused by these severe trials were so small that they Inspector declared the "bridge stood like a rock". From this point on the line passes in the direction of Nottingham Road over which it crosses by an arched bridge, and forward by embankments and viaducts of the River Maun, whence Mansfield is said to have derived its name. The viaducts are very neat and substantial piece of workmanship, consisted of nine arches, having an elevation of 50 feet, the length being 400 feet. The line from the viaducts to Mansfield station is on a curve and presents no noticeable features of special interest. The work throughout the line is of the most solid and durable kind, with which is combined an amount of neatness very creditable to the contractors. The strata of the line consists of sand and sandstone rock, the latter being so difficult to dislodge that 120 tons of powder was used in the cuttings. With the exception of a few slight alterations required to be made in some of the signals and points, the line was found perfectly satisfactory, and habitants of Mansfield with those of the districts through which the line passes, will be glad to know that that is fully intended to open it on or about the 1st of March.

In the event the line was fully open for traffic on 3 April 1871 and before the sinking of the pits, the Mansfield to Southwell and Rolleston Junction line was just a pastoral cross-country branch line with a very light service.

Brief timeline

Working by electric train tablet block came into force from Farnsfield to Mansfield North Junction on 27 October 1890, and the 1903 timetable showed that through trains from Newark to Mansfield departed at 8.15am, 11.00am on Thursdays only (ThO), and 3.35pm, returning at 9.43am, 10.55am (ThO), 3.35pm and 6.03pm (ThO). By the 1920 timetable this had been reduced to two through trains, departing Newark at 8.19am and 5.20pm, returning at 9.28am and 4.10pm. There were, however, more services between Southwell and Newark although a description of this is beyond the scope of this book, being amply covered in the Oakwood Press book, The Mansfield–Southwell–Rolleston Railway, by Robert Weston.

The tranquillity of the line was ended with the opening of three branches to serve the newly sunk collieries, coal traffic then being the lifeblood of the line, exiting in both directions from the branch.

Mansfield Colliery Junction to Mansfield Colliery opened on 11 January 1905, the next branch to open being that from Rufford Colliery Branch Junction to Rufford Colliery on 20 June 1912, the line being extended to Clipstone Colliery in the spring of 1929. A workmen's service operated from Mansfield to Rufford Colliery from 10 February 1918 until this was withdrawn with effect from 16 July 1928.

The Blidworth Colliery branch opened on 21 December 1925 and at the same time the route lost its passenger service on 12 August 1929. Electric key token block working in place of electric train tablet block was instituted between Farnsfield and Blidworth Junction from 20 October 1929 and the opening of the Mid-Nottinghamshire Joint Line from Farnsfield to Ollerton on 30 November 1931, gave the LMS access to Bilsthorpe Colliery.

The Mid-Notts Joint Line closed from Friday 7 September 1962 and at the same time the line between Bilsthorpe and Farnsfield was "temporarily taken out of use" by the engineer.

Southwell to Blidworth Junction closed to traffic from 1 May 1965, but Kirklington station remained open for goods until 25 May 1965. Blidworth Colliery closed in September 1928, reopened in September 1932 and the branch closed on 2 October 1966, leaving the colliery to be served via the former LNER branch. Blidworth Junction to Rufford Junction would close from 3 October 1966, and Blidworth Junction to Blidworth Colliery was "taken out of use" by the engineer on 24 June 1967. And finally for that period, Mansfield Colliery Junction to Mansfield Colliery closed from 18 July 1967, all the colliery traffic then using the former LNER line.

The last train on the Rufford to Clipstone Colliery Branch ran on 26 August 1983, that section of the branch then closing on 29 August 1983. The final train along the Rufford Colliery Branch ran on 14 October 1983, the branch being closed on 17 October

MANSFIELD, SOUTHWELL, and NEWARK.—Midland.

FmChesterfld, p.191	mrn	mrn	aft
Mansfield ....dep	6 15	9 35	3 40
Blidworth	6 32	9 48	3 52
Farnsfield .. arr	42	9 57	4 0
Farnsfield .. dep	48	9 58	4 1
Kirklngtn&Eding-	7 1	10 6	4 8
Southwell ....[ley	7 30	1013	4 14
Rolleston Jnc. 191	7 38	1021	4 23
191 Nottingham a	8 30	1125	5 10
Newark 191,121a	7 55	1030	4 35
191 Lincoln ..arr	9 30	[illegible]	5 40

From Retford, p.121	mrn	mrn (Thursdays only)	mrn (Except Thursdays)	aft
191 Lincoln ..dep	7 0	10 0	10 0	3 40
Newark ......dep	8 35	11 0	12 0	5 0
191 Nottingham d	8 5	....	1115	4 15
Rolleston Junc. ..	8 45	1115	1215	5 12
Southwell ....[ley	8 51	1126	1233	5 18
Kirklngtn&Eding-	8 58	1132	1243	5 25
Farnsfield .. arr	9 3	1142	1255	5 31
Farnsfield .. dep	9 4	1147	1 30	5 32
Blidworth [204	9 12	1155	1 45	5 40
Mansfld 194,195 a	9 25	1220	2 10	5 55

◊ **Above**: The 1877 Bradshaw's shows a service of three trains per day as per this extract. ***(Author's collection)***

1983 and at the same time so did the final remaining section of the Mansfield to Southwell line.

(Source *https://branchline.uk/rail_chronology/Mansfield.html)*

Proposed branches and new connections

The LD&ECR whose main line crossed the Mansfield to Worksop line at Shirebrook, had planned to build a branch to Mansfield and had got as far as producing Plans and Sections for the route in March 1896, and a second and different set in March 1897.

During the 1890s, a body known as the Mansfield Railway Commissioners had been established to report on the town's railway services. Although they had been actively engaged in providing better railway facilities, including retiming of some Mansfield to Nottingham trains, they were really hoping for another railway company to serve the town to encourage competition, drive down fares and improve communications.

November 1895 had seen a very ambitious scheme which would have placed Mansfield in a much more important position. According to an editorial in the Mansfield Reporter this project was intended to commence with a junction on the North Staffordshire Railway about four miles north of Burton, running through Ashbourne to Hopton and Wirksworth, connecting here with the High Peak Railway, and then on to Cromford, Matlock Bath, Ashover and Clay Cross, joining the MS&LR at Williamthorpe and thence, via Sutton-in-Ashfield and Mansfield to Retford. An alternative route from Clay Cross to Tibshelf, Mansfield and Retford was also proposed, but nothing more was heard of this venture. The Commissioners had approached the MS&LR and GNR with the hope of getting these companies to tap the town, they had little success and so instead turned to the LD&ECR, who appeared only too willing to construct a branch from their line near Warsop.

Studying deposited plans and a report on the proposed line which appeared in the Mansfield Chronicle of 4 December 1896, showed that the branch would have been split into two sections, Railway No. 1 being 4 miles 2 furlongs and Railway No. 2, 2 furlongs and 5 chains.

It would have left the LD&ECR main line at a point where the narrow gauge Sherwood Forest Railway is today, and on a rising gradient of 1 in 100 for 4½ chains it would then have almost paralleled today's A6075 Peafield Lane in a south-westerly direction towards Mansfield Woodhouse, on the level for 2 miles and 6 chains. Close to the junction of Peafield Lane and the A60 Leeming Lane, it would then have headed more-or-less south, crossed a 130-yard long 55-foot high viaduct over Rock Valley at a rising gradient of 1 in 100, and then levelling out would have crossed Pelham Street with a level crossing, where a large high rise building is today. It would then have passed Ratcliffe Gate where the Brown Cow public house is today, and terminated at Berry Hill Road (now Littleworth), close to its junction with Baums Lane and the later built Great Central Road.

As time progressed and the LD&ECR began to feel the difficulties of its financial position, some delay occurred in the carrying out of its project and eventually the whole scheme was dropped in the autumn of 1896 after the MR had agreed to offer running powers for goods and coal traffic to a goods depot that the LD&ECR, or their ally, the GER, would build in Mansfield. Other plans were produced for shorter branches in Mansfield which yet again led to nothing.

Above: "Crab" 4-6-0 42710 departs from Clowne with the 10.50 Blackpool to Radford on 1 August 1959. Regular passenger services on the Clowne branch had ceased in 1954 but excursions and summer Saturday holiday traffic continued. ***(R.J. Buckley)***

Clowne Branch

Right: The driver of 58047 collects the tablet from signalman Neil Baker at Elmton & Creswell Junction on 27 October 1987. The train is 6G62 14.20 from West Burton Power Station, destined for Seymour Yard. It would have arrived from the Worksop direction and run round its train at Creswell, before taking the Clowne Branch to Seymour. ***(Robin Stewart Smith)***

Below: Three tablets for the Clowne Branch, each showing different engraved wording. Left: A fibre tablet inscribed "Oxcroft Colliery Sidings No. 3 – Creswell Junction". The word "Oxcroft" has been stamped in a ground out section, and the "No. 3" is a later addition – the 'box was originally named Barlborough Colliery Sidings, but was renamed Oxcroft Colliery Sidings No. 3 on 9 January 1931 and the tablet being amended to suit. Centre: Another adapted fibre tablet, where the whole of the top line has been ground out to accommodate the new wording, but the "3" is still an addition. Right: This alloy tablet would have been for the Seymour Junction to Oxcroft Colliery Sidings No. 3 section but, after the closure of that 'box on 30 November 1969, it was amended to suit the section all the way to Elmton & Creswell Jcn.

Above right: Tablet machines in Seymour Junction; the one on the left is the Oxcroft instrument. A tablet machine can only issue one tablet at a time to prevent two trains occupying a single line section and, until a tablet is restored into a machine to clear the system back to normal, another cannot be removed. The Oxcroft Disposal Point (DP) Branch diverges at a ground frame (GF) on the single line between Seymour and Creswell and, because a train for the DP does not complete the journey to Creswell, the tablet machines are out of sequence with each other because there is effectively a tablet missing. A train for Oxcroft would be offered on to Creswell as normal and a tablet withdrawn from the main Creswell machine (right). This would be issued to the driver who then proceeds as far as the GF at Oxcroft Junction, where the tablet is placed in an instrument which unlocked the GF to allow the points to be set for the train to enter the sidings. Once the train is inside and the main line points restored to Normal, the GF tablet is removed (therefore locking it) and placed in another instrument which unlocks the left hand Oxcroft instrument in Seymour Junction 'box. This contains a tablet which is removed and put into the main Creswell machine, and the 3-5 (Train Cancelled) bell signal sent to Creswell to restore the system to Normal. For a train to depart the branch, the 5-2 (Release Tablet) bell signal was sent to Creswell to allow the removal of a tablet from the main machine. This would be placed back in the Oxcroft machine to allow the tablet to be removed at Oxcroft Junction and placed into the GF release to allow the points to be operated. Once out of the sidings and on the single line clear of the points, the GF was returned to normal, the tablet taken out and handed to the driver and then the train continued to Seymour. The tablet would be handed to the signalman, who placed it back in the main Creswell machine to restore the system to Normal. ***(Steve Ray)***

Above: The Clowne Branch was steeply graded from both ends to the summit at Clowne, and loaded coal trains subsequently required a banking loco. The driver of each train was given a token but the banking loco driver was handed a 17.5-inch long, wooden handled brass train staff inscribed "Elmton & Cresswell Junc. Clown Banking Engine Staff". Initially called Clown, the "e" was only added to the village and its railway features in the 20th Century. This staff dates from after 1887 as it has a single "s" in the word Creswell. It sold at auction in 2020. ***(All photos Author's collection unless stated)***

Right: A photo taken by Neil Baker from Elmton & Creswell 'box. Neil explains: "The rarest of rare birds on the Clowne branch, namely a loaded MGR from Seymour to Creswell. The Class 58 is being assisted by a blue Class 56, which would work the train forward to the power station and the Class 58 would return to Barrow Hill. The reason that loaded MGR trains did not use the branch very often was that they required banking due to the steep uphill gradient to Clowne. Apart from when the Worksop to Sheffield line was closed for engineering works to Brookhouse Viaduct for a fortnight in August 1981, I can only remember a couple of occasions when this happened. The next time a loaded train was assisted over the branch was also the last time this took place, on Friday 20 January 1989 when 7F72 Markham Colliery to Cottam Power Station was diverted due to engineering work on the 'Old Road'. The train engine was 58033, and 58031 was assisting on the rear. To save running round at Creswell, 58031 worked the train forward to Cottam and 58033 returned light to Barrow Hill. This took place just over a year after the more common empty MGR trains which ran from the Creswell direction to Seymour had finished running."

Above: A 2Z01 Inspection Special, comprising 31405 and Saloon DB999504, is seen leaving the Clowne Branch on 30 March 1988. Once on the main line, the engine then propelled the coach towards Shireoaks. ***(Both Neil Baker)***

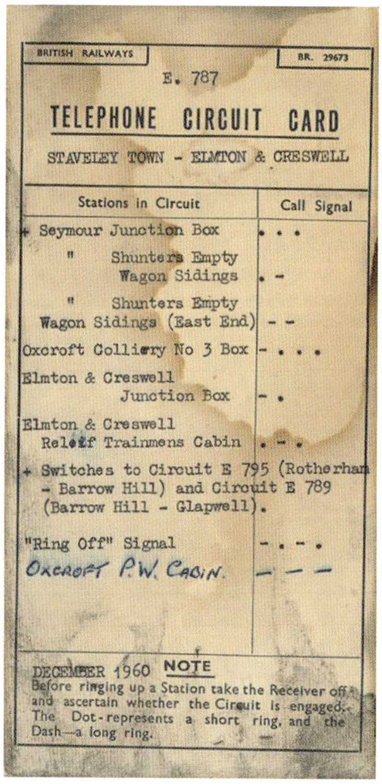

BRITISH RAILWAYS

BR. 29673

E. 787

TELEPHONE CIRCUIT CARD

STAVELEY TOWN - ELMTON & CRESWELL

Stations in Circuit	Call Signal
+ Seymour Junction Box	• • •
" Shunters Empty Wagon Sidings	• –
" Shunters Empty Wagon Sidings (East End)	– –
Oxcroft Colliery No 3 Box	– • • •
Elmton & Creswell Junction Box	– •
Elmton & Creswell Relief Trainmens Cabin	• – •
+ Switches to Circuit E 795 (Rotherham - Barrow Hill) and Circuit E 789 (Barrow Hill - Glapwell).	
"Ring Off" Signal	– • – •
Oxcroft P.W. Cabin.	– – –

DECEMBER 1960 NOTE

Before ringing up a Station take the Receiver off and ascertain whether the Circuit is engaged. The Dot-represents a short ring, and the Dash—a long ring.

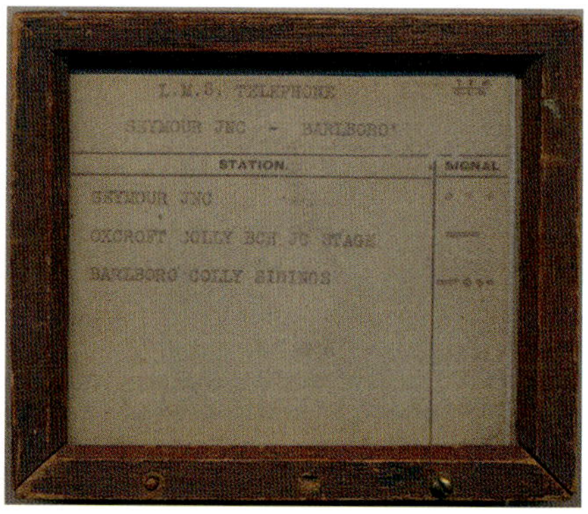

L.M.S. TELEPHONE

SEYMOUR JNC - BARLBORO'

STATION	SIGNAL
SEYMOUR JNC	• • •
OXCROFT COLLY BOX JC STAGE	–
BARLBORO COLLY SIDINGS	– • • •

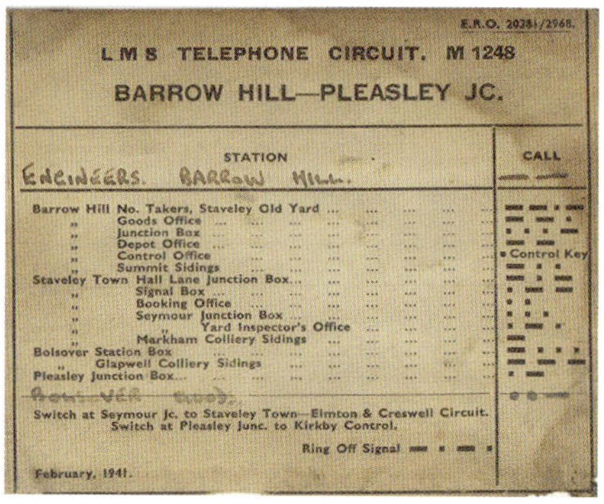

E.R.O. 20281/2968.

LMS TELEPHONE CIRCUIT. M 1248

BARROW HILL—PLEASLEY JC.

STATION	CALL
Engineers. Barrow Hill.	– –
Barrow Hill No. Takers, Staveley Old Yard ...	– – • –
" Goods Office ...	– – •
" Junction Box ...	• • • –
" Depot Office ...	– –
" Control Office ...	• Control Key
" Summit Sidings ...	– • •
Staveley Town Hall Lane Junction Box...	– • –
" Signal Box ...	• – –
" Booking Office ...	• •
" Seymour Junction Box ...	• • •
" " Yard Inspector's Office ...	• – •
" Markham Colliery Sidings ...	–
Bolsover Station Box ...	– • • •
" Glapwell Colliery Sidings ...	– – –
Pleasley Junction Box...	• –
Bolsover Goods.	• • –

Switch at Seymour Jc. to Staveley Town—Elmton & Creswell Circuit.
Switch at Pleasley Junc. to Kirkby Control.

Ring Off Signal – • – •

February, 1941.

Right: Three Telephone Circuit Cards that relate to the Clowne Branch and beyond. They showed the locations along the routes with telephones, together with their codes. The dot represents a short ring and the dash a long one; Seymour Junction was therefore three short rings. The card on the left is from Elmton & Creswell Junction 'box (one long one short ring) and was rescued by Neil Baker. The other two are from Oxcroft Colliery Sidings No. 3 and were rescued by the author just before demolition of the 'box. The top card dates prior to the renaming of Barlborough Colliery Sidings 'box in 1931, while the bottom card is dated February 1941. ***(Author's collection)***

Above: Elmton & Creswell Down Fixed Distant signal seen in the 1970s when it was still a Midland Railway Lower Quadrant style (**Left**) and just before tracklifting along the branch in 2011 (**Right**) when there was track beneath all that vegetation! ***(Left Derek Talbot, right Author)***

Right: Romanian-built 56019 trundles along the branch at Markland (near Clowne) on a dull day in August 1978. ***(Phil Sangwell)***

Left: Approaching Clowne, the MR line paralleled the LD&ECR line. The latter's station is seen extreme left. The MR branch is the left-most track which appears to have some wagons stabled on it, and the station is where the houses dip to the right of the LD&ECR station. Over to the right are the exchange sidings for Southgate Colliery which closed in January 1929 due to severe flooding. ***(Author's collection)***

Right: The Shireoaks Colliery Company's Southgate Colliery was situated on the Southgate estate close to Clowne station. In 1875 Miss Bowden cut the first sod, and sinking began in 1877; the Top Hard seam was reached in March that year at 321 yards. A 150-foot chimney was built in 1890, and by 1900 production was 600 tons a day from a 1000-foot deep shaft and a workforce of 400 men. The image shows the Gas House in the foreground and the gasometers on the right, with the colliery behind. It closed on 17 January 1929 due to severe flooding, but was reopened in 1955 to aid the construction of a link to the High Hazels seam at Creswell Colliery. This was abandoned in 1961, the shafts were filled and colliery was demolished. A pump house remains today, albeit now clad in metal sheeting. ***(Author's collection)***

Right: Timetabled passenger services ceased on 5 July 1954 and goods facilities in July 1960. Freight continued, as did excursions and summer Saturday holiday traffic – notably from Radford to Blackpool North. 12A Carlisle Kingmoor-allocated "Black 5" 4-6-0 45097 departs with the 1M01 10.50 Blackpool to Radford on 11 August 1962. On the following Saturday, 18 August, 45270 worked 1M01 for its last time via this route. Notice the former LD&ECR station over to the left, and that the sidings for Southgate Colliery have now gone. ***(John Spencer Gilks)***

Left: Clown Station as it appeared c1900 with a selection of staff posing on the single platform. ***(Author's collection)***

Below: On 4 July 1938 the station was renamed "Clown and Barlborough". It was renamed again on 18 June 1951 by BR, with an additional "e" to become "Clowne and Barlborough". ***(Author's collection)***

Below right: The final scheduled passenger train stopped here on 5 October 1954, but remarkably the station survived into the 21st Century until demolition in 2000. 56074 passes the station remains on 6 September 1978 with an empty wagon set from the Creswell direction, heading towards Barrow Hill. ***(Phil Sangwell)***

Below: A Midland Railway ticket for a journey from Clown to Chesterfield. ***(Courtesy Midland Railway Study Centre)***

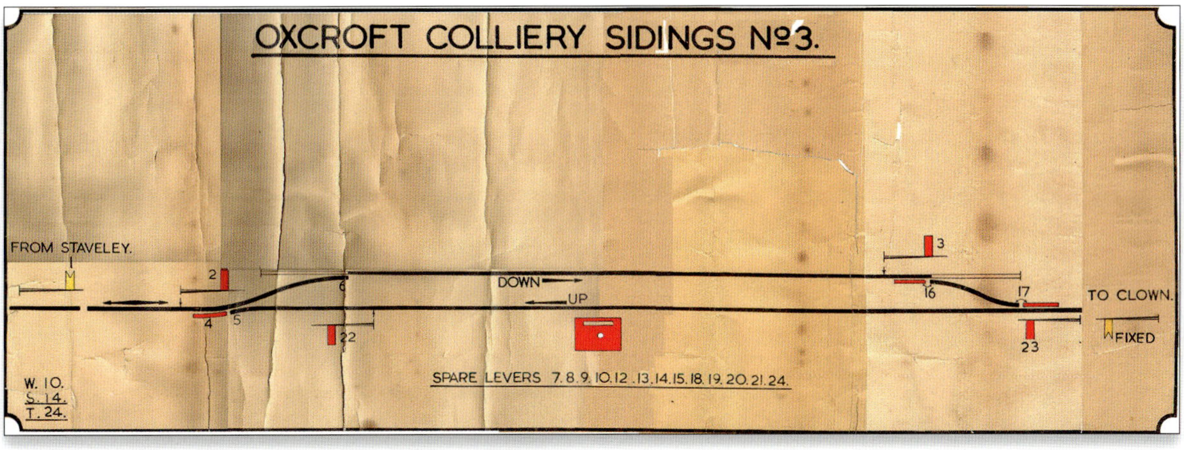

Above: This rather damaged diagram for Oxcroft Colliery Sidings No. 3 dates from 1951. On 2 February 1902 the 'box opened as a ground level style entitled Barlborough Colliery Sidings. It was raised up in August 1914, and was renamed on 9 January 1931. It had a 24-lever frame to control access to the colliery sidings and the passing loop but, on closure of the colliery and the removal of the sidings, it became a passing place only; subsequently, its working levers were reduced to ten. ***(Author's collection)***

Left: The signalman enacts a token exchange with the train crew, witnessed from a passing excursion heading towards Seymour. The 'box closed on 30 November 1969 but was left standing for several years afterwards ***(Pete Churchman collection)***

Left: The Staveley Company sank Barlborough No. 1 Colliery in 1871, and by 1878 the complex was complete with railway sidings, washery and brick works. It was purchased by the Oxcroft Coal Company in 1930 to develop the High Hazel seam, and became known as Oxcroft No. 3. It continued working until 1946 when severe geological and water problems affected production. Fortunately, a new face was developed which allowed the colliery to work until closure in 1949.

Right: This is the LD&ECR bridge over the MR Clowne Branch, dated 7 June 1934. The signal box controlled the LD&ECR's access to Barlborough Colliery. Originally named Barlborough Colliery Junction, it was renamed Oxcroft Colliery No. 3 in 1930; being on a different line ensured the two boxes were not confused. It was abolished on 5 April 1950. The sidings in the foreground were operated by the MR's Oxcroft Colliery Sidings No. 3 'box. Slayley Hill bridge is in the background. ***(Both Author's collection)***

Left: Photographed from the parapet of the closed LD&ECR line overbridge, 56015 passes beneath Slayley Hill bridge as it slogs up the 1 in 66 climb towards Clowne. Out of sight at the rear would have been the banking loco. ***(Phil Sangwell)***

Below: Just after passing Oxcroft Junction, 47060 & 47845 pass milepost 154 with the Branch Line Society's "The Barrow Hill Farewell" railtour on 23 March 1991. The image was taken from the Bolsover Road overbridge. ***(Author's collection)***

Below: With the now-disused line to Creswell in the foreground, and milepost 154 visible right-of-centre, 60011 "Cader Idris" takes the Oxcroft Colliery Branch on 29 March 1995. This one-mile branch opened in 1908 and was originally controlled from Oxcroft Junction signal box, which opened on 21 June 1908. It closed on 5 September 1915 and was replaced by a ground frame. ***(Author)***

Above: Oxcroft Colliery No. 1 survived until 27 February 1976, and Oxcroft Colliery No. 5 (a short-lived drift mine on the site of what would become Oxcroft Colliery No. 1 railway sidings) later became the Oxcroft Coal Disposal Point. 56131 "Ellington Colliery" is at the disposal point on 17 November 1995, having brought in and detached from a set of HAA wagons for loading. It will run to the other end of a waiting loaded set which will then make 7F35 for Ferrybridge. The method of working here was for the internal shunter to drag the empty wagons from the sidings and split them into sets of four or five to push beneath the loading screen. The wagons would then be pushed back into the sidings and the process repeated until all wagons were loaded.

Above: As viewed from the M1 Motorway embankment, 58006 is seen leaving Oxcroft with 7C75 to Drakelow "C" Power Station on 17 March 1994. ***(Both Author)***

Left: 56013 climbs the 1 in 182 gradient to join the Clowne Branch (descending at 1 in 66 from Clowne) as it leaves the Oxcroft Colliery Branch in the early 1980s. The signal is worked from the ground frame just behind the photographer. ***(Phil Sangwell)***

Right: 56089 worked the final train from Seymour Stocking Site on 28 January 1997 as 7H12 15.02 Seymour to Drax, which is on the left at Seymour Sidings. It is being passed by 58012 with 7B67 Oxcroft to West Burton. The 58 is on the Clowne Branch and the line to the right is to Bolsover. Seymour Junction 'box is behind the camera. ***(Author)***

Above: The first 'box at Seymour was called Clowne Branch Junction, and opened before August 1877. A second structure superseded it on 19 June 1888 and was renamed Seymour Junction. This was further replaced on 28 May 1928 by the 'box shown here. In this 28 July 1963 view, the next and final Seymour Junction incarnation – a BR Type 19 – can be seen in the background. ***(Mike King)***

Below: Looking west, the spoil heaps of Ireland Colliery tower over Seymour Junction. The houses on the left are in Poolsbrook. The fine signal gantry was lost when the area was re-signalled in 1982. ***(Author's collection)***

Above: A Barrow Hill-based Class 08 shunts the sidings at Seymour Junction on 13 April 1982. ***(RCTS GGR0138C Gordon Grubb)***

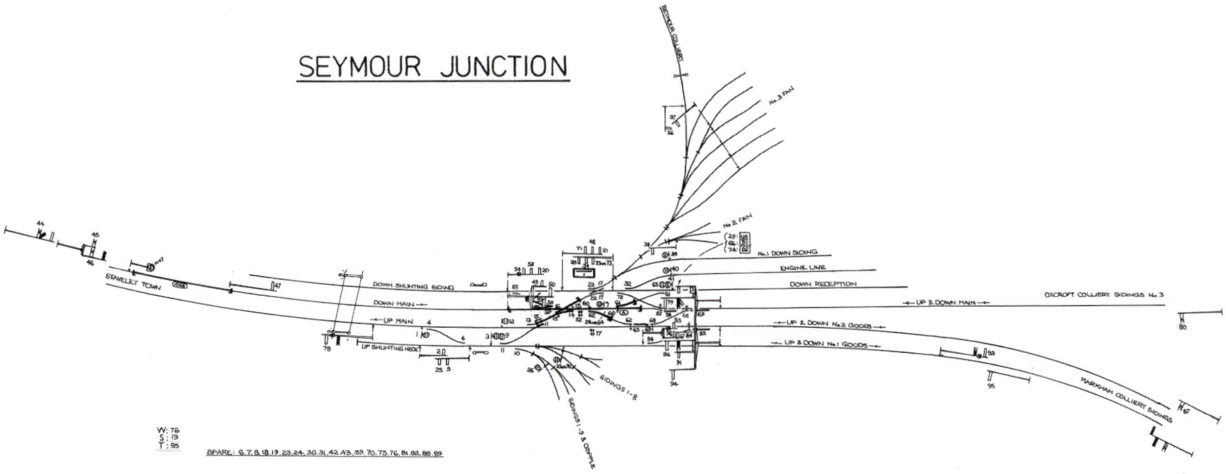

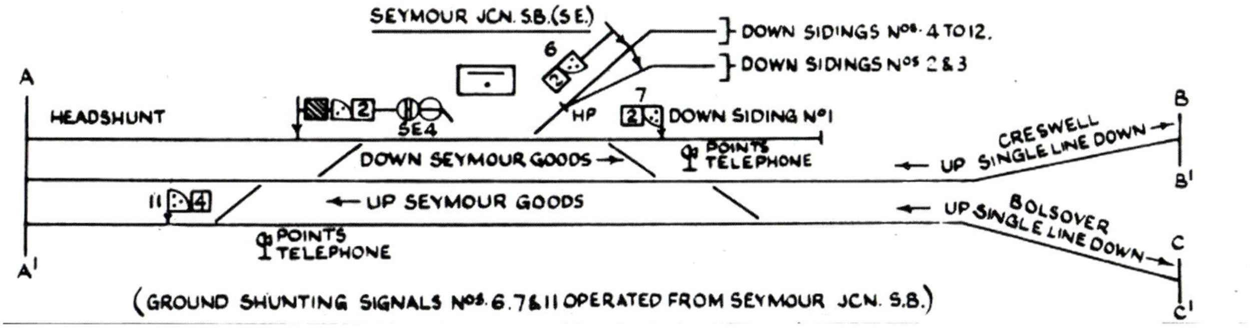

Centre & above: The layout at Seymour Junction as it was in 1968 when the 1963-built 'box still contained a 95-lever frame to control the steam-era layout. In 1982 the area was re-signalled and rationalised; all the sidings on the Up side were dispensed with and the much simpler layout only required a 25-lever frame. The area was prone to flooding so the opportunity was taken to move the relays from downstairs onto the operating floor, adjacent to the frame where floodwater couldn't reach them. The diagram of the re-signalled Seymour Junction is dated 15 August 1982. ***(John Hinson/Andrew K. Overton)***

Doe Lea Valley Line

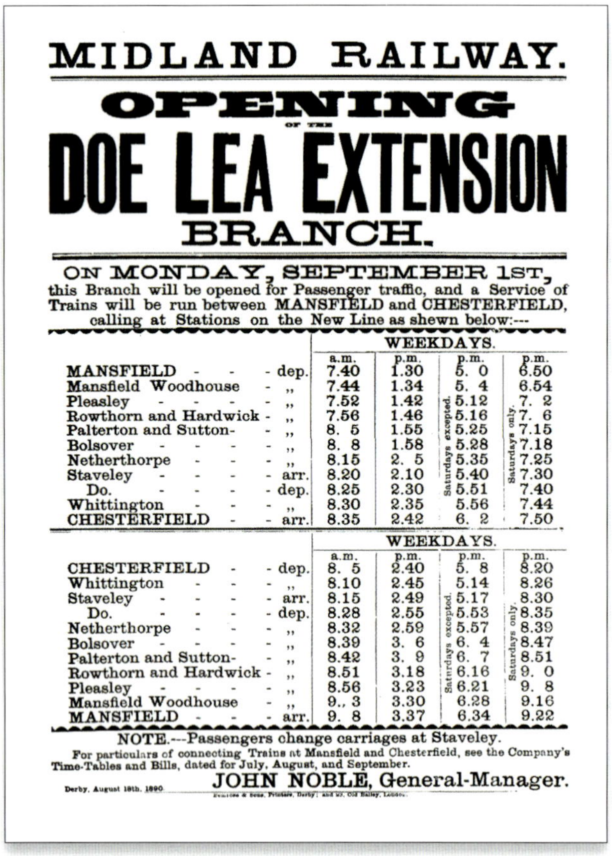

MIDLAND RAILWAY.

OPENING OF THE

DOE LEA EXTENSION BRANCH.

ON MONDAY, SEPTEMBER 1ST,
this Branch will be opened for Passenger traffic, and a Service of Trains will be run between MANSFIELD and CHESTERFIELD, calling at Stations on the New Line as shewn below:---

		WEEKDAYS.			
		a.m.	p.m.	p.m. Saturdays excepted.	p.m. Saturdays only.
MANSFIELD	dep.	7.40	1.30	5. 0	6.50
Mansfield Woodhouse	,,	7.44	1.34	5. 4	6.54
Pleasley	,,	7.52	1.42	5.12	7. 2
Rowthorn and Hardwick	,,	7.56	1.46	5.16	7. 6
Palterton and Sutton	,,	8. 5	1.55	5.25	7.15
Bolsover	,,	8. 8	1.58	5.28	7.18
Netherthorpe	,,	8.15	2. 5	5.35	7.25
Staveley	arr.	8.20	2.10	5.40	7.30
Do.	dep.	8.25	2.30	5.51	7.40
Whittington	,,	8.30	2.35	5.56	7.44
CHESTERFIELD	arr.	8.35	2.42	6. 2	7.50

		WEEKDAYS.			
		a.m.	p.m.	p.m. Saturdays excepted.	p.m. Saturdays only.
CHESTERFIELD	dep.	8. 5	2.40	5. 8	8.20
Whittington	,,	8.10	2.45	5.14	8.26
Staveley	arr.	8.15	2.49	5.17	8.30
Do.	dep.	8.28	2.55	5.53	8.35
Netherthorpe	,,	8.32	2.59	5.57	8.39
Bolsover	,,	8.39	3. 6	6. 4	8.47
Palterton and Sutton	,,	8.42	3. 9	6. 7	8.51
Rowthorn and Hardwick	,,	8.51	3.18	6.16	9. 0
Pleasley	,,	8.56	3.23	6.21	9. 8
Mansfield Woodhouse	,,	9., 3	3.30	6.28	9.16
MANSFIELD	arr.	9. 8	3.37	6.34	9.22

NOTE.---Passengers change carriages at Staveley.

For particulars of connecting Trains at Mansfield and Chesterfield, see the Company's Time-Tables and Bills, dated for July, August, and September.

Derby, August 18th, 1890. **JOHN NOBLE, General-Manager.**

Left: The Doe Lea Extension Branch opened to passenger traffic throughout on Monday 1 September 1890, as this poster extolled, with a weekday service of four trains each way. ***(Glynn Waite collection)***

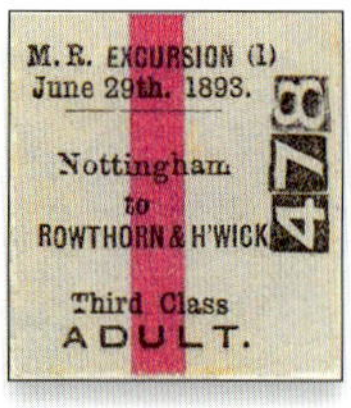

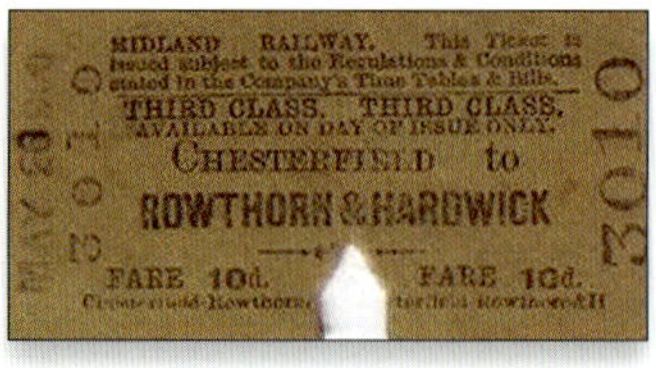

Above: The first station on the branch itself from the Mansfield direction was Rowthorn & Hardwick. These tickets are for journeys from either end of the route to Rowthorn & Hardwick – a MR Excursion from Nottingham dated 29 June 1893, and a Third Class from Chesterfield with a fare of 10d. ***(Both Glynn Waite collection)***

Below: It is thought no photographs survive of this station, but the 1904 Railway Clearing House Handbook of Railway Stations shows that it was capable of dealing with passengers, goods, livestock, horse boxes and prize cattle vans. This map shows there was a loop and siding, although the station was single line with just one platform. Gough's book does not mention a signal box, so access to the loop and siding was probably via a ground frame. ***(Map reproduced courtesy of the National Library of Scotland)***

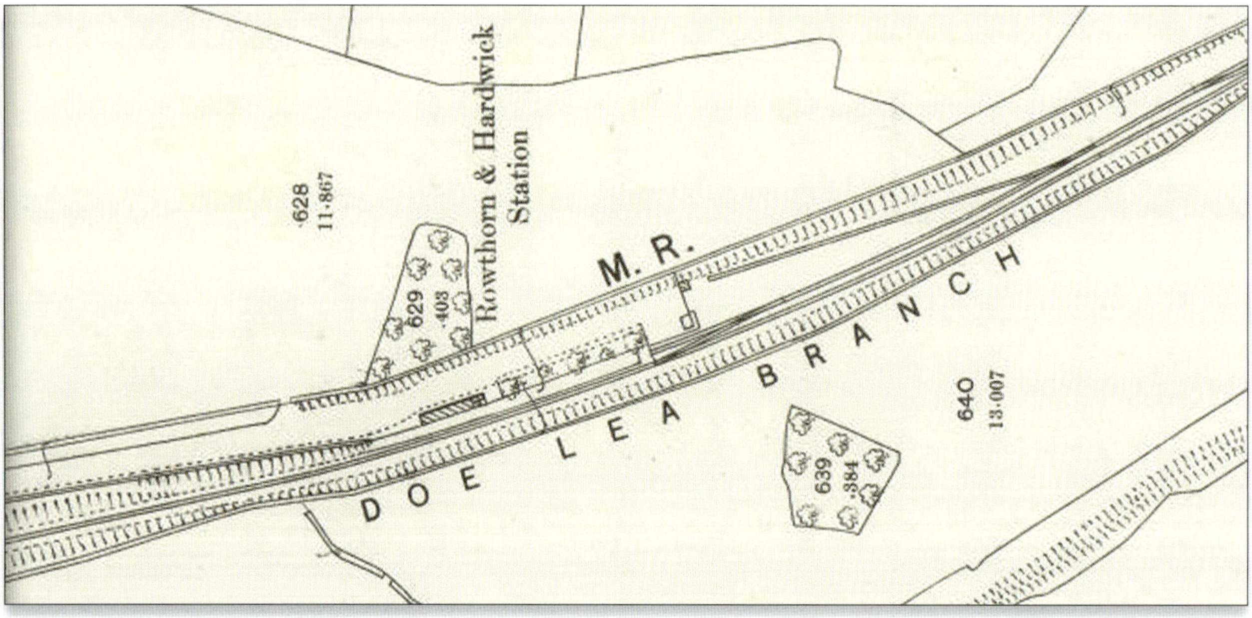

Right - opposite page: North of Rowthorn & Hardwick is Rowthorn Tunnel, the south portal being seen on 2 January 1924. The May 1941 Railway Magazine contained a letter and photograph from Mr J. Marshall which read: An Abandoned Midland Branch: On July 28, 1931 the Doe Lea branch of the late Midland Railway, from Pleasley to Staveley, was closed to passenger traffic by the L.M.S.R., and in part abandoned, and included in the abandoned section is Rowthorne tunnel. Mr. J. Marshall, draws attention to the characteristic Midland board at the tunnel entrance, giving its name and length, which is still in position. The tunnel is 929 yd. long, and though the south entrance is in good repair, the northern end has suffered from colliery subsidence, and looks on the point of collapse; the sides are bulging inwards, and masonry has fallen from above. Between here and the site of Rowthorn sidings three small underline bridges have been dismantled. Beyond here was situated Rowthorne and Hardwick station, little trace of which now remains. ***(John Alsop collection)***

MANSFIELD, TEVERSALL, ALFRETON AND BOLSOVER.

	WEEKDAYS.																			
MANSFIELD .. dep.	7 5	7 35	9 37	..	1 5	1 10	1 45	2 5	..	4 45	5 0	6 50	6 52	8 15	10 20	..	..	..	..	..
Mansfield Woodhouse	7 9	7 39	9 41	..	1 9	1 14	1 49	2 9	..	4 49	5 4	6 54	6 56	8 19	10 26	..	..	..	..	..
Pleasley	7 18	7 47	9 50	10 5	1 18	1 22	1 57	2 17	3 25	4 57	5 12	7 2	7 5	8 28	10 34	..	..	..	..	..
Teversall	7 25	..	9 57	Saturdays only.	1 25	Saturdays excepted.	Saturdays only.	2 25	Saturdays only.	Saturdays only.	Saturdays excepted.	Saturdays only.	7 12	8 35	Saturdays only.	..	..	..	..	..
Whiteboro' (for Hucknall Huthwaite)	7 30	..	10 2		1 30			2 30					7 17	8 40		..	..	..	..	..
Tibshelf & Newton	7 34	..	10 6		1 34			2 34					7 21	8 44		..	..	..	..	..
Westhouses & Blackwell	7 39	..	10 11		1 39			2 39					7 26	8 49		..	..	..	..	..
ALFRETON & South Normanton arr.	7 42	..	10 14		1 42			2 43					7 29	8 52		..	..	..	..	..
Rowthorn & Hardwick	..	7 53	..	10 12	Saturdays excepted.	1 28	2 3	Saturdays only.	3 32	5 3	5 18	7 8	Saturdays excepted.	Saturdays only.	10 40	..	..	..	..	..
Glapwell	..	7 58	..	10 17		1 33	2 8		3 38	5 8	5 23	7 13			10 45	..	..	..	..	..
Palterton & Sutton	..	8 3	..	10 22		1 38	2 13		3 51	5 13	5 28	7 27			..	..	..	..	..	..
Bolsover	..	8 6	..	10 25		1 41	2 18		3 54	5 17	5 31	7 30			10 51	..	..	..	..	..
Staveley Town	..	8 11	..	10 30		1 46	2 23		3 57	5 23	5 36	7 36			10 57	..	..	..	..	..
Barrow Hill & Staveley Works arr.	..	8 17	..	10 36		1 52	2 30		4 3	5 30	5 42	7 42			11 3	..	..	..	..	..
Barrow Hill & Staveley Works dep.	..	8 30	..	10 38	..	2 6	2 35		4 4	5 33	5 45	7 44			..	..	..	..	..	..
Whittington	..	8 35	..	..		2 9	2 39		4 8	5 38	5 50	7 49			..	..	..	..	..	..
CHESTERFIELD arr.	8 10	8 40	11 10	10 46	3 19	2 14	2 45	3 19	4 14	5 45	5 55	7 54	8 25	9 26	..	..	..	..	..	..

	WEEKDAYS.																			
CHESTERFIELD .. dep.	8 7	8 20	9 5	10 5	1 35	1 35	3 2	3 14	5 50	6 50	7 52	8 40	8 33	10 55	..	..	..	..	..	..
Whittington	..	8 26	9 10	..	..	..	3 8	..	5 55	6 54	..	8 45	..	11 0	..	..	..	..	..	..
Barrow Hill & Staveley Works arr.	..	8 28	9 13	..	..	..	3 10	3 24	5 59	6 59	..	8 48	..	11 3	..	..	..	..	..	..
Barrow Hill & Staveley Works dep.	..	8 35	9 25	..	Saturdays only.	..	3 15	3 26	6 7	7 1	Saturdays excepted.	8 49	Saturdays only.	11 8	..	..	..	..	..	..
Staveley Town	..	8 38	9 29	..		..	3 17	3 28	6 10	7 5		8 51		11 10	..	..	..	..	..	..
Bolsover	..	8 47	9 40	..		..	3 26	3 40	6 19	7 15		9 0		11 19	..	..	..	..	..	..
Palterton & Sutton	..	8 50	9 43	..		..	3 29	3 44	6 23	7 19		9 4		..	..	..	..	..	..	..
Glapwell	..	8 55	9 47	..		..	3 33	3 48	6 27	7 28		9 8		11 25	..	..	..	..	..	..
Rowthorn & Hardwick	..	9 1	9 52	..		..	3 38	3 53	6 32	7 37		9 13		..	..	..	..	..	..	..
ALFRETON & South Normanton dep.	8 30	..	Saturdays only.	11 8	2 2	3 0	Saturdays excepted.	Saturdays only.	Saturdays excepted.	Saturdays only.	8 29	Saturdays only.	9 16	Saturdays only.	..	..	..	..	..	..
Westhouses & Blackwell	8 34	..		11 14	2 6	3 4					8 33		9 20		..	..	..	..	..	..
Tibshelf & Newton	8 38	..		11 19	2 11	3 9					8 39		9 25		..	..	..	..	..	..
Whiteboro' (for Hucknall Huthwaite)	8 42	..		11 23	2 15	3 13					8 43		9 29		..	..	..	..	..	..
Teversall	8 47	..		11 27	2 19	3 17					8 47		9 33		..	..	..	..	..	..
Pleasley	8 55	9 7	9 57	11 33	2 25	3 23	3 43	3 58	6 37	7 48	8 53	9 21	9 38	..	..	..	..	..	..	..
Mansfield Woodhouse	9 5	9 14	..	11 40	2 38	3 30	3 52	4 5	6 46	8 0	8 59	9 29	9 45	..	..	..	..	..	..	..
MANSFIELD arr.	9 11	9 20	..	11 45	2 43	3 35	3 57	4 10	6 52	8 10	9 5	9 35	9 50	..	..	..	..	..	..	..

Trains shewn in italics run only as indicated.

Above: The Midland Railway timetable for July, August and September 1903, now showing a few more trains per week along the line.

Left: Undoubtedly the only reason for a station at Rowthorn & Hardwick was the proximity of Hardwick Hall, less than two miles by road, or less than a mile as the crow flies; in 1885 the hamlet of Rowthorne had less than 200 residents. Designed by Robert Smythson, an exponent of the Renaissance style, and built between 1590 and 1597 for Bess of Hardwick, Hardwick Hall is one of the earliest examples of the English interpretation of this style which, having slowly spread from Florence, came into fashion. Its arrival in Britain coincided with the period when it was no longer necessary or legal to fortify a domestic dwelling. This Midland Railway postcard extolls its virtues and gives the quote "more glass than wall", a well-known local saying that actually characterises one of the key features of Hardwick, namely the exuberant use of glass, an expensive and rare material for houses in 1590s England. Today it is owned by the National Trust and well worth a visit. ***(Both Author's collection)***

Above: Four staff members pose on a station barrow for the obligatory photo call at Glapwell station in Midland Railway days c1912. The station nameboard has been changed; the original blue enamel type with white lettering has been replaced with the later wooden style with screwed-on cast letters. There are various adverts on the station wall including one for Northern Ireland and one about Parcels. ***(Author's collection)***

Midland Railway.

OFFICE OF SUPERINTENDENT OF THE LINE,

DERBY, AUGUST 30TH, 1892

CIRCULAR No. 600.

OPENING OF GLAPWELL STATION.

This Station, which is situated between Rowthorn and Hardwick and Palterton and Sutton, has been opened for passenger traffic, and parcels, &c., may be entered to that Station accordingly.

Above: Glapwell was the final station to open along the Doe Lea Valley Line. This section of a Midland Railway notice dated August 30th 1892 announces its opening. ***(Midland Railway Study Centre)***

Left: Passenger traffic ceased on 28 July 1930 and the station was abandoned, along with the track southwards through Rowthorn Tunnel to Pleasley Colliery West. The station building found other uses and by the early 1970s was used by the Full Gospel Revival Mission as a meeting hall. It is seen here in 1974. ***(Author's collection)***

Left: The first Glapwell Colliery Sidings 'box, opened on 14 July 1890, was superseded by this one dating from 29 March 1925. This photo was taken on 29 March 1969, exactly 44 years later. The closure date is not recorded but was sometime between 1969 and 1978. The trackbed in front of the 'box was occupied by two tracks that by-passed the screens to the empty sidings; the Doe Lea Valley single line passed behind the 'box before closure in 1932. The photo was taken from an enthusiasts' special train on the lines into the loaded sidings. ***(Colour-Rail 25324)***

Right: Moments before the previous photo was taken on 29 March 1969, the photographer is observed by a shunter in his small cabin at the bottom of the image. ***(J.G.S. Smith/Author's collection)***

Above left: Tablet for the section between Bolsover and Glapwell, which sold at auction in September 2018 for £260. Bolsover 'box closed in 1978 and the Signal Alterations Notice for Saturday 6 May to Friday 12 May 1978 stated the following: "BOLSOVER CASTLE - MARKHAM COLLIERY SIDINGS TO GLAPWELL. The single line between Markham Colliery Sidings Signal box and Glapwell Colliery Sidings Ground Frame has been renamed Up/Down Bolsover and will be worked in accordance with the 'One Train Working' regulations. The authority for the single line will be a tablet labelled 'Markham to Glapwell'. The key for releasing Glapwell Colliery Sidings Ground Frame is kept at Markham Colliery Sidings Signal box." ***(Author's collection)***

Above: The Glapwell branch was used for several railtours. This is the RCTS "Dukeries Rail Tour" of 24 July 1960, which used 43145, 44590 & 64314 in sections. The first two mentioned can be seen here at Glapwell; the Route Reporting Code 320 is seen on the buffer beam of Ivatt Class 4 2-6-0 "Flying Pig" 43145. ***(H.K.Boulter/Author's collection)***

Above: In 1882 the Sheepbridge Coal and Iron Co sunk shafts close to Ault Hucknall, but named it Glapwell. At the time the village consisted of just 18 homes, but these were soon bolstered with the building of miners' houses. In July 1883, the Top Hard seam was reached at a depth of 300 yards. Glapwell No. 1 Colliery seen here was worked from 1882 to 1960, whilst Glapwell No. 3 Colliery alongside was worked from 1923 onwards. In 1954 Bramley Vale Drift Mine was also connected, and was worked until 1970. By 1930 there were 3,273 men employed, which dwindled slightly to 3,060 in 1949 and to 2,935 in 1950 (consisting of 2,338 below and 597 on the surface). New technology enabled the highest output from the pit in the years 1967/8 at 1,101,370 tons. Glapwell station is in the foreground, and special "Paddy Mails" were laid on to bring in the workers. These trains utilised coaches that were utterly worn out but, as men were not allowed by law to travel with the public in their dirty work clothes, the roughest stock had to be endured. The colliery closed on 30 June 1974, although the Merry-Go-Round circular issued for the week ending March 1976 showed Glapwell dispatching 2,500 tons of coal to West Burton Power Station, as 6G74 18.15 MWThO – probably to clear the remaining stocks. ***(Author's collection)***

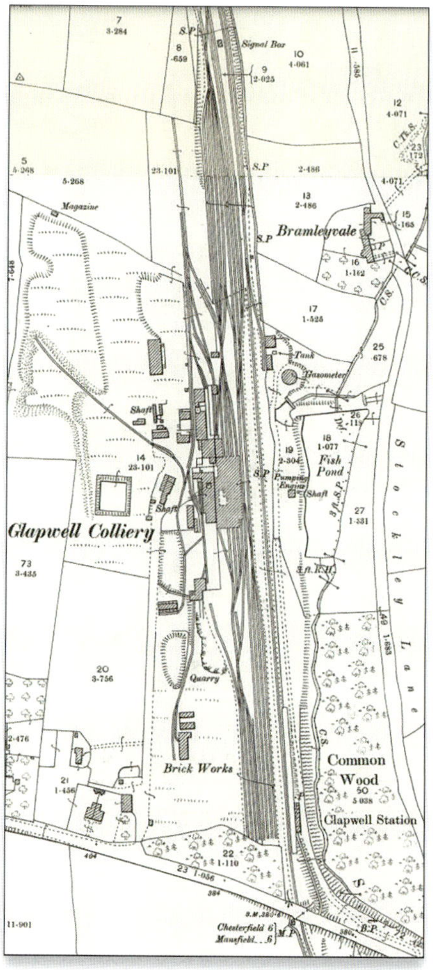

Right: Map of the Glapwell area. The station is bottom right. ***(Reproduced courtesy of the National Library of Scotland)***

Above: Contemporary postcard view of Glapwell Colliery. ***(Author's collection)***

Right: The RCTS "Dukeries Rail Tour" of 24 July 1960, with Fowler 4F 0-6-0 44590 leading Ivatt Class 4 2-6-0 "Flying Pig" 43145. A healthy number of loaded 16-ton wagons await collection from Glapwell Colliery Sidings as the participants of the tour wander around. ***(Colour-Rail 303934)***

Above: On 16 October 1965 the RCTS (West Midlands Branch) ran the "Midlands Locomotive Requiem" Rail Tour which utilised specially-prepared 4F 0-6-0 43953 from Nuneaton Abbey Street to Seymour Junction, where Clayton (Class 17) D8613 was attached. The train then ran along the Doe Lea Valley Line as far as Glapwell Colliery Sidings, before returning to Seymour Junction without the Clayton. The approach to Glapwell Colliery is seen, as viewed from the train. The conical tip was flattened after closure of the colliery and very little sign of it remains. ***(Dave Hill)***

Right: After arrival at Glapwell, the 4F ran round the train, while D8613 was uncoupled to follow the train back to Seymour Junction. The Claytons were a short-lived and unsuccessful class; D8613 was new to 41A Tinsley on 22 January 1965, and moved to 41E on 10 April 1965, before the whole class were transferred to Scotland. D8613 moved to 64B Haymarket on 28 May 1966. Condemned on 6 October 1971, it was scrapped in August 1975. ***(TOPticl Digital Memories – https://topsie.wixsite.com/topticl)***

Right: Glapwell Colliery No. 14, seen on 2 August 1959. Built by Hudswell Clarke Works as No. 1353 of 1919, it was new to the Sheepbridge Coal and Iron Company at Crosby Ironstone Quarries, Frodingham. In December 1925 it moved to the Sheepbridge Works near Chesterfield, and thence to Glapwell in August 1934. On Vesting Day 1 January 1947, Glapwell became part of National Coal Board Area 2, then NCB Area 1 from 1 July 1949. There are no disposal details available for the loco. ***(Andy Bailey)***

Right: Robert Stephenson & Hawthorns Works No. 7091 of 1943 at Glapwell Colliery on 19 May 1963, still wearing its War Department No. 75055. New to Longtown (MOD) but stored at Longmoor from March to December 1944, it went to France and Belgium between February 1945 and January 1947. On return to the UK it was initially stored at Ipswich MPD prior to sale to the NCB at Moor Green workshops. It was then moved around the following: Hartington Colliery (Staveley) (September 1947), Westthorpe Colliery (1948), Markham (1954), Creswell (April 1955), Glapwell (June 1955), Markham (late 1955) and Glapwell again (March 1960). Reportedly out of use at Glapwell by December 1965, it was sold for scrap to T W Ward on 30 November 1966. ***(RCTS Collection Jack Faithfull FA14735)***

Right: On a wet 20 June 1974, Brush Type 4 D1630 was sent to clear the remaining wagons in Glapwell Colliery Sidings, and is seen waiting to return to Seymour Junction. This loco became 47048 in March 1974, Class 47/4 No. 47570 on 31 October 1980, and latterly Class 47/8 No. 47849 on 31 January 1990. The loco was removed from service on 1 December 2001 and scrapped by C. F. Booth at Rotherham on 1 May 2002. ***(Phil Sangwell)***

Above: Palterton & Sutton station opened to passengers on 1 September 1890, and to goods 18 days later. It is seen during flooding in 1931, just after the end of passenger services, as Johnson 3F 0-6-0 3242 creates a splash with a coal train heading northwards towards Bolsover. Palterton & Sutton signal box opened on 11 August 1918 as an intermediate token station, but not a passing place as it was initially single track here, with a passing loop provided later. As mentioned previously the 'box closed on 31 July 1934, with a GF being provided in lieu of access to the Ramcroft Colliery Branch. The signalman can be seen observing the proceedings from the balcony, as a staff member on the platform is about to get his feet wet from the resulting bow wave!

Above: The loco crew look on at the photographer, who has moved to ground level to take another photo. The first wagon carries "Sheepbridge"; this would have been bright red with a black underframe, and white (shaded black) lettering. The Southern Railway (SR) 12-ton 8-plank open wagon behind is a long way from home, and would have carried a brown livery with white letters. No. 3242 was built at Derby in 1890, and at the beginning of 1948 was allocated to 18D Staveley (Barrow Hill), where it gained its BR number 43242. It moved to 18A Toton in January 1950, followed by 16C Kirkby in Ashfield and finally 21A Saltley in the week ending 10 January 1959. It was withdrawn in the week ending 4 August 1962. ***(Both courtesy Midland Railway Study Centre)***

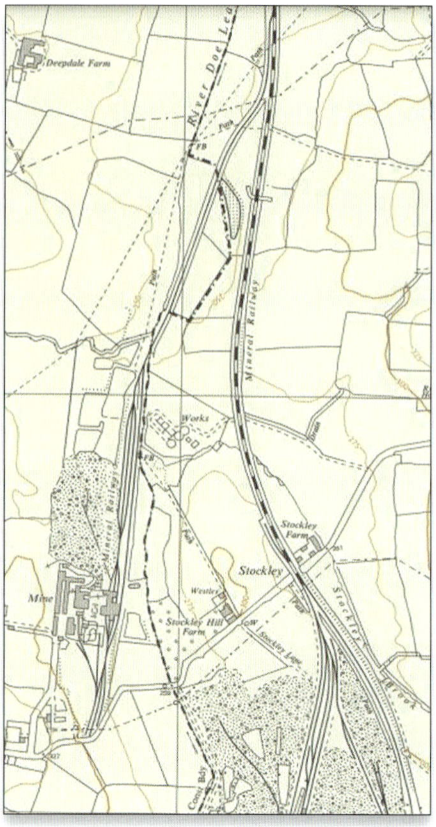

Above & right: The Ramcroft Colliery Company was formed by Charles Paxton Markham as a direct result of the war effort. The Top Hard seam was accessed at 152 yards deep, and it was proposed to further exploit the coal reserves of the Palterton and Heath areas of the Sutton estates. The MR began working the Ramcroft Colliery Branch on 16 September 1918 and a colliery workmen's train service was introduced. The MR also leased two pieces of land for sidings on 25 March 1919 for an annual rent of £37:2s:6d. The map shows Ramcroft Colliery and its branch diverging from the Doe Lea Valley Line; notice the proximity to Glapwell Colliery at the bottom of the map. The workmen's service was withdrawn on 3 October 1927, and the mine was mothballed in 1929. Palterton & Sutton signal box closed on 31 July 1934, colliery access being provided by a GF in lieu. Ramcroft reopened for coal production in 1939, and closed again in October 1966. The area was later opencast, the last remaining seams being removed from the Deep Ring Bell opencast operation. The land was returned to agricultural use afterwards. ***(Author's collection, map courtesy of the National Library of Scotland)***

Left: Looking rather diesel-esq in outline, this is actually a steam loco built by the Sentinel Waggon Works of Shrewsbury. Seen at Ramcroft, Sentinel No. 2 was Works No. 9580 of 1954, delivered new on 10 December 1954 to NCB East Midlands Division, Holmewood Colliery. ***(Colour-Rail 111499)***

Above: One of the many plates issued to commemorate closed collieries, in this case Ramcroft. ***(Janet Silk collection)***

Left: NCB No. 13 0-6-0ST seen at Ramcroft Colliery on 8 March 1964. This was Avonside Engine Co. Works No. AE1727 of 1916. ***(Transport Library HG2092/Horace Gamble)***

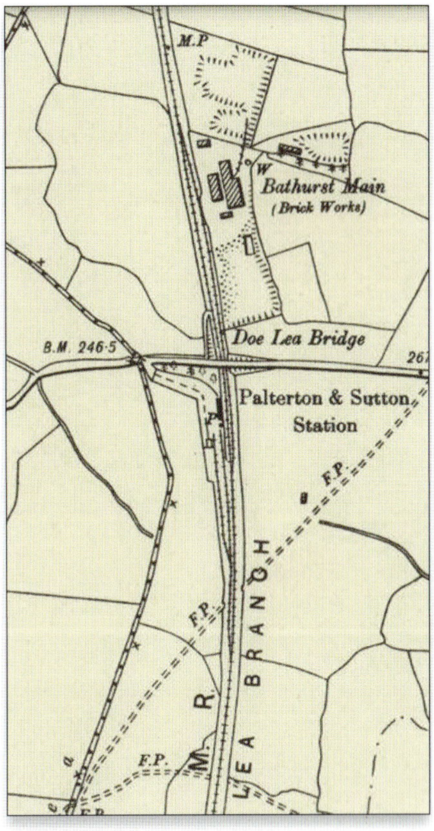

Above & right: The New Byron Brickworks are thought to have opened around 1850, making fireclay products from clay extracted by surface drift in fields to the south of the works and conveyed there by road. The works were originally named Bathurst Main Brickworks (as on this map), and was situated just north of Palterton & Sutton Station. By the beginning of the 20th century the fireclay from the adjacent area was becoming inferior in quality and its use was discontinued, although fireclay products continued to be made by female labour from imported fireclay. Building brick production began with appropriate material being quarried from the area immediately adjacent to the works. On the outbreak of WW2, and until 1942, the bricks produced were used to construct air raid shelters in Carr Vale and the surrounding area. In 1942 the brickworks closed and the premises were requisitioned for use as a sorting and storage depot for shell cases, although brick-making recommenced after the war. The company entered liquidation in 1958, and the works and land were acquired by the local authority for refuse tipping. The single line towards Bolsover is on the left, with the brick-loading siding on the right. By the time of the photo it was in use for wagon storage – notice the gap left in the rake of wagons for the foot crossing. ***(Map reproduced courtesy of the NLS, photo Author's collection)***

Left: The 16 October 1965 RCTS "Midlands Locomotive Requiem" railtour with 4F 0-6-0 43953 and Class 17 Clayton D8613 is seen passing the former brickworks on its way to Glapwell. Bolsover Castle dominates the hillside on the right. ***(J.S. Gilks)***

Below left: Just after the brickworks the line passed beneath the LD&ECR Bolsover (or Carr Vale) Viaduct. The Engineer of 28 February 1896 showed this engraving of the viaduct, which straddled the Doe Lea Valley and the Midland Railway line, with the following caption: "The Bolsover viaduct, of which the engraving on page 118 shows a portion only, the central part, which consists of eight semi-circular arches, each of 35-foot span. The greatest height, which is above the proposed Glapwell extension of the Manchester, Sheffield, and Lincolnshire Railway, is 80 feet from foundations to rail level. The foundations, which are of Portland cement concrete go down, on average, 20 feet and are founded on hard blue bind. The construction is of brick with brindle brick facings throughout, all angles, both in piers and arches, being bull-nose." Notice the mention of the MS&LR Glapwell Extension, which was never built. ***(Author's collection)***

Left & centre left: Bolsover Station signal box opened on 11 June 1893 as an intermediate tablet station. It is seen here not long before closure, which came on 23 April 1978. Looking north, Bolsover Station can just be discerned on the curve. After the signal box's removal, the run round loop points became hand operated, the loop remaining in use until the end of traffic from the coalite plant.

Below left: The 24-lever frame inside the 'box, with a tablet machine and auxiliary machines on their respective lockers. ***(All Bill and Jim Froggatt collection)***

Below: Signalman Brian Mitchell poses on the 'box steps. ***(Author's collection)***

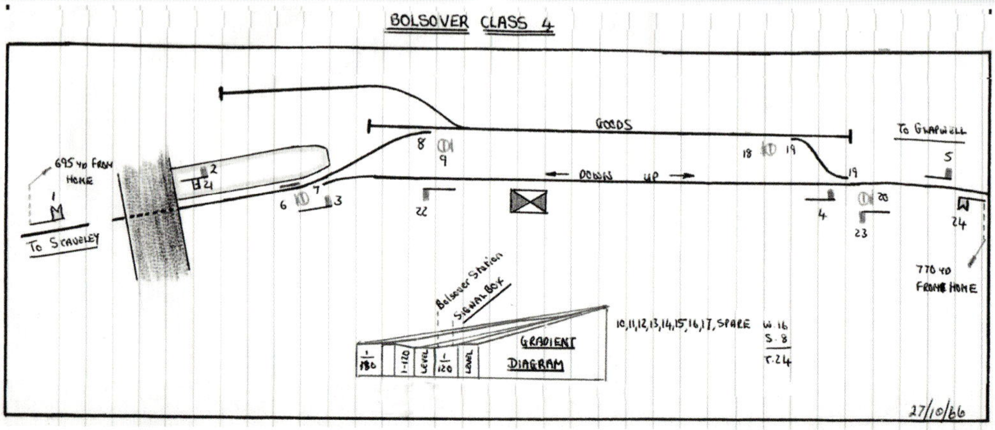

Above: Hand drawn diagram of Bolsover Station 'box, which was a Class 4 'box at that time. The diagram dates from 27 October 1966. ***(Malcolm Rush)***

Right: Bolsover Station opened without ceremony on 1 September 1890, and four staff members pose for their photo on a sack barrow. Epps's Cocoa, portrayed on the enamel advert, was founded in 1839 by homoeopathic chemist James Epps. He later owned a cocoa plantation in Jamaica and his own ship to transport the crop, the Epps Cocoa London factory occupying an area of about two acres. James Epps & Co acquired Taylor Brothers in 1908, and was bought by Rowntree in 1925. The factory was closed in 1931. After closure to normal passenger traffic, an unadvertised service continued to call until 14 August 1931. Pre-war excursions continued until at least 27 July 1939. Records show that a half-day excursion service called at Bolsover on 26 July 1949. The station gained the suffix "Castle" on 25 September 1950 to distinguish it from the nearby ex-LD&ECR "Bolsover", which became "Bolsover South". Goods facilities were withdrawn on 1 November 1962. Occasional specials continued to call at the station, such as one run to Chesterfield on 28 July 1977 in connection with the Queen's Jubilee celebrations, and there were yearly August excursions from 1978 until 1981 organised by Bolsover Miners' Welfare.

Right: Bolsover Station viewed southwards.

Right: The Midland Railway produced postcards showing interesting destinations close by their routes, including Bolsover Castle. This hand coloured postcard shows a gardener tending the flower beds at Bolsover Castle, with a very elegant lady looking on. The legend on the card reads "BOLSOVER CASTLE-Bolsover Station-MIDLAND RAILWAY". ***(All Author's collection)***

Left: The BR enamel station name board was purchased in a house sale for the sum of £5 by David Chandler. After its purchase it was stored out of sight at his house until the BBC Antiques Roadshow was staged at Bolsover Castle in November 2015. Here he stands proudly with his sign, which caused quite a stir at the event. After valuation and offers of purchase, the sign was eventually sold to Bolsover Castle for subsequent display. ***(Unknown)***

Right: Emerson Muschamp Bainbridge formed the Bolsover Colliery Co. Ltd in 1889, and secured a lease on land at Bolsover from the Duke of Portland. Shaft sinking began, and the Top Hard seam was reached at 356 yards' depth and production commenced in 1891. The Bolsover Colliery Co. also secured leases to mine at Creswell, Mansfield, Rufford, Clipstone and Thoresby, and by 1933 the company's mines were employing over 9,000 men. 4.5 million tons of coal were being extracted from the Top Hard, Waterloo and High Hazel seams by that time. In this 1900s postcard view of the colliery, a steam roller awaits further duties.

Left: Bolsover is seen here in 1938. ***(Both Author's collection)***

Below: Avonside 0-4-0ST Works No. 1999 of 1927 is seen at Bolsover Colliery on 8 March 1964. ***(Transport Library/ Horace Gamble)***

Below: English Electric Works No. D922 of 1965 is seen at NCB Bolsover Colliery on 23 May 1979. ***(Adrian Foster)***

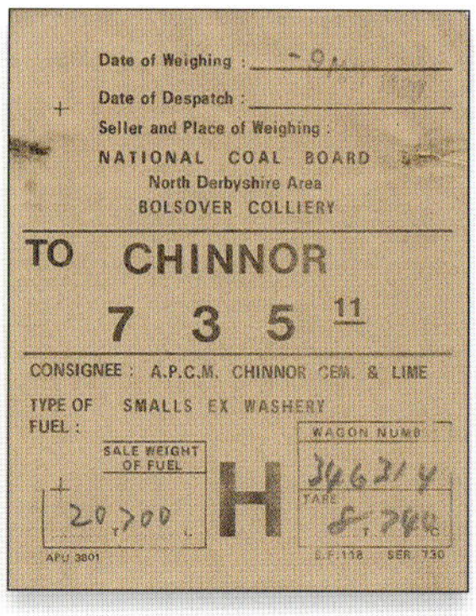

Right: Wagon labels from different eras: Left: A MR label from 1911; Right: An NCB from 1980. ***(Left Courtesy Midland Railway Study Centre/Right Author's collection)***

Right: Coalite smokeless coal was invented by Thomas Parker in 1904. The product is the residue left behind when coal is carbonised at 640 °C (1,184 °F). Darker and more friable than high temperature coke, it is easier to ignite, burns with an attractive flame, and is lighter than coal, making it an ideal fuel for open domestic fire grates. In 1936 the Smoke Abatement Society awarded its inventor (who died in 1915) a posthumous gold medal. The forerunner of the Coalite Company was formed with the building of a production unit at Barugh near Barnsley, followed in the 1920s by two more plants near Doncaster and at East Greenwich. In April 1937 the main manufacturing plant at Bolsover was opened by Prince George, Duke of Kent, at the time being the largest of its type in the world. Coal was delivered by rail, first from the nearby Bolsover Colliery and later from other sources. It was heated in eight large air sealed ovens called "batteries". Volatile constituents were driven off and condensed into coal oil and a watery fraction called ammoniacal liquor. Coal gas was used to heat the ovens and was also burned in the works boilers and furnaces. Any excess was flared off. The coal oil and liquor were piped over the road to the chemical works for processing into various chemicals. The residual Coalite solid fuel was cooled, sorted into various grades based on size, and stockpiled for distribution by road transport. By the 1950s older plants were closed with production concentrated at the expanded Bolsover and Askern plants. Further plants opened in Rossington and Grimethorpe. The coal oil and liquor from all these plants was processed at the central refinery at the Bolsover plant. In 1948 the name changed to the Coalite Chemical Company, and in 1952 the registered head office was moved from London to Bolsover. In 1956, after the introduction of the Clean Air Act, Coalite was licensed as an "authorised fuel". In 1978, the company merged with the Charringtons Coke distribution company, followed by the acquisition of the Falkland Islands Company. The acquisition in 1986 of Hargreaves Fuel distribution services marked the zenith of the company's fortunes; from there on it was downhill – the sale of solid fuel began to shrink in the 1980s as cheaper natural gas gradually took over the domestic heating market. After Askern works closed in 1986, Anglo United took over the company in 1989. Grimethorpe closed in 1994, and in 1997 the Falkland Islands Holdings subsidiary was floated off to become an independent company again. In 2002 Anglo was bought by a consortium of local businessmen, and soon after Coalite Chemicals Ltd went into administration and then receivership and, finding no buyers, closed down in 2004. For several years the site lay derelict before clearance of the heavily contaminated land began. The distinctive smell remained for several years, even when passing the site on the M1 Motorway. ***(Author's collection)***

Below: Coalite No. 2 was a Peckett 0-4-0ST, Works No. 1921 built in 1936. It is seen here stabled between duties (**top**) and working in the Coalite plant on 8 March 1964. ***(Top Author's collection, bottom Transport Library/ Horace Gamble)***

Left: The Coalite cruciform logo as seen on the Bolsover office building. ***(Author's collection)***

Above: Having visited Glapwell and left the Clayton behind, 4F 0-6-0 43953 returns the RCTS "Midlands Locomotive Requiem" special along the branch on 16 October 1965. The Coalite plant is on the right, with another access point into the sidings. This was controlled from the single-lever Distillates No. 1 GF, just out of sight to the left. The eagle-eyed may be able to spot Bolsover Castle lurking above the spoil heaps of Bolsover Colliery. ***(Transport Treasury MM3049)***

Below: 35 years later, 58025 passes the same spot on 20 July 2000 with 6Y42 empties from Bolsover Coalite to Worksop. The trees have matured in the interveining years and the spoil heaps have been flattened somewhat, revealing more of Bolsover Castle on the skyline. ***(Author)***

Above: Bolsover Coalite (or Distillates No. 1 GF) single-lever GF as seen on 18 July 1992. ***(Andrew K Overton)***

Above: Load Haul-liveried 56055 is viewed from the former Buttermilk Lane Bridge on 21 June 2000 with 6Y42 Bolsover Coalite to Worksop. The Coalite Chemical works dominate the background. ***(Author)***

Left: Markham Colliery Sidings was the final signal box along the Doe Lea Valley before reaching Seymour Junction, controlling access into Markham Colliery. The original 1890 'box was at ground level, and was raised in height on 27 April 1919. It was replaced on 28 October 1928 by a new 'box, seen behind 47278 as it leaves the colliery with another load of "Black Gold". ***(Phil Sangwell)***

Above: The signalman stands at the top of the steps watching the photographer take his photo (**left**), and the well-kept frame inside (**right**). Around half of the levers are white, denoting they are spare. Notice the small suitcase on the cupboard top, no doubt containing the signalman's mashing tackle and snap! ***(Both Phil Sangwell)***

Left: In 1882 the Staveley Company leased 5,000 acres of coal reserves on the Sutton Estates from William Arkwright for a period of 63 years. By 1885 Markham No. 1 Colliery was in full production, Markham No. 2 being sunk in 1886. Another shaft was sunk at Doe Lea Bridge, which became Markham No. 5 Shaft. On Nationalisation in 1947, Markham came under the control of the National Coal Board. On 1 September 1967, Markham 1, 2, and 4 were merged into one Markham mine, which closed on 2 July 1993 after 109 years – one of Derbyshire's last deep mine closures.

Right: On 23 April 1989 The Institution of Mining Engineers ran the "Notts & North Derbyshire" railtour, which visited all the area's collieries. The train consisted of three Tyseley-based DMUs. It is seen on the approach to Markham Colliery Bunker, which was commissioned on Sunday 19 July 1970.

Below: The Doe Lea Valley and Elmton & Creswell via Clowne lines meet at Seymour Junction, where a 4F 0-6-0 and a WD 2-8-0 stand at the head of trains in the sidings. The wagons curving off to the left of the 'box are on the Seymour Colliery branch. *(All Author's collection)*

Pleasley Junction to Pleasley West

Right & below: Timetables reproduced from the May 1926 Bradshaw's Guide: Mansfield to Teversall and Alfreton & South Normanton (on the Erewash Valley Line); Mansfield to Clown, Bolsover, Staveley Town, Sheffield Rotherham, Eckington and Chesterfield Midland. ***(Author's collection)***

MANSFIELD, TEVERSALL, and ALFRETON AND SOUTH NORMANTON.—Midland.

Miles	Week Days.	mrn	aft	aft
	Mansfield .... dep.	6 58	2 0	5 15
1½	Mansfield Woodhouse	7 2	2 4	5 19
4½	Pleasley	7 12	2 14	5 29
7	Teversall	7 20	2 22	5 37
8½	Whitebore'	7 26	2 28	5 43
9½	Tibshelf and Newton	7 30	2 32	5 47
11½	Westhouses & Blackwell 476 . [477	7 34	2 37	5 52
12½	Alfreton & South Normanton . arr.	7 38	2 40	5 56

Miles	Week Days.	mrn	mrn	aft	aft
	Alfreton & South Normanton dep.	7 54	10 33	3 5	6 37
1½	Westhouses and Blackwell	7 58	10 38	3 10	6 42
3	Tibshelf and Newton	8 4	10 44	3 16	6 48
4½	Whitebore'	8 9	10 49	3 21	6 53
5½	Teversall	8 15	10 55	3 28	6 59
8½	Pleasley 480	8 24	11 4	3 39	7 9
11½	Mansfield Woodhouse 522	8 34	11 12	3 50	7 18
12½	Mansfield 473, 480, 481 ...... arr.	8 37	11 17	3 53	7 21

For other Trains BETWEEN Mansfield and Pleasley .... PAGE 480

MANSFIELD, CLOWN, BOLSOVER, STAVELEY TOWN, SHEFFIELD, ROTHERHAM, ECKINGTON, and CHESTERFIELD.—Midland.

Miles from Sheffield	Week Days.	mrn	mrn	mrn	mrn	mrn	aft	aft	aft	aft	aft	aft	aft	aft	aft	aft	Sundays. mrn	aft
	Mansfield .... dep.	6 45	7 23			Calls at West Tinsley on Saturdays at 12 3 aft.	1 5	1 15			1 45	3 58	4 48			Calls at Catcliffe on Saturdays at 9 41 aft.		
	Mansfield Woodhouse	6 49	7 27				1 9	1 19			1 49	4 4	4 52					
	Shirebrook	6 55						1 25				4 10						
	Langwith	7 0						1 30				4 15						
	Elmton and Creswell	7 24						1 37				4 33						
	Clown	7 32						1 45				4 41						
	Pleasley		7 37				1 17				1 59		5 3					
	Rowthorn and Hardwick		7 44				1 23				2 6		5 10					
	Glapwell		7 49				1 28				2 11		5 15					
	Palterton and Sutton		7 54				1 33				2 16		5 20					
	Bolsover †		7 58				1 36				2 20		5 24					
	Staveley Town	7 42	8 7				1 44	1 55			2 29	4 51	5 33					
—	Sheffield .... dep.				8 35	11 55	Except Saturdays.		Saturdays only.	1 20	Saturdays only.			5 20	7 34	9 30	8 25	3 50
1	Attercliffe Road				8 39	11 59				1 24				5 24	7 39		8 29	3 54
3	Brightside				8 44					1 29				5 29	7 44		8 33	3 58
3½	Wincobank and Meadow Hall				8 47					1 32				5 32	7 47			
5	Holmes				8 51					1 36				5 36	7 51			
—	Rotherham * .... dep.																8 48	4 12
8½	Treeton				8 59	12 13				1 44				5 44	7 59	9 45	8 57	4 20
9½	Woodhouse Mill				9 4	12 18				1 48				5 49	8 4	9 50	9 2	4 25
12½	Killamarsh				9 10	12 24				1 55				5 55	8 10	9 56	9 8	4 31
14½	Eckington and Renishaw			8 13	9 15	12 28				2 0				6 0	8 15	10 1	9 18	4 36
17	Barrow Hill & Staveley Works	7 50	8 12	8 20	9 22	12 35	1 48	2 1	2 4	2 10	2 35	4 57	5 40	6 7	8 23	10 10	9 20	4 43
18	Whittington	7 54		8 24	9 26	12 39				2 14	2 39	5 0	5 44	6 10	8 28	10 13	9 23	4 46
20½	Chesterfield § 446, 477 .. arr.	8 0		8 30	9 32	12 45			2 15	2 20	2 45	5 6	5 50	6 16	8 32	10 19	9 30	4 52

Miles	Week Days.	mrn		mrn	mrn	mrn	aft	aft	aft	aft	aft	aft	aft	aft	aft	aft	aft	aft	aft	aft	Sundays. mrn	aft
	Chesterfield .... dep.	7 44		8 14	9 10	11 15	1 43			2 50	3 13	3 22	5 45	5 58	6 18			8 25	10 50	8 20	7 47
2½	Whittington	7 50		8 20	9 16	11 21	1 49			2 56	3 19		5 51	6 4	6 24			8 31	10 56	8 26	7 52
3½	Barrow Hill & Staveley Works	7 53	8 23	8 30	9 20	11 25	1 53	2 5	2 12	2 59	3 23	3 28	5 54	6 6	6 27		6 33	8 35	10 58	8 29	7 56
6½	Eckington and Renishaw	8 0			9 27	11 33	2 1	Except Saturdays.	Except Saturdays.	Saturdays only.	3 31	Saturdays only.	6 1	Saturdays only.				8 42	Saturdays only.	8 35	8 2
8½	Killamarsh	8 6			9 32	11 38	2 6				3 36		6 6					8 49		8 40	8 7
11½	Woodhouse Mill	8 12			9 38	11 44	2 12				3 42		6 12					8 54		8 46	8 13
12½	Treeton	8 16			9 42	11 48	2 17				3 46		6 16					9 0		8 50	8 17
16	Rotherham * .... arr.	Calls at Catcliffe at 8 20 and West Tinsley at 8 27 mrn.																			
15½	Holmes				9 50	11 56					3 54		6 25					9 12		8 59	8 26
17½	Wincobank and Meadow Hall					12 1					3 59		6 31					9 17			
17½	Brightside				9 55	12 6					4 2		6 34					9 20		9 7	8 34
19½	Attercliffe Road	8 36									4 8		6 40					9 25		9 12	8 39
20½	Sheffield ‡ 461 .... arr.	8 41			10 2	12 13	2 32				4 12		6 44					9 32		9 16	8 43
5½	Staveley Town		8 29	8 36				2 11	2 18	3 5		3 35			6 33		6 39				
8½	Bolsover †			8 46				2 20				3 46					6 49				
9½	Palterton and Sutton			8 50				2 24				3 51					6 54				
11	Glapwell			8 53				2 29				3 56					6 59				
12½	Rowthorn and Hardwick			9 0				2 35				4 2					7 6				
14½	Pleasley 478			9 7				2 43				4 8					7 15				
9½	Clown 522		8 45						2 33	3 20					6 46						
12½	Elmton and Creswell 479		8 52						2 40	3 27					6 52	7 48					
15	Langwith		9 8						2 46	3 33						7 54					
16½	Shirebrook		9 14						2 51	3 38						7 59					
19½	Mansfield Woodhouse		9 21	9 17				2 52	2 58	3 45		4 17				8 7	7 28				
21	Mansfield 478, 481, 482 arr.		9 24	9 20				2 55	3 2	3 48		4 22				8 10	7 29				

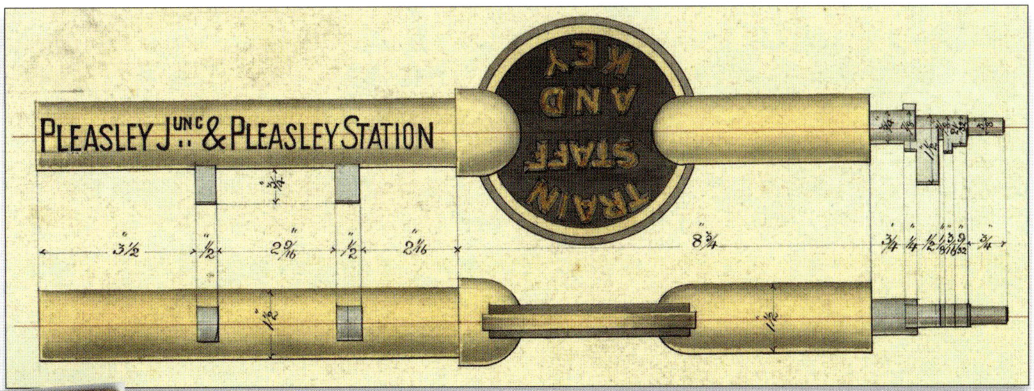

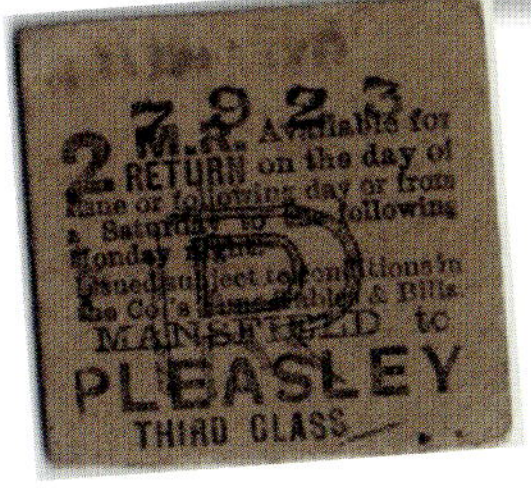

Above: Drawing for the original Midland Railway Train Staff and Key, for the section between Pleasley Junction and Pleasley Station. ***(Courtesy, Midland Railway Study Centre, Derby)***

Left: Undated half Edmondson ticket 7923 ordinary 3rd class return half Mansfield to Pleasley. ***(Courtesy Midland Railway Study Centre)***

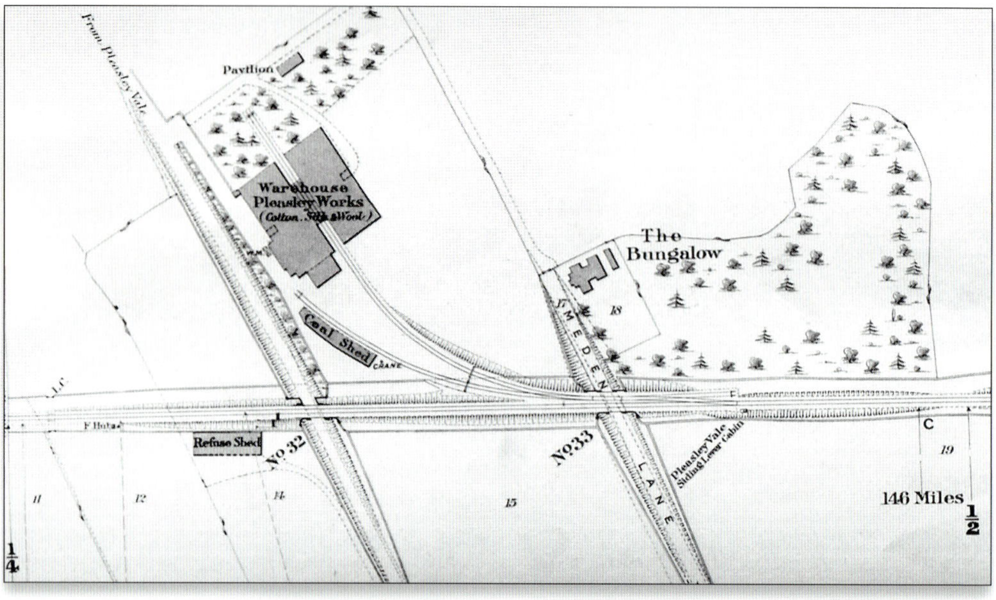

Right: This section of MR plan shows the Pleasley line and the connections into the Pleasley Works Cotton, Silk and Wool warehouse (otherwise known as Hollins Siding) at Bridge No. 33. Notice the mention of Pleasley Vale Lever Cabin, which would have been a GF. ***(Dave Phillips collection)***

Right: In 1784 William Hollins & Co Ltd inaugurated a factory at Pleasley Vale, which became the first in the world to take in raw cloth material at one end and send out the finished garment ready for sale at the other. The mill buildings seen here were built in the mid-19th century and later developed the Viyella cloth, winning large contracts from the government to provide cloth during World War II. The Pleasley to Tibshelf line can be seen coming in top right and curving off bottom right; the factory's sidings midway between were known as Pleasley Vale Sidings. ***(Author's collection)***

Left: At 144m 49ch the five arch Pleasley Viaduct took the line over the valley of the infant River Meden. Unfortunately, the proximity of Pleasley Colliery had a detrimental effect on the structure owing to subsidence. This photo was taken after the arches had been strengthened with wooden supports, a feature that remained until the end. The story goes that, after BR structural engineers completed a survey on it in 1964, the viaduct was blown up in 1965! Their reasoning was that, although it was decreed to be structurally sound and would be safe for at least the next 50 years, the railway that used it had closed so it may as well be demolished! ***(Author's collection)***

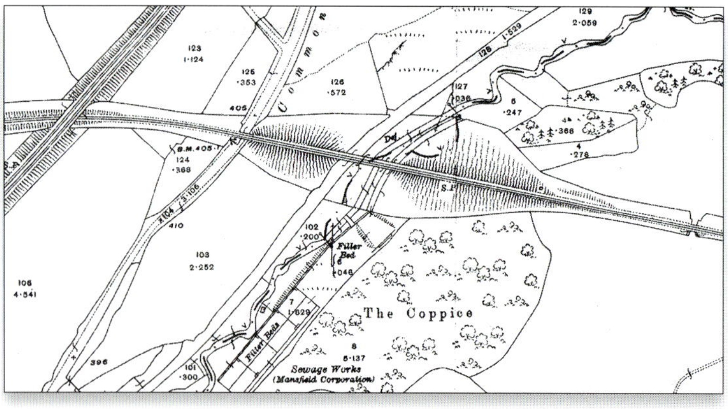

Left: A 1914 map of the line showing the location of the viaduct. Notice that the MR line then passes beneath the GNR line to Pleasley. ***(Reproduced courtesy of the National Library of Scotland)***

Above: This view shows Pleasley Station signal box on the northbound (Mansfield side) platform. The 'box opened on 29 April 1886, but closed on 13 December 1925 when the line through the station was singled by the LMS and the northbound platform dispensed with as an economy measure. ***(John Alsop collection)***

Right: The staff of Pleasley station pose for the usual photo call in Midland Railway days. It opened without ceremony on 11 May 1886 with the start of passenger services on the branch. Initially four trains each way were provided between Mansfield and Alfreton but, with the opening of the Doe Lea Branch on 1 September 1890, services more than doubled with a further four trains a day from Mansfield to Chesterfield via Mansfield Woodhouse, Bolsover and Barrow Hill. In the background, the chimney of Pleasley Colliery looms out of the murk. ***(Author's collection)***

Left: The now-single platform station is seen in May 1950, long after regular passenger services had ceased (from 28 July 1930). Even after closure to passengers, the station was given the suffix "West" in 1950 to differentiate it from the nearby GNR station, which became "Pleasley East". It remained in use for goods traffic until 1 September 1952, and for excursion traffic until 1964. ***(Author's collection)***

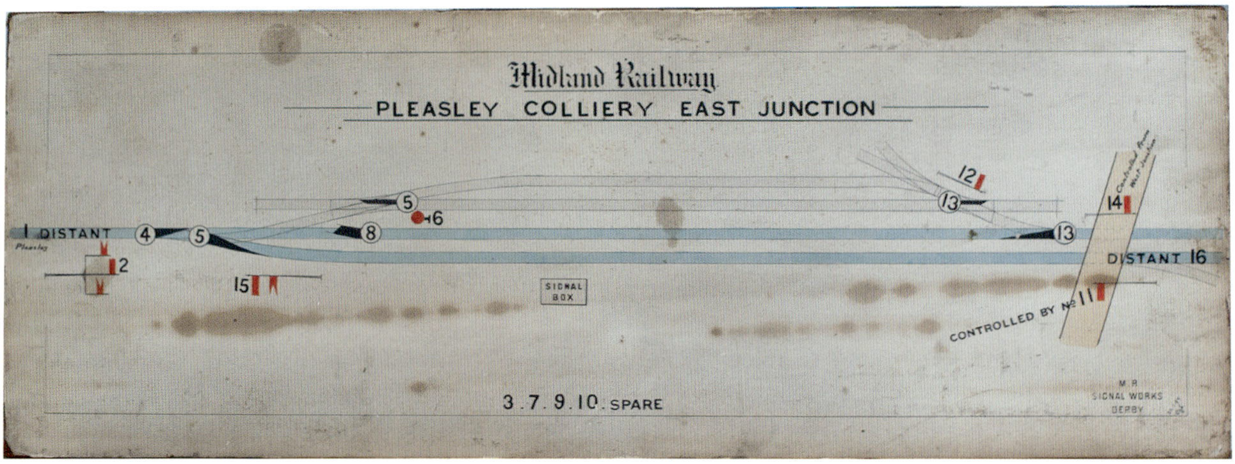

Above: A great survivor – the signal box diagram from Pleasley Colliery East Junction. This 'box opened on 27 July 1890, and closed on 22 October 1939 when Pleasley East Ground Frame replaced it. The 'box was situated on the north side of the line, so on the diagram Pleasley Station was to the left and the overbridge on the right of the diagram is the former Longhedge Lane. The diagram sold at auction in 2022. ***(Courtesy Simon Turner, G.W. Railwayana Auctions)***

Right: On 16 March 1968 the Railway Enthusiasts' Club ran "The Collier No. 2 Rail Tour" from Nottingham Midland to Annesley Mansfield, Mansfield Colliery Junction (Mid), Rufford Junction (Mid), Bentinck Colliery Sidings, Pinxton, New Hucknall Colliery, Westhouses & Blackwell, Tibshelf South Junction, Skegby Junction and Pleasley East GF. The 3-car DMU, comprising two unidentified Class 105 "Cravens" vehicles and Class 104 "BRC&W" vehicle 50495, is seen at the Ground Frame. ***(FA12103 RCTS Photo Archive, collection of Jack Faithfull)***

Left: The four roads of Pleasley Colliery Sidings, seen from the Longhedge Lane bridge. The wagons in the distance show the curve for the former Doe Lea Valley route to Glapwell, Bolsover and Seymour Junction, while the route to Tibshelf is straight ahead. The section of route to Tibshelf, Teversall and Westhouses will be discussed in a future book. ***(PG01830 RCTS Photo Archive, collection of Peter Green)***

Above: In 1872 a lease was granted to the Stanton Iron Company for the extraction of coal from the Top Hard seam. Sinking commenced during 1873, and the Top Hard seam was eventually reached in February 1877. This view of the colliery from the south-west in the early 1900s shows several MR emblazoned wagons in the otherwise almost empty sidings.

Above: A second view, this time from the north-west. The MR line was behind the spoil heap on the left, while the GNR Leen Valley Extension was on the far right. By the late 1950s all output was from the combined Deep Hard / Piper workings to the south-east but, despite high output, the surface infrastructure was deteriorating. As a new surface drift and coal processing plant had opened at nearby Shirebrook, the decision was made to transfer all output underground there and coal-winding at Pleasley subsequently ceased. The shafts remained in use for man riding and materials until the colliery's closure in 1983. The downcast shaft was filled but the upcast initially remained for some time to supply air to Shirebrook. The baths, washery, screens etc. were demolished over a period, but the remains were fortunately given a preservation listing in 1986, saving them from demolition. The Friends of Pleasley Pit preservation group was formed in 1995, and today open days are held and the pit is well worth a visit. ***(Both Author's collection)***

Mansfield East to Rufford Junction

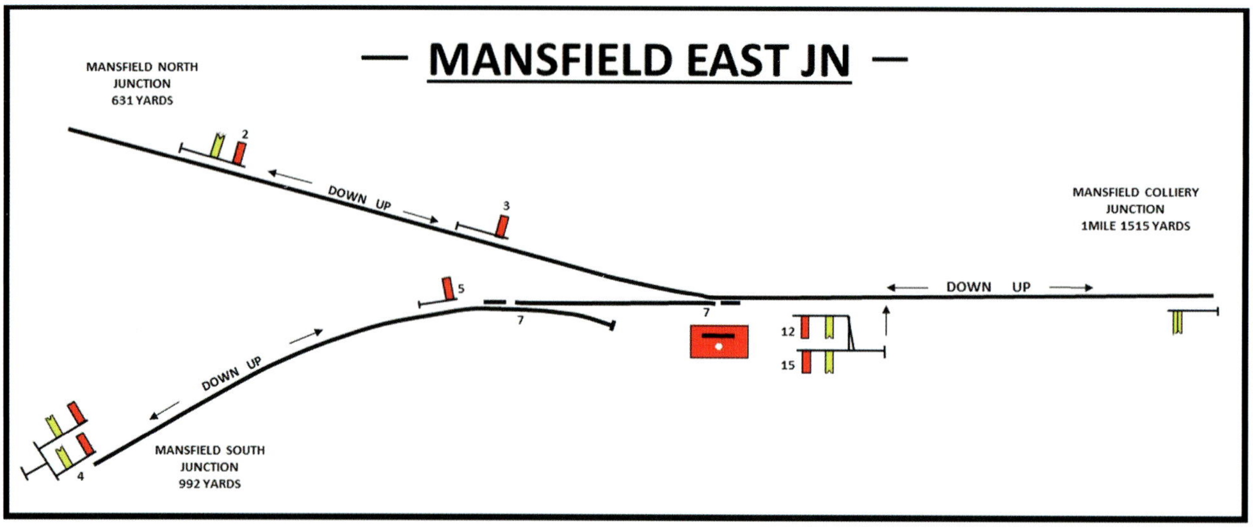

Above: A representation of the diagram at Mansfield East Junction. The line from Southwell to Mansfield North Junction opened on 3 April 1871 and Electric Train Tablet Block was introduced from 27 October 1890. Mansfield East Junction opened on 28 January 1906 as a single-storey type. It was raised in height on 30 November 1913, and closed on 11 December 1966. ***(Author)***

Above: At Mansfield East Junction, No. 12 signal is "Off" for an approaching train to take the curve towards Mansfield North Junction on 11 August 1964. No. 7 trap points are in the foreground, and the eagle-eyed will spot someone stooping down on the right – maybe a driver or fireman of a waiting train picking blackberries? ***(Transport Treasury PY10073M A)***

Above: Mansfield East Junction on 11 August 1964, viewed from inside the 'box. The route right is towards Mansfield North, while 8F 2-8-0 48098 and brake van are taking the left route towards Mansfield South. ***(Milepost 92½)***

Right: On Saturday 12 May 1956, the fireman of Mansfield-based 8F 2-8-0 48442 prepares to hand the single line tablet for the section of line from Mansfield Colliery Junction to the signalman who, in turn, is holding out the single line tablet for the short section from Mansfield East Junction to Mansfield South Junction. ***(Jack Cupit/Neil Baker collection)***

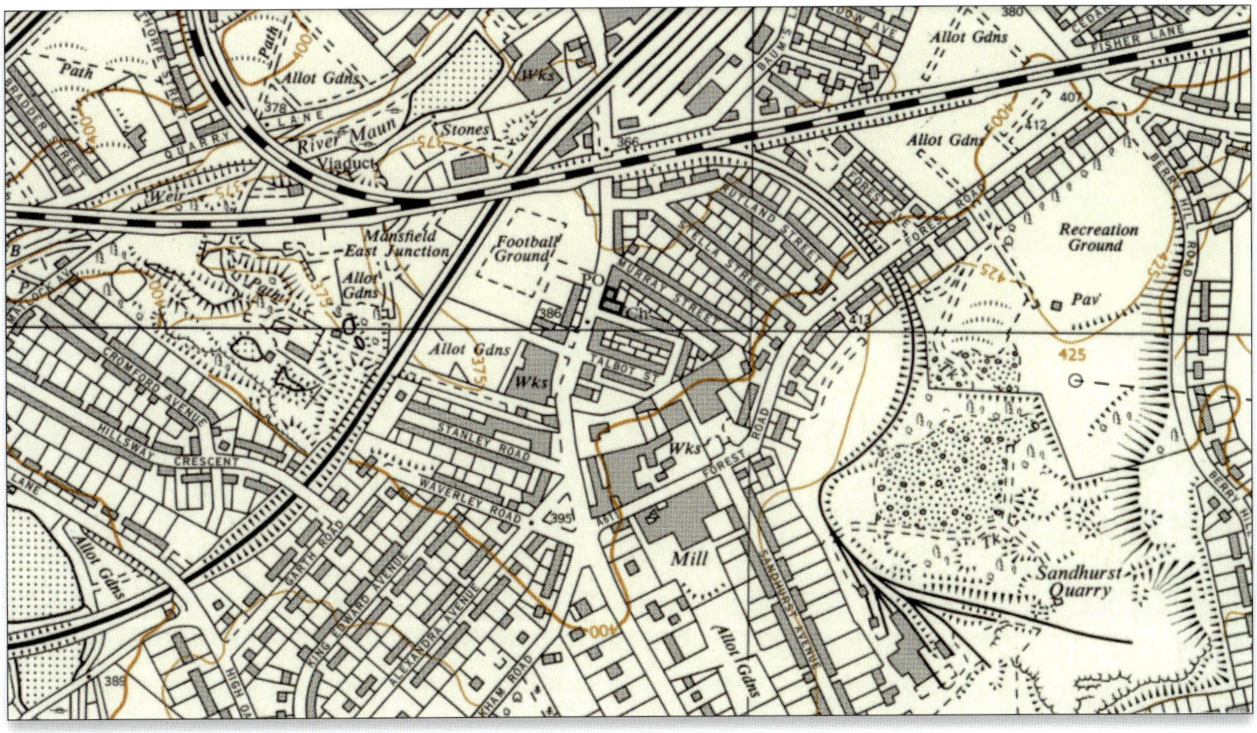

Above: There were several sand quarries in Mansfield, some of which had internal rail systems. This map shows the single lines from Mansfield North and South Junctions converging at Mansfield East Junction, then heading off top right towards Mansfield Colliery Junction. The line into Sandhurst Quarry can be seen curving off down to the sidings and working faces, passing in a cutting beneath Forest Road. The line from bottom left to top centre is the Mansfield Railway line from Kirkby South Junction to Clipstone West Junction. Mansfield Station Goods Yard is at the top of the map. ***(Reproduced courtesy of the National Library of Scotland)***

Left: Sandhurst Quarry from the air, with access from the main line curving beneath Forest Road at top left. Lines of wagons await loading beneath the sand "cliff" in the top left quarter of the image, and the route of other sidings can be discerned. ***(Author's collection)***

Right: This is Hudswell Clarke 0-4-0ST EMPRESS, Works No. 472 of 1896, at Sandhurst Quarry in the early 1950s. Originally named "Patsy", it was sent on long term hire as new to Pinxton Collieries Ltd, Pinxton & Brookhill Colliery Railway. It was returned to Hudswell Clarke circa February 1902 and sold on to Mansfield Standard Sand Co, Sandhurst Quarries, as EMPRESS on 23 April 1902. Rebuilt in 1941, it was scrapped between 1956 and 1959. ***(Transport Treasury MP80318)***

Right: There was another sand quarry at Berry Hill, with sidings alongside the single line. The view east from Windsor Road Bridge shows an unidentified Class 25 shunting the sand sidings. The loco has propelled from Mansfield to just beyond the GF, and has left some wagons on the single line. Having uncoupled, it has entered the sidings via the GF points with four empty sand wagons and a couple of Conflat Ls for loading. ***(RCTS PG00752 Peter Green collection)***

Left: The view in the opposite direction, looking west towards Mansfield East Junction. Having left the wagons seen above on the single line, the Class 25 has drawn forward beyond the access points, and the guard has just operated the single-lever ground frame to the right to give access to Berry Hill Quarry sidings. Notice Mansfield East Junction's Distant signal beyond the loco. ***(RCTS Peter Green collection)***

Right: 20169 at Mansfield Standard Sand Co, Berry Hill Quarry Sidings on 3 May 1979. This train would have travelled to Sherwood Colliery Sidings South with the two Railfreight 45-ton "VCA" vans and a brake van. After running round, it would have then returned to Mansfield South Junction and propelled to Berry Hill Sidings. The ground frame is just beyond Windsor Road overbridge. The two "VCA" vans and brake van were left on the running line whilst 20169 entered the sidings to collect some vans and open wagons.

Left: Turning around towards the sidings, we see bagged sand for the loco sanding system being hand-loaded into the vans. Some open wagons were shortly added to the rear before the consist re-joined the two "VCA" vans and brake van. The train proceeded back to Mansfield South Junction and thence Kirkby Summit where the "VCA" vans (containing tinplate) were shunted and left at the Metal Box Company site at Oddicroft Lane, Sutton-in-Ashfield. The lorry is a Ford "D" Series. ***(Both Malcolm Rush)***

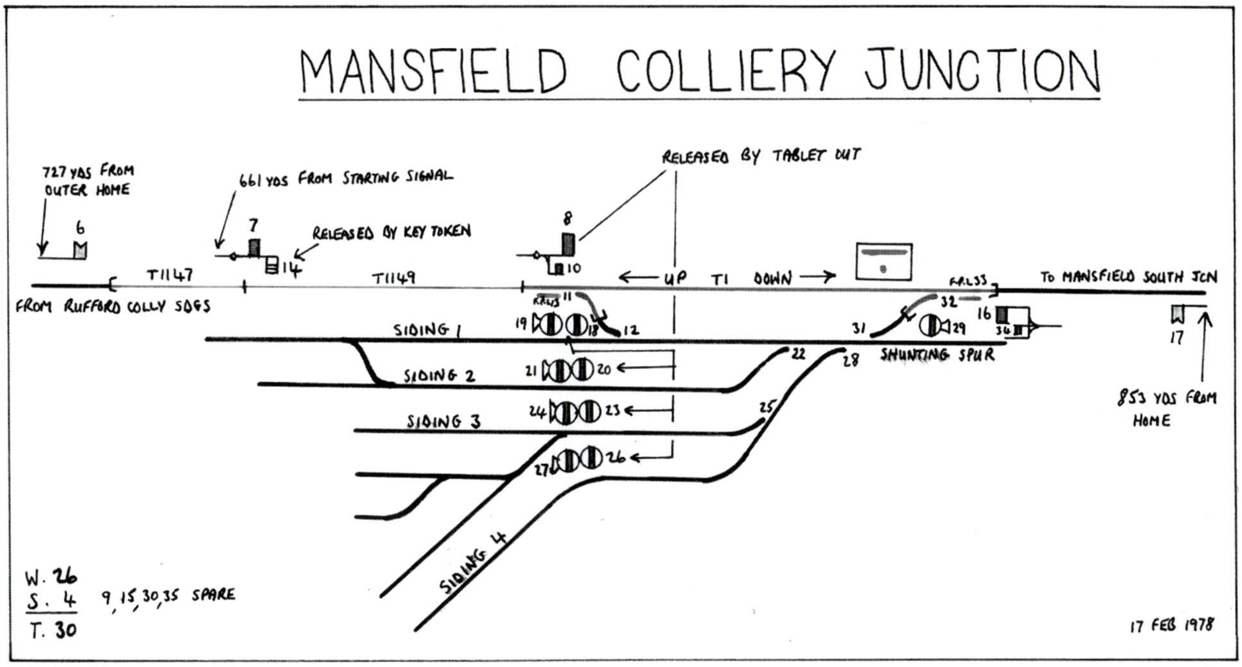

Above: A hand-drawn diagram of Mansfield Colliery Junction as of 17 February 1978. The Mansfield (or Crown Farm) Colliery Branch was closed on 18 July 1967, and all output went via the former GCR-worked Mansfield Railway; the branch then became another siding. Between 1978 and 1982 the sidings were reduced to just Nos. 1 and 2.

Right: This is the view from Oak Tree Lane bridge looking east towards Ratcher Hill Sand Quarry, as 20160+20166 pass Mansfield Colliery Junction with 9T11 Clipstone Colliery to Avenue Coking Plant on 25 February 1981.

Below: Originally named Mansfield Colliery Sidings, this 'box opened on 28 January 1906 and controlled the branch to Mansfield Colliery with Electric Tablet Working. From 25 January 1909, the method of working the branch was altered to working as a siding and, on 7 April 1929, the 'box was renamed Mansfield Colliery Junction. That same year, a new frame was installed: Levers 1–5 were of the Turnover double-wire style, while levers 6–35 were standard REC 4½-inch Tappet. At an unknown date, but probably after 1955 but before 1966, the Turnover levers were abolished and removed. The 'box closed on 15 October 1983. Here 44004 "Great Gable" propels its train into the sidings on 17 September 1979. The train had originated at Rufford Colliery and was bound for Avenue Sidings, but the loco was suffering from a lack of engine power and so the train was recessed in the sidings. *(All Malcolm Rush)*

Left: Another Class 44, this time 44002 "Helvellyn", trundles past Mansfield Colliery Junction on 3 June 1977 with an Up coal for Toton while a pair of Class 20s wait in the sidings. This loco was withdrawn in February 1979 and scrapped at Derby Works in October 1979. The the empty doll on the signal gantry was formerly occupied by No. 35 signal, which was for the route direct onto the Crown Farm line. *(Syd Hancock)*

Above: This was the first of the Bolsover Colliery Co. Ltd collieries in Nottinghamshire. Sinking began in February 1904, and coal was reached in May 1905. Although officially named Mansfield Colliery, it soon became known as Crown Farm, or Crownie, due to its proximity to the land of Crown Farm. The colliery was first served from a branch (opened January 1905) from the MR Mansfield to Southwell line, but was later also served by the GCR-worked Mansfield Railway between Clipstone and Kirkby South Junction, which ran along its northern side. As mentioned previously the MR connection closed in 1967, the Mansfield Railway then taking all traffic. ***(Author's collection)***

Above: A couple of steam shunting locos seen at Mansfield Colliery: (**Left**) Hawthorne, Leslie & Co. 0-4-0ST "Diana" Works No. 3912 of 1937. This loco was scrapped on site in 1975. (**Right**) Peckett 0-4-0ST "Victory" Works No. 2092 of 1947, delivered new to NCB Bolsover Colliery Co, Rufford Colliery. It was moved c1951 to Mansfield Colliery, to Sherwood Colliery October 1954 and back to Mansfield Colliery c1954/55. It was scrapped in 1967. ***(Both Andy Bailey collection)***

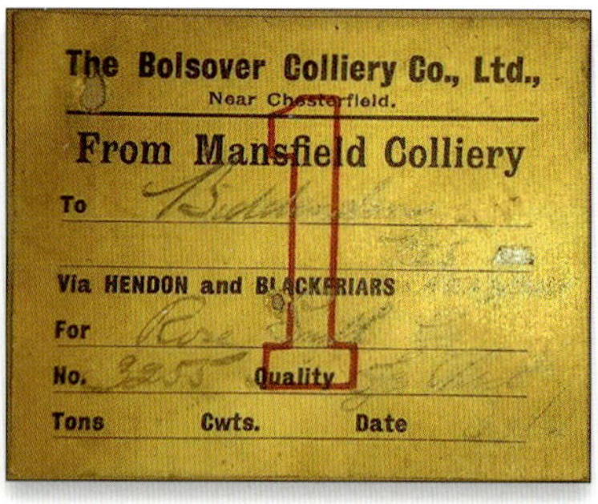

Far left: A Bolsover Colliery Co. Ltd wagon label for wagon No. 3255, from Mansfield Colliery to Biddenden (in the borough of Ashford in Kent) via Hendon and Blackfriars.

Left: Crest of the Bolsover Colliery Company Limited. ***(Both Author's collection)***

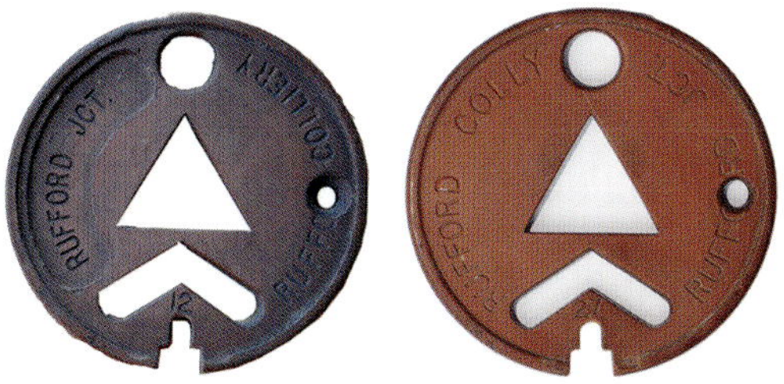

Here we see a series of single line tokens and tablets for the section of route between Mansfield Colliery Junction and Rufford Colliery, which shows the changing sections as 'boxes closed or were renamed.

Above left: Single line steel and brass Key Token No 13, engraved both sides MANSFIELD COLLY JCT-RUFFORD JCT. This was post-April 1929, when Rufford Colliery Junction and Mansfield Colliery Sidings signal boxes were renamed Rufford Junction and Mansfield Colliery Junction.

Far left and left: Tablet for the Rufford Colliery to Rufford Junction section. Notice that the tablet has had Rufford Colliery Jct ground out and replaced with Rufford Jct, again post-April 1929. The tablet alongside is a newer example, as it shows the later location name.

Left: When Rufford Junction 'box closed in June 1968 the section then became Mansfield Colliery Junction to Rufford Colliery, and this Token reflects that. Originally it would be painted green, traces of the paint remaining. ***(All courtesy Simon Turner GW Railwayana Auctions)***

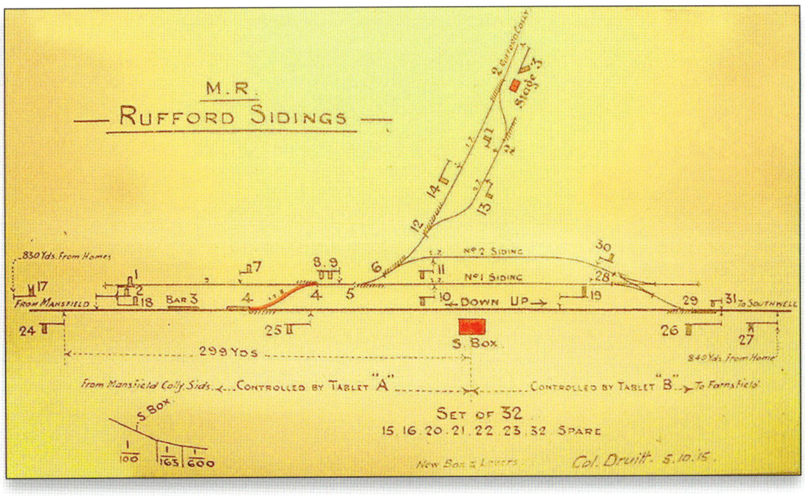

Right: As we have seen previously, the single line signalling section (prior to any colliery branches being opened) was Mansfield North Junction to Farnsfield. Mansfield Crown Farm with its new branch was the first to open in 1906, followed by the sinking of Rufford Colliery in 1911 and its requirement of a second new branch. The MR did not require construction powers to build the Rufford Branch, and a GF was provided for access from the single line to sidings for construction traffic prior to the construction of a signal box. This would have been adjacent to what later became No. 29 points. The branch opened on 20 June 1912, and on 21 March 1915 a new signal box and connections were provided. This is the original track layout sketch of Rufford Sidings, as inspected by Col. Druitt on 5 October 1915. The 'box is recorded as having a 32-lever frame, of which 7 were spares. The sketch shows a new connection through No. 4 points (in red) to enable direct access to the branch and sidings from the Mansfield direction. The GF would have been abolished with the opening of the 'box. Although the 'box became a token point to shorten the sections, trains were unable to pass here until new lines and pointwork were installed in 1917. The 'box was re-named "Rufford Colliery Junction" on 1 January 1929, and a new 60-lever frame was commissioned on 17 February 1929 with the first five levers being of the "new pattern turn-over" type (as at Mansfield Colliery Sidings). The 'box was renamed again on 7 April 1929 to "Rufford Junction"; there is some doubt, however, as to whether the 'box actually carried the former name. ***(Author's collection)***

Above: This east-looking view from Helmsley Road Bridge (to the left of the above diagram) towards the former Rufford Junction shows a pair of unidentified Class 20s heading towards Mansfield with 8F36, which will have originated from Rufford or Clipstone Colliery. The shunt neck shown on the left of the diagram once came as far as here. ***(Clyde Hatter)***

Left, below & bottom: The Railway Enthusiasts' Club's "The Collier No. 2" railtour of 16 March 1968, which we previously saw at Pleasley, travelled as far as Rufford Junction as the line forwards to Blidworth Junction had shut on 3 October 1966. Notice the distinct lean to the 'box which may have hastened its demise; it closed just three months later on 16 June 1968. The signalling section subsequently became Mansfield Colliery Junction to Rufford Colliery. ***(Left Clyde Hatter collection/ others Jim Hatcher)***

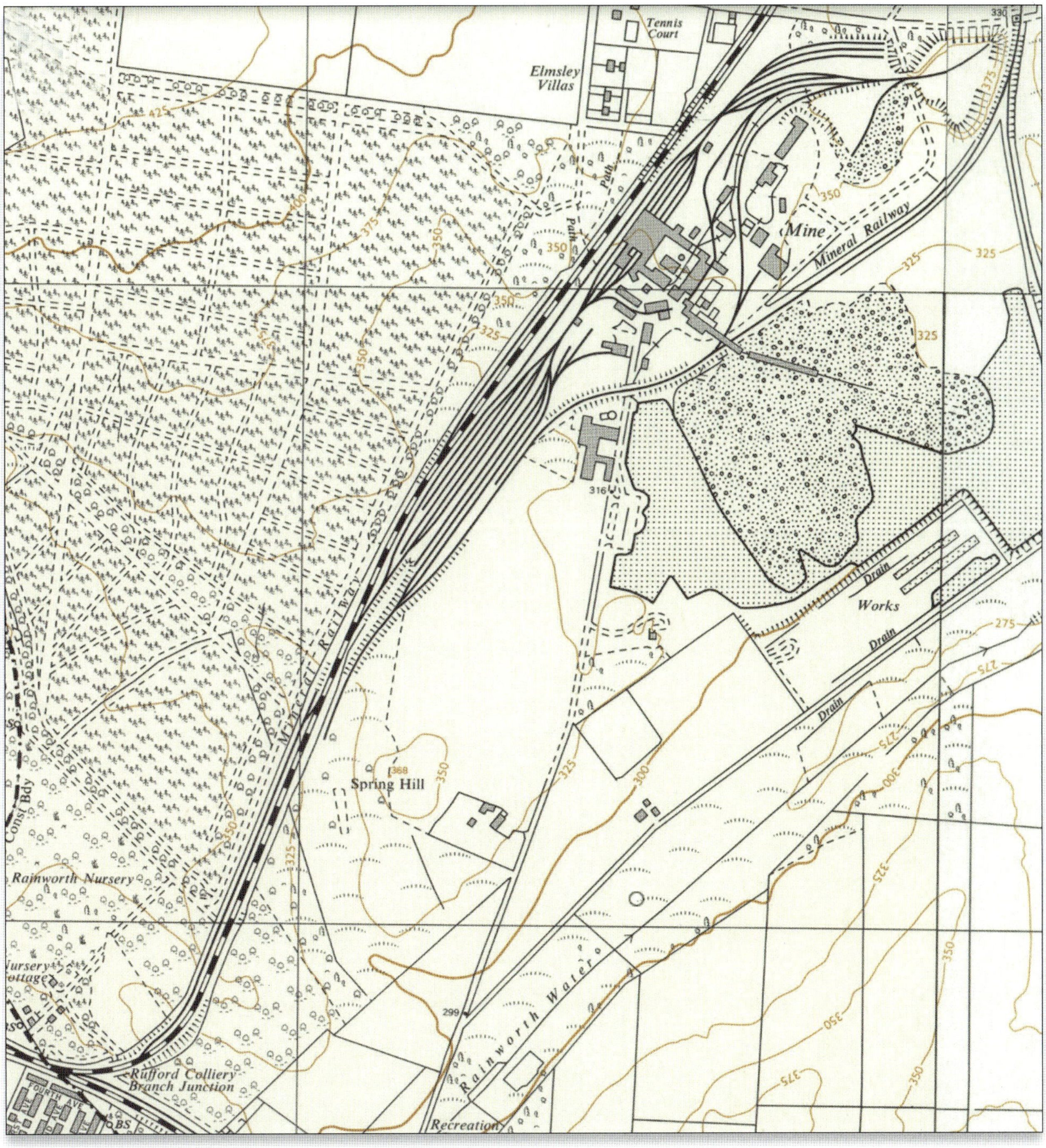

Above: Map of Rufford Colliery Branch from Rufford Junction to the colliery. The MR lines are shown black & white while the other lines are colliery lines. The GCR branch comes in top right, while the MR branch continues off the top of the map to Clipstone Colliery. ***(Reproduced courtesy of the National Library of Scotland)***

Left: A view from the gantry which supported Rufford Junction's No. 40 home signal and Rufford Colliery's fixed distant. The two loops which started at Rufford Jct and ended at Rufford Colliery are visible on each side of the main running line, and one of the winding towers of Rufford Colliery can be seen top left. ***(Clyde Hatter)***

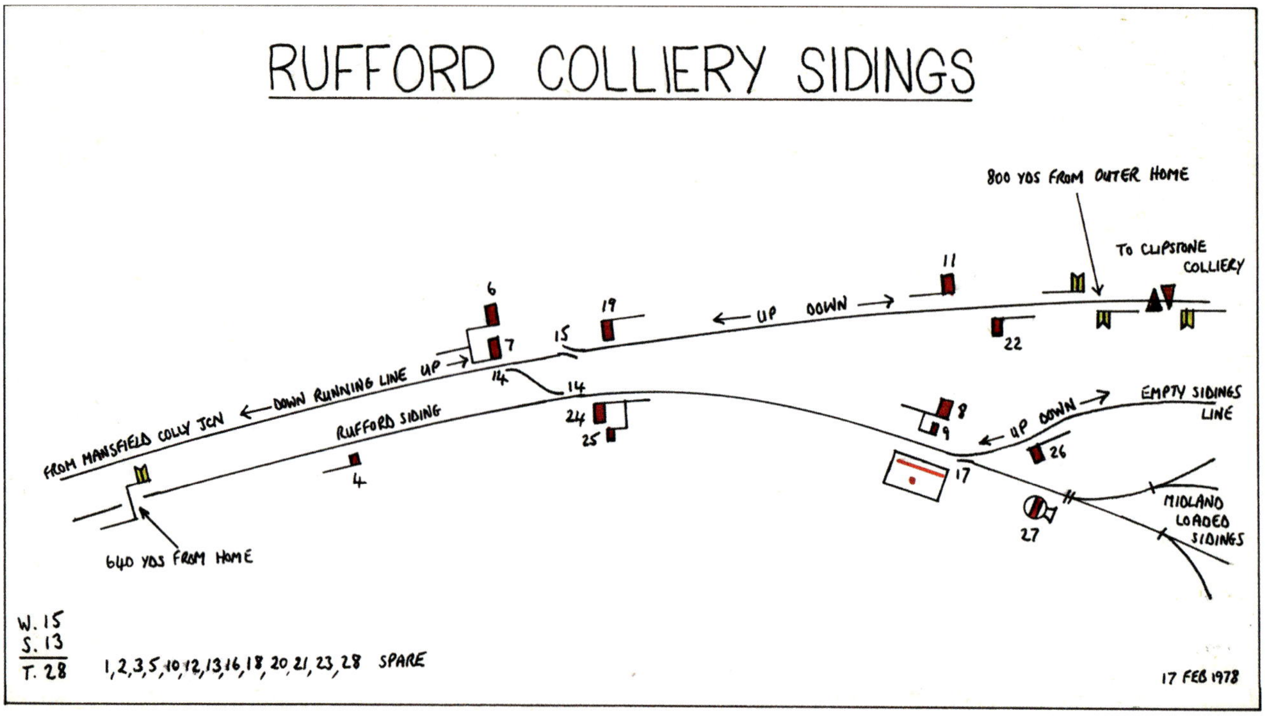

Above: Hand drawn diagram of Rufford Colliery Sidings, dated 17 February 1978. In his excellent book "The Midland Railway A Chronology", John Gough records that on 10 February 1918 "Rufford Colliery" 'box was opened, and that a replacement "Rufford Colliery Sidings" 'box opened in December 1928. Tablet working was introduced on the Rufford Branch in 1928, and the Clipstone Colliery Branch opened on either 29 December 1928 or 1 February 1929. The Signalling Records Society records that: "c.1927 a new contractor's siding for the Clipstone branch was laid", and "c.1929 a junction for Clipstone Colliery branch brought into use". The branch was just over three miles long and cost £109,000 to build. On 11 December 1973 the LMS-built Clipstone siding at Rufford Colliery Sidings was abolished, and on 29 November 1981 Rufford Colliery Sidings 'box was abolished. A new GF was then brought into use utilising the former 14 points, and No Signalman Key Token working was introduced from Mansfield Colliery Junction. Over 11/12 December 1983 a link was formed between the LMS Clipstone Colliery Branch and the former GCR Rufford Colliery Branch, allowing all inbound and outbound traffic to use the former GCR lines and enabled the closure of Rufford Colliery to Mansfield South Junction by the Midland route.

Right: Rufford Colliery Sidings 'box seen on 17 February 1978. Although the lower quadrant signals were of ex-MR origin, it is doubtful they would be new as, by 1928, the LM&SR had been established. Could they have been recovered from elsewhere? Possibly the reason they survived was that the box was Eastern Region and the ER probably didn't want to spend money upgrading at that site.

Right: Having deposited their wagons at Mansfield Colliery Junction, 20158 & 20164 propel a brake van towards Clipstone Colliery on 17 September 1979. No. 6 signal directs them towards Clipstone Colliery, passing en route Rufford Colliery on their right. *(All Malcolm Rush)*

Above: In 1911 the Bolsover Colliery Co. Ltd leased land from Lord Savile and sank two shafts to access the Top Hard seam, which was reached in October 1913. The seams were under part of the Rufford Abbey Estate, from which the colliery therefore took its name. ***(Author's collection)***

Right: RS&H 0-4-0ST No. 1 NCB (Works No. 7642) was sent new to Rufford Colliery in 1950, and is seen with the driver posed on the footplate on 19 May 1959. It moved to Blidworth after February 1961, then to Warsop Colliery between December 1964 and May 1966. It was scrapped by William Bush Ltd, Alfreton by April 1967. ***(RCTS FAI4154 collection of Jack Faithfull)***

Left: Ruston & Hornsby No. R3 of 1959 shunts N.C.B. wooden internal user wagons at Rufford Colliery on 26 March 1982. The wagons still carry the former Bolsover red livery, but with NCB markings. ***(Dave Peachey)***

Above: Clipstone Colliery in 1930. ***(Author's collection)***

Left: The staff for the Clipstone Colliery Branch is exchanged for the key token to Mansfield Colliery Junction. 20164 & 20158 pass with a Clipstone Colliery to Mansfield Colliery Junction train on 17 September 1979. The staff, marked "Clipstone Branch", was a homemade wooden affair which also carried a key for Elmsley Level Crossing further along the branch. ***(Malcolm Rush)***

Right: Stanier 8F 2-8-0 48192 is seen on the LMS single line from Clipstone Colliery to Rufford Colliery Sidings circa 1960. The loco, formerly from 17D Rowsley, was transferred to 16B Kirkby-in-Ashfield in the week ending 11 July 1959. Moved to 40E Colwick in December 1965, it had spells at Sutton Oak, Springs Branch, Stockport Edgeley and Heaton Mersey. It was condemned from the latter in the week ending 30 March 1968. ***(Derek Wilson)***

Left: The train crew and shunters have a conversation at Clipstone Colliery on 23 June 1972 as a pair of Class 20s wait in the London Midland side Loaded Sidings. ***(RCTS Photo Archive PG01240 collection of Peter Green)***

Above: Steam at Clipstone Colliery: (**Left**) Hawthorn Leslie 0-4-0ST "Clipstone No. 2", Works No. 3630 of 1925, is seen on 19 May 1959 during an enthusiast visit to the colliery. (**Right**) On loan from BR is 41J Langwith Junction-allocated J69 No. 68556, seen in 1960. ***(Left RCTS FAI4161 collection Jack Faithfull, right Derek Wilson)***

Right: Yorkshire Engine Co. 0-6-0ST, Works No. YE2521 at Clipstone Colliery on 16 March 1969. It was new in 1952 to the Appleby-Frodingham Steelworks at Scunthorpe as their No 9. Displaced by diesel traction in the 1960s, it was sold to the NCB and deployed at Clipstone Colliery. After withdrawal it was presented to the National Coal Mining Museum (NCM), and subsequently loaned to a number of sites (including a few years at Barrow Hill Roundhouse) before its return to the NCM. The NCM has since loaned it to Rocks by Rail, the Living Ironstone Museum at Cottesmore. ***(Transport Library/Horace Gamble HG2012)***

Below: New headstocks built by Head Wrightson and new Markham electric winding engines were commissioned in 1953. The headstocks were the tallest in Europe at the time and the winding engines were of the Koepe friction type, which enabled deeper coal seams to be exploited. 58007 departs from Clipstone Colliery on 13 June 1994 with 7G37 for West Burton, along the former Mansfield Railway access. The MR empties line once crossed beneath just in front of the loco. ***(Author)***

Welbeck Branch

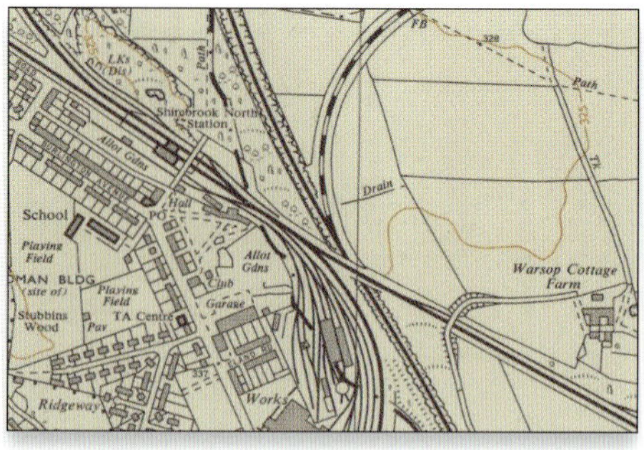

Right: In 1912 the GCR built a 2¾ mile branch from the former LD&ECR line to serve Welbeck Colliery, taking two years to build at a cost of £29,433 and opening on 19 April 1916. Despite the MR line being relatively close to Welbeck, the company ironically had no interest in the Welbeck traffic. At the Grouping in 1923, however, the London, Midland and Scottish Railway (LMS) had other ideas and wished to cash in on the movement of coal from the colliery at Welbeck. Subsequently as provided for in an LMS Act of 1926, they built a 3¼ mile long-branch line from the main line just north of Shirebrook Junction, then to the north of Church Warsop, to Welbeck. This map shows the branch curving off towards top right. Due to the earthworks required, this branch cost £63,000 and opened in January 1929 – but it could be deemed as a failure since most of the coal still went via the original branch. ***(Reproduced with the permission of the National Library of Scotland)***

Right: BR closed the LMS branch in 1959 but retained it at the colliery end for shunting purposes and wagon storage. This is the north-looking view in the cutting approaching Shirebrook, where the Welbeck Branch connected to the main line through Spring Control No. 29 points. The signal on the left is the Up Main Intermediate Home No. 33 with Shirebrook Station's Distant signal beneath. The branch signal post held the Up Colliery Branch Inner Home No. 38 and a Fixed Distant for Shirebrook Station. ***(Author's collection)***

Right: In the mid-1960s Bridge No. 5 over Wood Lane was removed, though the remains of the abutments can still be seen today. ***(Eric Hill collection)***

Left & below: The cuttings were used for landfill and most of the branch east of the A60 road was covered by the colliery waste tip. Bridge No. 6 was infilled but both parapets are still in situ, although one is hidden by bushes. ***(Old Warsop Society/Author)***

The Midland Railway Killamarsh Branch

Although the Killamarsh Branch was closed long before Worksop PSB opened, it almost had a connection with the GCR line as it allowed the Midland Railway (MR) to serve Kiveton Colliery. It is therefore felt there is justification for inclusion of the branch in the story, additionally because, as a child, your author walked sections of the trackbed around Kiveton. Another passion I had in the 1970s was collecting Victorian bottles from closed rubbish tips, one of which was situated close to the line at Norwood. On a dig there one day the remains of the branch were also explored which, at that time, still served the Yorkshire Tar Distillers site.

Origins

Norwood Colliery (also referred to as Holbrook No. 2 Colliery) was sunk by the Sheepbridge Iron & Steel Company in 1865. The MR constructed its Killamarsh Branch to serve it under the Midland Railway (Branches Etc.) Act of 1866; this opened on 1 October 1868 and connected with the MR "Old Road" at Norwood Sidings, to the north of Killamarsh Station. A signal box was provided in 1875 to control access to the branch; initially named "Norwood Sidings", it was renamed "Killamarsh Branch Sidings" between October 1876 and August 1877. It was replaced by a new 'box on 14 September 1890.

The branch curved away eastwards and passed beneath a farm track, then crossed the River Rother on a low girder bridge. Norwood Siding followed shortly after, probably installed to serve a brickworks. Initially the branch terminated at Norwood Colliery, 70 chains (7/8 of a mile) from the main line junction.

In 1874 the MR sought additional powers to extend the line to serve West Kiveton Colliery and Kiveton Park Colliery. Opened on 19 August 1878, this section involved the driving of the 300-yard-long Norwood End Tunnel to penetrate a ridge. The railway tunnel paralleled the much longer Chesterfield Canal's Norwood Tunnel alongside, and at the eastern end it passed beneath Coal Pit Lane before opening out into a deep cutting, beyond which Kiveton Park Colliery came into view. Due to ground movement beneath the tunnel over the years, distortion occurred which was rectified by the insertion of iron ribs.

With the construction of the Derbyshire Lines of the MS&LR (later GCR) and the LD&ECR Beighton Branch, new overbridges crossed the Killamarsh Branch, whilst the GCR Waleswood Curve curved off north-eastwards on an embankment.

West Kiveton was in fact part of Kiveton Park Colliery; the shafts were Kiveton Nos. 3 and 4 sunk in 1874 although West Kiveton had its own headgear and surface buildings, which were used for men and coal. Up until 1928, miners resident in Killamarsh used the West Kiveton shafts to gain access to the Barnsley Seam workings, but just two years later the whole area was abandoned.

KILLAMARSH AND KIVETON PARK							
(Staveley No. 1 Trip).							
				EMPTIES			
				pm			pm
KILLAMARSH	dep	...	...	1:30	...	...	3:55
Norwood Colliery	arr	...	...	1*40	...	...	...
	dep	...	...	2:10	...	...	...
KIVETON PARK	arr	...	...	2:20	...	...	4:15
* Yorkshire Tar							
KIVETON PARK	dep	...	...	3:00	...	...	4:55
Norwood Colliery	arr	...	...	...	...	...	5*15
	dep	...	...	...	...	...	5:35
KILLAMARSH	arr	...	...	3:20	...	...	5:45
* Yorkshire Tar							

By 1898 there was a connection and sidings for the Derbyshire Chemical Works, close to the connection to Norwood Colliery. This later became Ellison and Mitchell's Works, and was eventually to become the Yorkshire Tar Distillers plant.

The 7 May 1945 Working Timetable for the branch is represented in the table, and as Norwood Colliery closed in 1945 the times shown for trains are actually at the Yorkshire Tar Distillers siding. After World War II, T. W. Ward opened their Killamarsh Scrapyard immediately east of the LD&ECR overbridge, with its own rail connection from the single-track branch. This scrapyard specialised in cutting up wagons and locos, dispatching over 300 steam locos in its time.

Closure

Killamarsh Branch Junction 'box closed in July 1959, and the majority of the branch closed on 19 May 1961. The track was severed at the Yorkshire Tar Distillers siding at 155 mile 41 ch. Ward's Scrapyard continued to trade, and locos for cutting up were stored at Killamarsh Branch Junction sidings until space in the yard was found for them.

In November 1967, the M1 Motorway opened on an alignment that took it directly over Norwood End Tunnel, resulting in the loss of its westernmost portion. The east portal has also been buried under landfill. The final section from Killamarsh Branch Junction to the Yorkshire Tar Distillers plant was abandoned on 15 November 1972, and the remains of the line around Killamarsh were lost when opencast mining started and the Rother Valley Country Park was created.

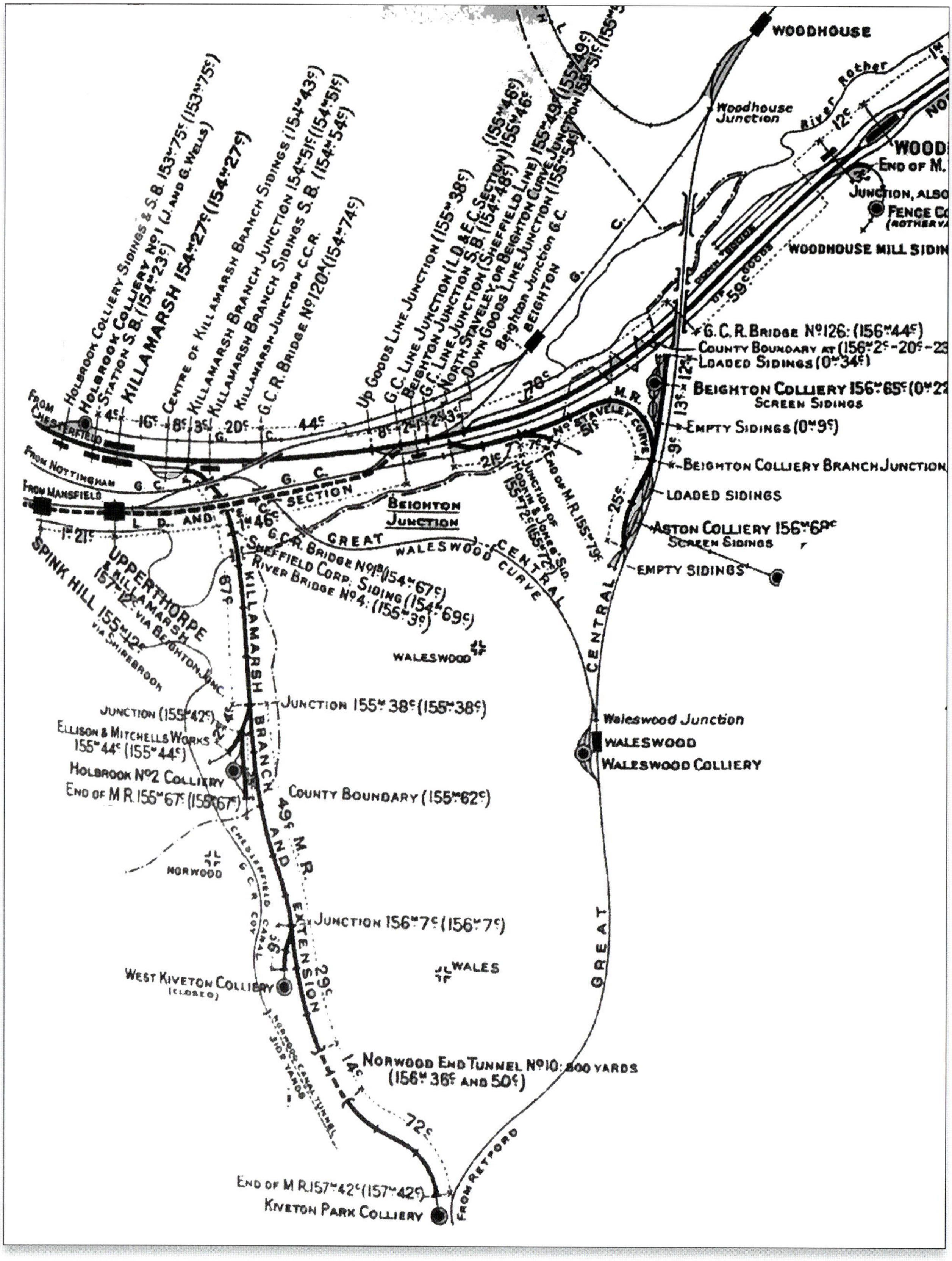

Above: Midland Railway map of lines around Killamarsh and Beighton, showing the Killamarsh Branch on the left. The map is oriented west at the top and east at the bottom. ***(Author's collection)***

Right: A larger-scale map of the junctions and lines in the Killamarsh area. Killamarsh Branch Junction is bottom left, diverging from the Old Road. The GCR Main Line is the centre route, with the LD&ECR Beighton Branch on the right. The fan of sidings is T.W. Ward's scrapyard. ***(Reproduced courtesy of the National Library of Scotland)***

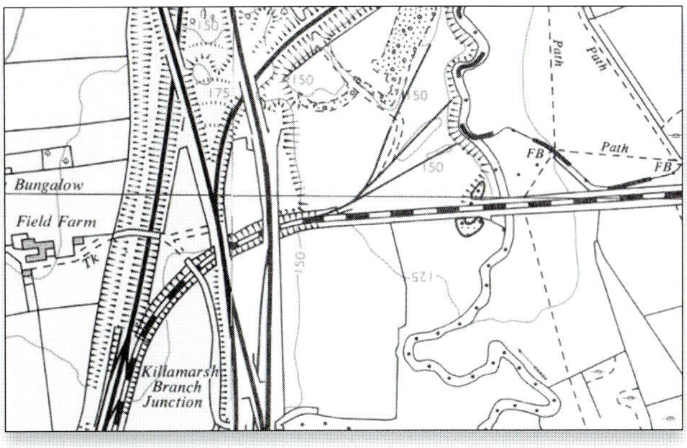

Below: The view from the former LD&ECR Beighton Branch overbridge sees Ivatt 4MT 2-6-0 43153 shunting T.W. Ward's Killamarsh scrapyard. The scrapyard connection would have been controlled from the single lever ground frame adjacent to the loco, which was released by an Annett's key on the train staff originally issued from Killamarsh Branch Junction signal box. ***(Alan Rowles)***

Below: The Killamarsh Branch, photographed on 24 July 1960 from the RCTS "Dukeries Railtour" passing over the LD&ECR overbridge. The single line heads towards Norwood Colliery (just visible top right), while to the left is T.W. Ward's scrapyard. Former Midland Railway 4P 4-4-0 41120 was one of over 300 locomotives cut up in the scrapyard's lifetime.

Below: A wider view of the yard shows at least 12 locos being dealt with, including examples of 0-6-0 and 4-4-0 and a selection of tank locos at the end of the line waiting their turn. ***(Both Lawson Little)***

Above: A closer view of 4P 4-4-0 No. 41120 being scrapped at T.W. Ward Ltd on 25 July 1960. Behind is 2F 0-6-0 58190. ***(FA10711 RCTS collection Jack Faithfull)***

Left: The Yorkshire Tar Distillers Ltd site at Killamarsh used its own internal shunting loco; Black Hawthorn 0-4-0ST Airdrie, Works No. 1074 of 1894. It is seen on 19 May 1963. ***(RCTS FA14741 collection Jack Faithfull)***

Right: Another 19 May 1963 view of Airdrie at the Yorkshire Tar Distillers' Killamarsh Works. ***(RCTS RH01212 collection Roger Hateley)***

Above: An early postcard artist's impression of Norwood Colliery. ***(Author's collection)***

Right: A view from above the east portal of Norwood End Tunnel looking eastwards towards Kiveton, showing the deep cutting and steep gradient of the line at that point. The conical spoil heap of Kiveton Park Colliery is just visible on the horizon. ***(Alan Rowles)***

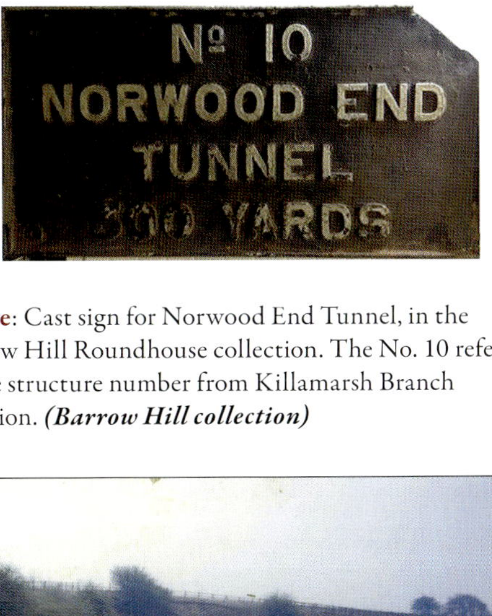

Above: Cast sign for Norwood End Tunnel, in the Barrow Hill Roundhouse collection. The No. 10 refers to the structure number from Killamarsh Branch Junction. ***(Barrow Hill collection)***

Above: The west end of Norwood End Tunnel after track lifting. ***(Author's collection)***

Above: The low bridge over the infant River Rother. ***(Alan Rowles collection)***

Above: Found too late to be included in Volume 1, here is another shot of Kiveton Park Colliery from the GCR side, showing Kiveton Park Colliery West signal box, which closed on 8 August 1926. This is the view down Colliery Road looking towards the pit, the MR line would be behind the houses. Two young children go about their business as they are watched by three waistcoat clad men, meanwhile a passenger train takes the curve towards Kiveton Park Station on the extreme left of the image.

Below: A view of the Midland Railway side of Kiveton Park Colliery with 3F 0-6-0 No. 3318 doing a spot of shunting in the yard. Coupled to a 3250-gallon tender the loco was built in February 1892 and was allocated to Derby in 1948, being withdrawn from there in August 1958. Notice the Kiveton wagons on the left and the A.E. Lawton of Stockport wagon on the right. There are plenty of pit props on hand, as can be seen between the loco and the wagon. The GCR main line as featured in Volume 1 would be over to the far left of this image. ***(Both Richard Allsopp collection)***

Chapter 4

Changing times Into the 1930s and the War years

Throughout the next two decades there were few changes to the status quo, one change being new sidings for Shirebrook Colliery coal traffic being authorised in 1927, built at a cost of £33,000 and ready for use by December 1928. The spoil gained from the construction, about 40,000 cubic yards, was transported to Rolleston for use in building a new curve.

The 1930s saw a few more changes as mentioned previously, it being agreed by the LMS that the passenger services from Mansfield to Alfreton & South Normanton and Mansfield to Staveley (Barrow Hill) via the Doe Lea Valley Line would be withdrawn from 28 July 1930, citing more convenient omnibus services as the reason. The Bradshaw's Timetable for 1920 shows that there were three trains from Mansfield to Alfreton and four in the return direction per day, hardly a busy service! The September 1930 Railway Magazine ran a paragraph stating:

Particulars of LMSR train alterations include intimations as to the closing for passenger train working on various sections and passenger stations. The services thus affected are those between...... Mansfield and Alfreton via Teversal; and Mansfield, Barrow Hill and Chesterfield via Bolsover. As a result the following stations will be closed for passenger traffic: Teversal and Tibshelf and Newton; Pleasley, Rowthorn and Hardwick, Glapwell, Palterton and Sutton, and Bolsover.

Then the May 1931 edition of Railway Magazine held a letter from Mr. J. D. Mawhood extracts of which read:

On to 28 July 1930, passenger trains were withdrawn from the Mansfield Woodhouse to Westhouses and Blackwell line via Pleasley; thus Pleasley, Teversal and Tibshelf and Newton stations were closed. This line has been very un-remunerative, and for some time prior to its closing there had been only one train daily between Mansfield and Westhouses, which left at 6:58 am. In the reverse direction two trains have been worked daily. The same day saw the closing of the Mansfield–Pleasley–Staveley Town LMS branch, with result that Rowthorn and Hardwick, Glapwell, Palterton and Sutton and Bolsover stations were closed. I travelled over this line on the last day on which passenger trains ran, and found very few people on the train which only consisted of two coaches. Both routes carry a very heavy mineral traffic, as they serve a number of collieries that lie directly on the route. Practically the whole of the ground formerly covered by these branches is served by bus services, in which the railways companies are interested.

The 1930s saw the LMS instigate a Sundays only railmotor service from Mansfield to Whitwell. The pre War, 3 July to 24 September 1939 times were as in the table. Could this service have possibly been to allow visitors to the Welbeck estate?

The railmotor used was most likely the same one that plied the Sutton Junction to Sutton Town branch a distance of ¾ mile during the week, known as the "Penny Emma". That branch didn't have a Sunday service and so this would probably give the option to utilise the railmotor on the Whitwell turns. Apparently the term "Penny Emma" comes from the fare of 1d (one penny), and the initials of the Midland Railway....MR...Emma!

Railmotor Sunday timetable
3 July – 24 September 1939

Depart	Time	Arrive	Time
Shirebrook	12.05	Mansfield	12.14
Mansfield	2.09	Whitwell	2.32
Whitwell	2.37	Mansfield	3.03
Mansfield	4.31	Whitwell	4.54
Whitwell	5.10	Mansfield	5.36
Mansfield	8.10	Whitwell	8.33
Whitwell	8.45	Mansfield	9.11
Mansfield	10.01	Whitwell	10.24
Whitwell	10.30	Mansfield	10.57
All times are pm			

War declared

The declaration of WW2 on 3 September 1939 saw many changes to the railway timetables countrywide, the end of timetabled passenger services between Mansfield and Sheffield, via the LD&ECR spurs, came on 10 September 1939, and these would never be reinstated. The final timetable saw departures from Mansfield at 10.28am, (10.30 SO) 12.55pm, 4.10pm and 7.15pm, and Sheffield at 9.43am, 3.25pm, 6.28pm and 11.14pm.

The Sunday Mansfield to Whitwell railmotor was withdrawn for the duration, timetables showed it running in 1939, but it had ceased by 1944 (more than likely earlier). In 1944 the Mansfield to Worksop service consisted of five return trips per weekday, with two extra on a Saturday, there was also a 4.10pm Shirebrook to Whitwell (Saturdays excepted) but curiously there was no return service shown! Also shown was an 8.31pm Mansfield to Elmton & Creswell, returning to Mansfield at 9.30pm.

The Government Evacuation Scheme had been developed during the summer of 1938, with the aim of ensuring the safety of millions of children from the South. Between 1940 and 1941 the German Luftwaffe began their air attacks on Britain and the safety of those in the areas being bombed was a priority. The evacuated children would be spread far and wide and in June 1940 children and teachers from the east coast port of Lowestoft were evacuated by rail some 200 miles to Creswell where they were welcomed with open arms.

Posters soon began to appear at stations asking "Is your journey really necessary?", produced by the Railway Executive Committee to remind passengers to avoid making unnecessary rail journeys during wartime. The transportation of servicemen and war supplies and munitions had to take priority over passenger journeys, and the railway timetable books included adverts about the movement of coal and munitions.

The towns along the Mansfield to Worksop route were spared the horrors of air raids, apart from the occasional sound of stray enemy aircraft. The sound of exploding bombs on Nottingham could be heard and the red glow as Sheffield was blitzed could be

◊ **Above**: Adverts from the 1944 Bradshaw's along with an "Is your journey really necessary?" poster. ***(All Author's collection)***

seen from Mansfield. There was, however, at least one occasion when a train was attacked by a lone fighter bomber.

Kirkby-based fireman Lol Stacey tells the story of the day when he was firing 4F 0-6-0 3239 during the summer of 1940 bound for Shirebrook Colliery Sidings. When he arrived there the driver went off to brew a cuppa, leaving Lol, his fireman, to rake over the engine's fire and wash down the cab. Suddenly, Lol says:

Out of the blue – a stray German aircraft zoomed across Warsop Vale and, spotting the smoke from our locomotive, opened fire with its cannons. Lumps of coal were blown into the air and then, making a second pass, "Jerry" punched holes in the tender side and I was hit in the leg.

Lol collapsed on the footplate in a pool of blood, thus becoming one of the first local casualties. He was rushed to Mansfield General Hospital where he recovered from his injuries, and later went on to become foreman at Kirkby loco depot.

Before we move on, here is a story told by Alf Green, a clerk at Whitwell, about the railways of Whitwell from 1946.

September 3rd 1946 – the day I started work at Whitwell station. At 25 years of age, I was starting a new job after 4½ years in the British army which took me around the British Isles, France, Belgium, the Netherlands, Germany, Egypt, Palestine, Jordan and Iraq.

Firstly, I will tell you about the condition I was in having travelled around so much. I was unable to settle down and I found the job to my liking as I wasn't tied down too much. I had a lot to learn in the job, as it was not as simple as it looked. The work consisted of a variety of jobs, and time was essential.

In September 1946 the railways were privately owned. Whitwell station was under the London Midland & Scottish Railway until it was nationalised in 1948. This made little difference, except freight came under Nottingham and passenger came under Sheffield. Our main customers were the Whitwell Colliery and the Steetley Quarry, we also dealt with the Steetley Colliery and the Shireoaks Colliery. Other business came from the Duke of Portland and the Welbeck estates.

Prior to nationalisation we had to deal with traffic out of Manton Colliery that was sent via the London Midland routes, all traffic coming into Whitwell, Steetley and Shireoaks from all routes except Eastern and GC as we knew it, was dealt with at Whitwell. Invoices had to be cleared. After nationalisation it became easier as we then dealt with all traffic into Steetley and Whitwell.

I should have started with the staff before going into workings etc. One station master, Mr Harold Doxey covered our station, Steetley Sidings and Midland Sidings at Shireoaks Colliery. Mr C Kenyon was the goods clerk, Miss Barwell from Creswell was the passenger clerk, and on the platforms we had two porters covering days and afternoons. Miss Edna Lee was the porter and I took the vacant position. We had a yard porter who dealt with colliery traffic and station yard traffic in the signal box were Mr J Leese and Mr H Harvey who worked days and afternoons alternately. Mr Gerry Charlesworth was the permanent way ganger with five plate layers with him – Mr C Hardwick, Mr J Patterson and Mr H Faulkner. The goods shed, though little used, contained a crane which was a manual thing. Years ago the weighbridge existed and was half way down the goods yard on the right hand side. It was still standing the last time I went down the path, but the weighbridge was taken out a long time ago.

At Steetley Sidings we had one signalman, one shift and one porter covering the sidings traffic from Steetley Company limited, Steetley refractory bricks and Steetley Colliery. At Woodend signal box there were two signalmen and a porter signalman, he had to take over from the day man and work until the afternoon man came on duty. He also had to work Shireoaks Colliery signal box. If he did 50% of his time in the signal box he got a signalman's wage, if not, a porter signalman's pay. Outside was a permanent way gang of four men. Our area was joined to Worksop at Woodend, and to Creswell at the west end of the tunnel.

Service of trains – passengers started at 5.58 am and finished at 10.15 pm Monday to Saturday. Sunday, there were four trains during the day. This was known as a push+pull service, but it only ran for a short time, though in the summer we had excursions most Sundays, the Whitwell Middle Club and Hodthorpe Club excursions, plus various others went by train.

The passenger line was closed in 1964 by Mr Beeching, and Whitwell was the only station in the Doncaster area that was closed. Freight traffic continued to run. Freight traffic had subsidised passenger traffic for years. Until the Steetley transport was formed we dealt with a lot of traffic from Steetley.

After about two years as a porter at Whitwell, I passed my clerical exams and became a station clerk. I was then posted to Clowne and Barlborough. In 1952 Clowne station was closed and I was sent back to Whitwell. During the time I spent away from Whitwell, Mr Kenyon had retired and I took his position.

The station continued to work well, Whitwell Quarry opened up in 1960 approximately, and for a while traffic poured out, including traffic going into Europe.

In recent years, British Rail have given the station buildings to the Midland Railway Museum at Butterley, it was taken down brick by brick and rebuilt at Butterley where it bears a plaque to this effect.

I have attempted to give you the basics of the workings at Whitwell station but it wasn't all dull stuff. The public came in from time to time and brightened our day, bringing parcels, livestock and obtaining travel tickets and information. In the winter his Grace, the Duke of Portland used to visit us about once a week. He would knock on the office door, with cap in hand and he would fall down the step inside the office! He would enquire about his sugar beet that his tractor driver was busy loading day after day. For about three months we would despatch approximately 15–16 wagon loads per week. Welbeck estates dispatched potatoes, carrots and animals from time to time. Fertiliser and seed potatoes were also received.

Whitwell Quarry dispatched their traffic to all the steel works in the country. Train loads of traffic went to Hawarden Bridge.

Before central heating came to working class houses, coal would be despatched to all parts of the country, but the use of gas, oil and electricity took away much of this business. It became very noticeable that we were sending train loads of coal to the power stations, and the odd wagons of traffic were disappearing.

A lot of incidents occurred during my time at Whitwell station, some years ago we had the Liverpool mounted police band come to the station and they did a show at Welbeck Abbey. Everything went marvellously until they came to reloading the horses for the return journey. The drum horse took nearly two hours to get into the horse box, in the attempts to get him in his box, he kicked two large stones off the station wall. As a result the train was very late departing. On another occasion, we had a consignment of maggots arriving off the last train, they had to be left in the office overnight; the next morning they were all over the floor and walls. One night a customer was sending some small birds away and opened the box letting them all out in the office.

I worked under five station masters, including Mr Doxey, Mr Sigsworth and Mr Robinson. We cultivated station gardens during Mr Sigsworth's reign and won several prizes in the garden competition. For one of the trips to the seaside from one of the clubs, we decorated the station with loads of buntings under the orders of Mr Sigsworth.

After closure in 1964 the traffic was dealt with at Worksop, in 1966 the clerk was withdrawn from Whitwell and placed in Worksop and I took a position in Worksop in 1968. A Mr Lindley was the last clerk to work at Whitwell.

And the 1950s

After the war had ended the railways were in a dire state, little investment or maintenance having been carried out whilst the war was on, "make do and mend" being the watch phrase. The "Big Four" had been financially squeezed by rules that forced them to carry freight at rates that were often unprofitable, and competition from an emerging road sector that had been prioritised for public investment.

The rail network had then been worn to the bone in supporting the war effort and considerably damaged by bombing, and rail safety had become a serious concern. There had been two major accidents within two days in October 1947, resulting in 60 fatalities, this contributing to that year being the second deadliest in British railway history. To restore the network and rolling stock to anything like its pre-war state was well outside the financial capabilities of the "Big Four", and as the steel, coal, iron, electricity and telecommunications industries had been nationalised, it seemed that the only way forward was for the fate of the railways to be the same.

As such in 1948 the government took the decision to nationalise the railways, and the "Big Four" companies were merged into one as British Railways. As well as new signage, from 1 June 1951 British Railways saw fit to add suffixes to stations in towns that were served by former rival companies, i.e. the LNER and LMS, such as Mansfield and Shirebrook. Mansfield (LMS) became Mansfield Town to differentiate it from the former LNER station, which became Central. Meanwhile in Shirebrook the LNER had renamed the former LD&ECR Langwith Junction, to Shirebrook North on 2 June 1924, so BR rather oddly gave the suffix "West", to the former LMS Shirebrook, oddly because the station was actually on the east side of the village!

As an aside, and to complete the Shirebrook stations story, The Great Northern Railway also had a station in Shirebrook on their Leen Valley Extension Line. This had opened on 1 November 1901 as Shirebrook, but was renamed Shirebrook South at the same time as Langwith Junction got its name change. This station closed to timetabled passenger traffic on 14 September 1931.

Timetabled freight traffic over the "New Found out" connections between Shirebrook West and Shirebrook North (the former Langwith Junction) had ceased by 1946, and the connections were lifted by 1951.

In 1958 the regional structure based largely on the "Big Four" company boundaries was amended to a geographic one. The nature of the change led to it being often referred to by the term "Penetrating Lines" as the lines that penetrated another geographic region were the ones transferred. The changes were implemented from 12.01am on Saturday 1 February 1958. Regional boundaries between the Eastern and London Midland Regions changed with the Eastern Region gaining more territory, with the new boundary being at milepost 154, between Sherwood Colliery and Shirebrook Sidings.

As previously mentioned, the 8.14am Chesterfield Midland to Elmton & Creswell (arrive 8.50am) and 4.23pm Elmton & Creswell to Chesterfield (arrive 5.04pm) services ceased to operate after 7 August 1954, although the summer Saturday Blackpool trains continued until 18 August 1962.

Finally for that decade, 2 November 1959 saw the ex-LMS line from Shirebrook Junction to Welbeck Colliery closed by the Eastern Region, all traffic then being concentrated on the former LNER connections at Welbeck Colliery Junction.

Passenger services end

The biggest blow to the line came when the Beeching Plan reared its ugly head in early 1963. Proposals were made to end passenger traffic along the Worksop–Mansfield–Nottingham line in the autumn of 1963; however, it didn't quite happen in that timescale. Closure notices announced the withdrawal of passenger trains along the line from June 1964 and although withdrawal was approved the Nottingham Evening Post for Saturday 27 June 1964 reported that:

"Hardship" of line closure

The withdrawal of local passenger train services between Nottingham Midland and Worksop could inflict hardship on various categories of passengers, says the Transport Users' Consultative Committee for the East Midlands area. The Committee announced today that in their report to the Minister of Transport they had made "certain suggestions" for alleviating the hardship.

The proposed axing of passenger services on the line and closure of certain intermediate stations was the subject of a public enquiry at Mansfield on March 11 when the committee heard many objections.

The objections only delayed the inevitable and it was to be Saturday 10 October 1964 when the end finally came. The 16 October edition of the Worksop Guardian reported:

END OF THE LINE

Musical send-off For Last "Midland" Passenger Train From Worksop.

Tickets dating back to the old LNER/LMS days were issued as souvenirs to enthusiasts travelling by the last scheduled passenger train on the Midland region branch from Worksop to Mansfield and so to Nottingham on Saturday night. The service has been axed under the Beeching plan.

Booking clerk, Mr. Ernest Fotheringham, of 88 Valley Road Worksop, said the tickets had been in the office since about 1925. For the journey from Worksop to Mansfield they now cost 3/9 second class single.

When the train left right on time at 8.7pm, it carried a larger contingent of passengers than for many years past – from Worksop at any rate.

TRUMPET FANFARE

And as Driver Ken Wilcox have a long farewell blast on the deep-throated siren of 2-6-4 tank engine No. 42284, the sound was augmented as the train pulled out by a trumpet fanfare by some of the passengers. They and others leaned out of the carriage windows and exchanged waves with people remaining on the platform to see the end of an era in Worksop railway history dating back to the old "Midland" days.

Driver Wilcox, of 29 The Downs, Wilford, Nottingham, a regular engineman on this route during his 25 years as fireman, passed fireman and driver, when asked how he felt about the closure said: "One can't help regretting it after so many years on this road."

Similar regret at the severing of the Worksop–Nottingham rail link was expressed by Fireman M. Whitt, who, with 18 years railway service and many trips on the same run, lives at 17 Failsworth Close, Clifton Estate, Nottingham, and Guard Herbert Briggs, of 63, Richmond Avenue, Ilkeston – 31 years on the railway.

The train was seen away from the Worksop East signal box by signalman Tom Wilson, 95, Prince Charles Road, Worksop, and the recoupling of the engine after the reversal procedure so familiar at Worksop, was carried out by Porter D. Hooley of 67, Dadley Road, Carlton-in-Lindrick, under the supervision of Assistant Station Foreman D.A. Griffin, 27, Queensway, Worksop. The operation was watched by Porter Harry Crookes, of 18, Welbeck Street, Worksop, who has himself carried out similar duties for many years.

The loading of parcels – these too, seemed a larger batch than usual – was in charge of Leading Parcel Porter A. Jackson of 4, Clinton Street, Worksop.

FIRST CLASS

Among those making the journey were Mr. George Whetton of Oakholme Avenue Worksop, who paid 5s 4d. for two first-class tickets to Creswell, and two young enthusiasts, 13-year-old Brian Fretwell of the welfare institute, and 11-year-old Graham Whawell of 13, Shakespeare Avenue, both of Creswell, who had travelled in on an earlier train, and then gone on to Retford for an afternoon's trainspotting. Amongst those watching the final departure from the platform was Mr. Charles Henry Crowther, of "Swanage", Watson Road, Worksop, who, aged 71, is an old North Eastern Railway man – he started his career at Leeds in 1906.

"BEECHING MUST GO"

While this was, of course, the final departure from Worksop, there was a still later train from Nottingham as far as Creswell. This left Nottingham Midland Station without incident at 10.25, but when it reached Mansfield a small group of revellers marked its departure by letting off fireworks.

NOISY SEND OFF

The noisy send-off was for what was now the 11.14 Mansfield to Creswell train, with Driver Arthur Bosworth, NUR Branch secretary, and Notts. County Councillor, on the footplate.

Somebody had chalked "Beeching must go" slogans all over the engine and coaches. Driver Bosworth, a staunch critic of the closure, sounded a defiant toot on the whistle as the train steamed away towards journey's end.

Quite a few railway enthusiasts were aboard for the final run.

The shutdown brought closure to 12 intermediate stations from Radford to Whitwell. The only one reprieved is Kirkby-in-Ashfield East, which stays open until Mr. Marples decides the fate of the Kirkby–Highbridge (sic) branch.

The last train from Nottingham departed at 10.25pm and Mansfield at 11.14pm, terminating at Elmton & Creswell where it arrived for the final time at 11.36pm. It was reported that a small group of revellers marked the departure by letting off fireworks and the Nottingham Evening Post for Monday 12 October 1964 ran the following story:

FIREWORKS AT SHUTDOWN – Defiant blast end trains last journey.

The last passenger train on the Nottingham–Mansfield–Worksop service left Platform six of Nottingham Midland station without incident at 10.25 pm on Saturday, but when it reached Mansfield a small group of revellers marked his departure by letting off fireworks.

The noisy send-off was for what was now the 11.14 Mansfield to Creswell train with Driver Arthur Bosworth, NUR branch secretary and Nottinghamshire county councillor on the foot plate.

Somebody had chalked "Beeching must go" slogans all over the engine and coaches. Driver Bosworth a staunch critic of the closure sounded a defiant toot on the whistle as the train steamed away towards journeys end.

Quite a few railway enthusiasts were aboard on the final run, amongst them was 18-year-old Stephen Randall of Shakespeare Avenue, Mansfield Woodhouse, who paid a sixpenny fare for the mile and a half journey to his home station, "just as a sentimental goodbye."

The shutdown brought closure to 12 intermediate stations from Radford to Whitwell. The only one reprieved is Kirkby-in-Ashfield East which stays open until Mr Marples decides the fate of the Kirkby–Pye Bridge branch.

At Worksop tickets dating back to the old LNER/LMS days were issued as souvenirs to enthusiasts travelling on the last scheduled passenger train to run on the Midland region branch line from Worksop to Mansfield and Nottingham. The tickets, said booking Clark Mr Ernest Fotheringham, of Valley Road, Worksop, had been in the office since about 1925. The train carried a larger contingent of passengers than for many years past. Driver Ken Wilcox gave a farewell blast on the siren of 2-6-4 tank engine number 42284 and the sound was augmented by a trumpet fanfare from the passengers.

The closure of the line for passenger traffic left Mansfield with the unfortunate tag of being the largest town in the country without a railway station.

Freight only

With the closure to passenger traffic the Nottingham to Worksop line became freight only between Radford Junction and Shireoaks

Junctions, and, serving many collieries along its route, a busy one at that. However, other than the Warsop Curve at Shirebrook, which only allowed traffic to travel southwards off the LD&ECR, there were no other connections between the former LD&ECR lines and the Midland Railway lines at Shirebrook.

As such with the advent of the power stations at West Burton and Cottam there was an inevitable surge of traffic from the collieries along the LD&ECR at Ollerton, Thoresby, Welbeck etc. and more traffic from the Mansfield Railway routes, particularly Mansfield Concentration Sidings, wishing to travel northwards. To do this they had to travel over the former LD&ECR line through Langwith via Clowne to Beighton and Woodhouse Junction, before they were able to gain access to the GC line. After running round at Woodhouse they could then head east to the power stations.

As traffic grew and train weights increased the gradient on the Langwith to Beighton line restricted the length of trains. In the mid-60s as the M1 Motorway was being built towards Barlborough it would have become necessary to provide a bridge over the Beighton Branch. To avoid this it was thus decided to provide a spur from just north of Langwith Colliery signal box on the LD&ECR Beighton Branch, to just south of Norwood Siding signal box on the MR line, thus enabling the line from Langwith Colliery to Spinkhill to be closed, and consequently saving the costs of bridging the line. The new spur came into use on 11 January 1967.

In 1974 the ex-LD&EC bridge over the MR at Shirebrook came up for renewal and the Eastern Region decided to construct a single track spur, commencing at the old LMS Welbeck Branch cutting and joining the LD&ECR just west of Warsop Junction. This spur came into use on 11 November 1974 and enabled the closure of the ex LD&ECR line west of the MR line, and the former Beighton Branch as far as Norwood Junction. The result of this new spur caused the reinstatement of the Down "New Found Out" spur from Shirebrook Junction to Langwith Junction to serve the W. H. Davis wagon works at Langwith Junction.

Shirebrook West diesel depot

The main locomotive depot and works of the LD&ECR was at Tuxford, but in 1895 this company also provided a brick-built two-road structure at Langwith Junction situated on the south side of the line, a few yards from the ends of the platforms of Langwith Junction station. Later extended it would take over the work of Tuxford Junction depot when this closed on 2 February 1959. Formerly all steam, the first diesels to arrive at Langwith Junction were 350hp shunters to take over the local shunting duties from steam. The first main line diesel to arrive was D5567, which was given trials as colliery pilot and on trip workings during the first week of February 1960.

Langwith was to have been converted to a diesel depot by September of 1962; however, progress was delayed and by November of 1962 there were still approximately 40 steam locos in use. The diesels were initially serviced in the old carriage shed at Langwith Junction, fuelling being accomplished from rail tankers which were pressurized with air to force the fuel out and into the locomotives' fuel tanks.

Because of growing operating difficulties being experienced in the maintenance of the new diesels in the filthy environment of the working steam depot, another solution had to be found. As such it was decided to convert the goods shed at Shirebrook West station into a temporary fuelling and servicing point, for the daily servicing of the twelve Brush locomotives and maintenance of ten shunting locomotives from the steam depot, which were, however, still stabled at Langwith.

This shed was single road and only able to accommodate one loco at a time. Inside a pit had been constructed to allow the fitters access to the underside of the diesels and staging was erected alongside the pit road, for high level access. Fuelling was accomplished with the aid of rail borne tankers stabled in the goods yard. By the end of 1963 it became clear that a purpose-built diesel servicing and fuelling depot was required at Shirebrook West and the Eastern Region was authorised to build a new depot to replace the steam depot and primitive diesel servicing facility.

This new depot was to be built on the site of the Shirebrook West goods yard and was to be of the standard Eastern Region design of the time, consequently, the temporary facilities in the goods shed were closed, the goods shed demolished and the yard, along with the former MR Warsop Colliery Branch access, which ran alongside the goods yard, lifted. Langwith Junction steam depot closed in February 1966 and the diesel depot then became the signing on point for the 240 footplate men formerly employed at Langwith.

Trains from Warsop Main Colliery had been utilising the former LD&ECR access but in doing so had to undergo a double reversal to gain access to travel to the north or south. To alleviate this in July 1976 the former MR Warsop Colliery Branch was reinstated, and as the branch ran alongside the rear of the depot building, because of congestion at the depot at weekends it was necessary to stable seven or eight locomotives on the branch end alongside the depot building. This would remain a feature of the depot right up to 1991.

Colliery closures

Production at Langwith Colliery ceased on 4 August 1978 after 99 years of service, this being due to dirty and thinning reserves of coal which were becoming expensive to mine; however, coal continued to be mined on a small scale for several months afterwards, salvage continued until 1979 but the shafts were kept pumping to prevent Creswell Colliery from flooding. Seam thickness in the Clowne seam had reduced to just 2 feet 9 inches, but in 1977–78, the last full financial year of operation, the colliery produced 405,161 tonnes of coal with a workforce of 580 men. Although the colliery had closed the "Toton" type signalling for the RLB wasn't decommissioned until Langwith Colliery Sidings box was closed on 6 June 1981 and the RLB seemed to linger on for quite a while before demolition was undertaken.

Concentration of loading facilities continued with Steetley Colliery merging with Shireoaks Colliery from 13 March 1983 and a 1,500-tonnes capacity steel bunker (instead of the conventional reinforced concrete rapid loading bunker) was built at Shireoaks at a cost of £1¾m, which included a stacking and reclaiming scheme. This required a new connection off the Woodend Junction to Shireoaks West Junction line which had been singled in 1979, in order to allow trains to run round. This emulated the original Midland Railway connection onto the single line, as it was when the line was first built.

The Miners' Strike of 1984 would see a huge change in the fortunes of the collieries then still in existence on the section of line between Shirebrook and Worksop, and one by one they succumbed to closure. On Tuesday 3 June 1986 the announcement was made that coal production at Whitwell Colliery would cease at the end of June, the Mansfield & Sutton Recorder newspaper reported:

Continuing heavy losses of around £8 million over the last year show that there is no viable future for Whitwell Colliery, the cost of producing coal is £69 per ton against a selling price of £42.

Of the workforce of 750, those transferring to other collieries numbered 389, the majority of the remainder (aged over 50) accepted early retirement. Coal traffic continued from the washeries until 31 March 1987 when coal from High Moor

Colliery was transferred to Kiveton Park Colliery for loading, the last worker finishing in July 1987. The steel headwork of No. 1 shaft was demolished on 20 March 1987 followed by the more difficult headstock of No. 2 shaft, which had been encased in reinforced concrete. The final act of demolition was by an explosive charge, fired at the base of the structure on 10 April 1987, the shafts being filled in and sealed off.

Warsop Main Colliery was closed on 25 August 1989 after 95 years, No. 2 shaft was abandoned on 4 April 1991 and No. 1 shaft on 28 April 1991. The Rapid loading bunker was demolished by explosion on 25 September 1991, the first headgear was demolished on 23 October and the second on 28 November 1991 after which the shafts were filled with limestone chippings and concrete, and finally capped with concrete.

Production ceased at Creswell Colliery with the loss of 700 jobs on 30 September 1991, the 1977-commissioned rapid loading bunker was demolished in June 1992, and Shirebrook Colliery was the penultimate colliery to close in the North Derbyshire Coalfield when it finished production on 7 May 1993; its bunker was demolished on 25 July 1994.

New train crew depot

Along with the run-down of the British mining industry in the early 1990s came the plan to concentrate train crews from Shirebrook and Barrow Hill at a new purpose built train crew depot at Worksop. This was opened by East Midlands Freight on 11 February 1991, upon which all men from Shirebrook and Barrow Hill were transferred. This resulted in the closure of Barrow Hill Depot and the transfer of weekend stabling of locomotives to the downside holding sidings at Worksop. From that time locomotives would only be seen at Shirebrook for refuelling and "A" exams.

Shirebrook Depot finally closed its doors on 28 September 1996, after a life of a little over 31 years. During 1998 the depot building was taken over by Bremick Plastics as a factory unit, the tracks leading into the depot being torn up and buffer stops erected. Never again would the building be host to diesel locomotives.

Just after the turn of the century Bremick Plastics ceased use of the building and the vandals and thieves took over, totally trashing it, with all the glasswork smashed and electrical installations stolen. The pointwork from the main line to the shed road sidings was removed in 2006 and in May 2008 all the remaining former shed roads were removed. By early 2009 the shell of the building looked fit only for demolition, and the oil and fuel tanks, cycle sheds and the former weigh house had been removed or demolished. However, yet another chapter was to be written when the site came up for auction in mid-2009, it being reported to have been sold for an estimated £130,000 to Top Cat Furniture Stores. The main shed underwent a clean out and the whole building was reclad in metal sheet for use as a furniture storage building, a task it continues to do today.

The Robin Hood Line project begins

In the late 1980s a consortium led by Nottinghamshire County Council (NCC), and including Derbyshire County Council (DCC), the Districts of Ashfield, Bassetlaw, Bolsover, Gedling, and Nottingham City Council, was formed to look into the possibility of restoring passenger services between Nottingham and Worksop. The local authorities had considered that the early implementation of the project was essential for their transport objectives, not to mention for social, economic and environmental reasons. This reflected the fact that the route passed through the heart of the coalfields which were suffering heavy job losses due to the downturn in mining and other industries.

The commencement of the project in early May 1988 saw test digs begin to unearth the filled-in Kirkby Tunnel, this really being the starting block for the project to reopen the route through to Nottingham. This led to a report being published in June 1988 about the condition of the tunnel, something which could have seen an end to the project before it had really begun. Fortunately the findings gave the green light when it was shown that the tunnel was structurally sound and in remarkably good condition, something of a surprise really after speculation that mining beneath it would have severely damaged the structure. This report saw BR's estimate for bringing the tunnel back into a useable condition reduce to £250,000, a quarter of what was previously thought.

With the project now gathering pace NCC set aside up to £6m for the reopening scheme to Mansfield, with further progress being dependent upon government and European grants, of which £13m would come from the government, £6m from the European Union while British Rail contributed £0.5m. NCC and DCC were to be responsible for rehabilitating the closed route infrastructure while the district councils took responsibility for the stations and car parking.

By 1990 it was being reported that the first seven miles of the line between Nottingham and Hucknall could be reopened within 18 months; however, the four-mile section between Linby and Kirkby Summit could take up to five years because of the lack of BR resources to reinstate this missing route. The sites for the stations in the Mansfield area were also chosen which involved negotiation with BR for land at Mansfield Woodhouse, and with British Coal for the use of land on the former Sherwood Colliery spoil heap as a car park. Ashfield District Council approved plans for reopening of the passenger station at Hucknall on the original site, with the new Sutton-in-Ashfield station site being north of the level crossing instead of the original site to the south. The station at Kirkby-in-Ashfield would have to be constructed on a totally new site, following the closure of part of the original MR route through the town, which had been done to eliminate a level crossing.

The name "The Robin Hood Line" was first agreed during a Rail Forum in Mansfield at which representatives from local authorities were present. It was envisaged that a half-hourly service would operate, with alternate trains being extended from Worksop to Retford, thus linking Nottingham with the East Coast Main Line. Earlier in the year the BR Rail Bill to authorise the rebuilding of the line was given its third reading in the House of Commons.

Moving into 1991

The decision to provide financial support to reopen the Robin Hood Line was formally taken by NCC on 2 July 1991. It was to be a four-stage project at a cost of £10m, with a target date of 1998 being projected for the reopening as a through route. However, it was expected that at least half of the cost would be spent on work around Kirkby and the reopening of the tunnel. By late 1991 it was expected that the Regional Railways Civil Engineers would begin work on the project in the early part of 1992, with expectations that Phase 1 between Nottingham and Newstead would be operational from October 1993.

A spanner was thrown in the works when on 27 November 1991 a Bill was deposited in Parliament for the construction of the Greater Nottingham Rapid Transit system, of which Line One would have an impact on the Robin Hood Line from Wilkinson Street, where the tramway would cross the railway, and then follow it as far as Hucknall.

Phase 1 of the project began on 30 June 1992 when a ceremony was held to cut the first sod at the site of Hucknall Station, to officially inaugurate the start of work on the reopening of the line, with NCC Councillor Terry Butler and David Mcintosh, Regional Railways District Manager (East Midlands), officiating.

Trains begin to run

As with many rail reopening schemes, in early 1993 the government pleaded poverty for further expansion of Phase 2 of the route. The £6m funding from the government to match that of NCC's contribution, was put on hold when the Public Transport Minister Roger Freeman told NCC that funding for large projects would not be available "for some time". He did, however, give NCC permission to borrow a further £367,000 required to build a station at Bulwell.

January 1993 saw track alterations at Bestwood Park Junction to single the track onwards to a new passing loop just north of Newstead station. The services would be terminating at Newstead in the interim period and after passengers alighted the train would move forward to the buffer stops where drivers would change ends to return the train to Nottingham. Because of the gradient in the station at Newstead and the fact that the driver would have to change ends here, the DoT rule stated that an unattended train could not be stabled on a gradient without applying handbrakes. As such the turn-back had to be on the level so the trackbed was lowered to achieve the level section.

Phase 1 was completed at a cost of £2.7m and 27 April 1993 saw 156411 convey dignitaries and press from Nottingham to Newstead and return, then a Robin Hood Line Fun Day was held on Saturday 8 May 1993 when over 1,500 people took the opportunity to travel along the route, before 156411 broke the banner at Hucknall station to introduce full services from 17 May. The passenger service was well received by the public with loadings exceeding expectations.

Phase 2 work starts

A new Bulwell station opened on 24 May 1994 and work on clearing topsoil on the approaches to Kirkby Tunnel began early in the year in preparation for reopening through the tunnel. The cuttings at either end of the tunnel had large amounts of material removed, some of which was used to fill the former GCR cutting to the north of the tunnel; breakthrough of the tunnel workings occurred in October. The new Kirkby Lane End Junction with the line from Pye Bridge was created over the weekend of 5 & 6 November 1994.

Mansfield stations

A £2m contract for the construction of Mansfield and Mansfield Woodhouse stations was let in early September 1994, work beginning at Mansfield on 19 November 1994. Over the years since closure of the station the road system had changed in Mansfield: the original station was now on the north side of the A6009 Mansfield inner ring road, which had cut through the trackbed of the line. The Grade II listed station buildings were in use as a nightclub and so couldn't initially be incorporated into the works, but during an eight-day blockade a new subway was dug and March 1995 saw work begin to lengthen the platforms at the new station which were required to be long enough to accommodate a HST set with a view to accommodating London services. As these would now have to cross the ring road, four 108-foot long, 70-ton "U" shaped beams were laid across the roadway to accommodate the platforms. Fortunately the former station building later became available and is now in use once again.

The new Mansfield Woodhouse station was to be built a few yards north of its original site, the Phase 2 station making use of the still-extant former goods shed on an island platform, the goods shed side becoming the terminating platform for trains from Nottingham.

The first movement over the reinstated track through Kirkby Tunnel to Kirkby Lane End Junction, took place on 24 September 1995 when Class 58 locos 58003 and 58030 performed signalling checks. The first move through the reopened tunnel took place just after 18.00 when 58030 ran through.

Phase 3 opens

In preparation for the Robin Hood Line opening, closure of Shirebrook Sidings 'box came on 17 January 1998, its functions being taken over by the 320-yard distant Shirebrook Junction signal box.

The costs were continuing to rise with the total reaching £23m with Phase 3 funding still being sought, and a further £3.5m was required in addition to £1.5m already in place, in order to build stations at Shirebrook, Langwith, Creswell and Whitwell.

Phase 3 saw the addition of a through platform at Mansfield Woodhouse, along with new stations at Shirebrook, Langwith-Whaley Thorns, Creswell and Whitwell, all except Langwith constructed on the sites of the original stations. The total cost for this final phase came in at £5.3 million. The final phase was opened by the Transport Minister, Dr Gavin Strang, on 11 May 1998. Class 150 Sprinter units 150016+150110 were used to convey guests, who were shown the new stations between Mansfield and Whitwell, after which they were met by dignitaries on arrival at Worksop. Speeches were made at Creswell on the return run to Nottingham.

Ten successful years

The Robin Hood line celebrated ten years of operation in 2003, during which time it had carried over seven million passengers, with around 3,500 users a day, and was announced as being Central Trains' fastest growing passenger train service. To celebrate the ten years of operation, Central Trains revinyled Class 170 "Turbostar" 170513 in a one-off Central Trains/Robin Hood livery of green and red.

From the May 2003 timetable the Midland Mainline franchise, which primarily worked between Nottingham/Sheffield and London St. Pancras, introduced a diagram for one of their Class 170s between Nottingham and Worksop, as a fill-in turn from their usual Nottingham to London St. Pancras runs. This service was the 17.26 Nottingham to Worksop, returning as the 18.52 Worksop to Nottingham, and was the only time Midland Mainline units were seen along the route.

Change of franchise and Sunday services

Central Trains became part of the East Midlands Trains franchise from 11 November 2007 and with it came a change of rolling stock which saw Classes 150/170 replaced by Classes 153, 156 and 158.

In 2008 a campaign for additional funding was led by Nottinghamshire County Council (NCC) who managed to attract 10,000 names on a petition of passengers who pledged to support a new Sunday service. Mansfield was quoted by its local MP as "the largest town in the UK not to have a Sunday rail service".

NCC agreed to pay 90% of the £217,000 per annum costs of the service until at least May 2011, but it was hoped that the Department for Transport (DfT) would continue to fund it on a permanent basis, if the service was well patronised. In figures being quoted it was said that there should be around 1,800 passengers per day by 2010. The timetable offered resulted in the introduction of ten trains each way between the hours of 09.30 and 19.30, running from Nottingham and Mansfield Woodhouse from 14 December 2008, four of these continuing to Worksop.

Unfortunately, soon after the service started, some East Midlands Trains crews refused to work their Sundays and EMT services were decimated over a number of Sundays. There were also a number of "bustitutions" due to engineering work and as such passenger usage was less than expected, with growth only seen between Mansfield and Nottingham. In the event NCC decided to reduce the funding and prioritise running a reduced service between Nottingham and Mansfield Woodhouse only from 22 May 2011, with the number of return workings reduced from ten to eight, and the Worksop services withdrawn. Although there have been calls for reinstatement of a Sunday service, none have yet materialised.

Robin Hood Line extension?

Around the same time as the Sunday services were being mooted, calls came for an extension of Robin Hood Line services along the former LD&ECR line from Shirebrook. After the end of coal traffic to High Marnham the line from Thoresby Colliery Junction was kept open and fully maintained as the Network Rail High Marnham Test Track, and in mid-2009 NCC commissioned a feasibility study to consider a plan to extend the Robin Hood Line along this route, by extending the current hourly service between Nottingham and Mansfield Woodhouse to Ollerton, calling at Shirebrook, Warsop and Edwinstowe, close to Center Parcs Sherwood Forest holiday resort.

NCC met with the rail minister Claire Perry in March 2016 to press for the scheme to be adopted, a report produced in February 2016 suggested that the likely costs of reinstatement, including the rebuilding of the three stations, would be between £18.9M and £24.5M, with signalling accounting for more than half of that figure. Operating costs were estimated to be some £1.6M per year, with revenue from fares expected to be a little over half of that, and the rest to be found from subsidies. A condition of the awarding of a new East Midlands franchise for operating the line in 2019 was that the operator was required to produce a business case for the extension to Ollerton; however, once again there has been no progress on this at the time of writing.

Proposals for the removal of Whitwell Tunnel

In 2011 Lafarge Aggregates the then owners of Whitwell Quarry, announced plans for the removal of the 544-yard long Whitwell Tunnel, the proposed scheme diverting the line away from this tunnel, and routing it in the open approximately 70 metres to the south-east, parallel to the existing tunnelled section.

The reasons for this was that the land surrounding the tunnel, both to the north-west and the south-east, was part of Lafarge Aggregates Whitwell Quarry. This quarry is one of only two in the UK at which high quality dolomitic limestone is extracted, this being a high purity limestone that is burnt in kilns and then used in the manufacture of steel and refractory products, and Whitwell is recognised as a source of national importance for this mineral. Lafarge wished to remove the main reserves in the quarry, but these then comprised of those associated with the railway tunnel, and to access these would mean removing the tunnel.

Lafarge already had planning permission from Derbyshire County Council to extract the limestone around the tunnel, but in order to remove the stone the proposal was to build about 1200 metres of new trackbed in the quarry base, which would run on previously quarried land to the south-east of the existing line. The new route would begin at a point just after bridge 68 Southfield Lane Whitwell, rejoining the existing line at a point just north of bridge 65, A616 Sheffield Road in Creswell. Bridge 67 a farm access bridge would be lost. The diversion was designed to be permanent with the line eventually running in a cutting following restoration of the quarry site after exhaustion of the stone.

Plans showed that initially the rock surface would be prepared and followed by the construction of a bridge over a new quarry underpass, to allow quarry vehicles to access either side of the line. After laying new ballast over most of the new line with the exception of the connections at either end, new tracks and signalling would be laid and connection of the new line to the existing line would occur over a weekend blockage period. Once complete rail traffic would immediately operate on the new line with a line speed of 60mph. However, it was proposed that the new section of line would be suitable for upgrading to 75mph. Lafarge project manager David Atkinson said:

The impact on rail users will be minimal as only two short weekend closures will be necessary to connect up the new track. Once operational, the diverted line will not affect train service quality or timetables and with the diversion in place, all rail passengers would notice is that the dark of the tunnel would be replaced by an open air, very brief view of our quarry.

Once the new line was in use the tunnel would immediately be sealed to prevent any trespass and possible colonisation by bats and other species, with demolition of the tunnel lining and removal of the track shortly after.

Network Rail agreed in principle to the diversion and were liaising closely with Lafarge, the tunnel removal benefiting Network Rail as the maintenance costs would be dispensed with and they would be left with a brand new section of trackwork. The application for the plans was expected to be submitted to the Infrastructure Planning Commission on 1 April 2011 and if a development consent order was issued for the diversion, then Lafarge would be able to begin work on the project in 2012. Projections based on current production estimated it would take five to six years to extract the stone around the tunnel and complete the diversion of the railway track.

All that being said, planning approval for the extraction of the stone in the vicinity of the tunnel expired in 2019 and an email in August 2022 to the Senior PR and External Communications Officer at Tarmac (now the operators of the quarry) enquiring about progress, elicited the following response:

Following an agreement with Network Rail, the railway tunnel is to remain in situ and the planning permission shows the tunnel is being retained.

So, it seems the project to remove the tunnel is now dead.

Coal no more

The movement of coal over the line ceased from Thursday 17 September 2015 when the last coal train left from Thoresby Colliery for Cottam Power Station, thus bringing down the curtain on loaded coal trains along the LD&ECR and former MR routes. With the downturn of coal movement nationwide the requirement for coal wagons lessened, and as such they could be seen stored at several locations. Two sets of Freightliner coal wagons were stabled for a while in the sidings at Thoresby Colliery Junction, but the last one was removed on 8 February 2018, after which the sidings were deemed out of use, and all the access pointwork was removed by Network Rail.

That was the last coal wagon move along the two routes and indeed with the exception of redundant coal hoppers heading to the W.H. Davis wagon works at Langwith Junction for conversion to other uses, there have been no coal movements over the Mansfield to Worksop line since.

Today

The line has gone from passenger and freight, to freight only, then back to passenger and freight, and now primarily passenger only. Elmton & Creswell signal box hangs on by the skin of its teeth, having been switched out of circuit for many years, and only opens for maintenance purposes; its days are numbered and once it has gone that ends the semaphore signals along the MR route.

Apart from the former LD&ECR lines (the Network Rail High Marnham Test Track) and the W.H. Davis wagon works branch, the former MR access to Langwith Junction, all the connecting branches have gone, and now just the basic main line remains. Where Mansfield had goods yards and many sidings, now just a double track line exists.

The passenger usage of the stations was hit hard by the Covid19 Pandemic in 2020–21, Whitwell for instance went from 19,790 entries/exits in 2019–20, to 4,862 in 2020–21, and Creswell saw 39,550 in 2019–20, down to 10,664 in 2020–21. Mansfield, the busiest of the stations had a footfall of 409,000 in 2017–18, falling to 396,000 in 2019–20, but a huge drop to 92,192 in 2020–21. By 2023–24 these figures had risen back to 10,426 for Whitwell, 40,532 for Creswell and 313,788 for Mansfield.

The latest on the Robin Hood Line was the announcement that services will be cut at Whitwell and Langwith-Whaley Thorns to two-hourly. The 2 February 2022 edition of the Worksop Guardian reported:

Outrage as "horrendous" train timetable changes will see services to villages near Worksop cut in half

Angry residents have hit out at changes to the Robin Hood Line which will see services to villages near Worksop cut in half. East Midlands Railway has proposed a change to off-peak calling patterns on the Robin Hood Line which are to be put into effect from Sunday, May 15. The changes on the line, which services between Worksop and Nottingham, will see half of calls at Langwith-Whaley Thorns and Whitwell stopped.

EMR said it has been working to identify long term issues which have affected the punctuality of the Robin Hood Line, and found that "the most robust option to improve performance in the short term" involved alternate hourly omission of calls at Langwith-Whaley Thorns and Whitwell, due to "the lowest customer demand."

It is likely that the Robin Hood Line has a secure future ahead of it, but alienating prospective passengers is not the way to go!

Above: Central Trains 170510 arrives at Creswell with 2W23 17.57 Nottingham to Worksop on 30 May 2003. The original station building still stands today, but notice that the platforms are now slightly staggered and, if brought back into rail use, the building would not be on the platform!

Left: The W.H. Davis wagon works still produces new and rebuilt wagons. 66778 "Cambois Depot 25 years" awaits departure from Shirebrook on 21 December 2021 with 4D21 13.29 Shirebrook Davis & Son to Doncaster Down Decoy. ***(Both Author)***

Shirebrook Junction

Above: Shirebrook Junction looking north. The 'box opened on 1 January 1899 with a 16-lever frame. The line curving right is the Warsop Curve, built to connect the MR with the LD&ECR at Warsop Junction. It was brought into use eight days later, with goods traffic commencing from 16 January and passenger traffic on 20 March. The tracks either side of the main line were known as "The New Found Out", built in 1904 to connect the MR with the LD&ECR at Langwith Junction (renamed Shirebrook North in 1924, see the author's books about the LD&ECR for more information: *https://www.fonthill.media/search?type=product&q=chris+booth*). This involved reframing the 'box in September 1904 with sufficient levers to work the connections; this image post-dates the work. ***(British Railways DY15396)***

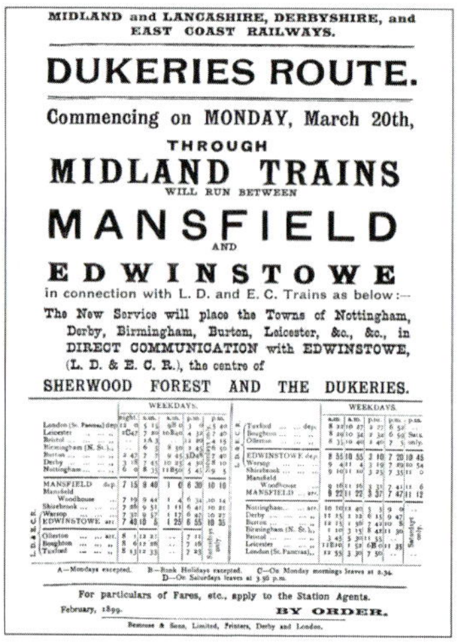
MIDLAND and LANCASHIRE, DERBYSHIRE, and EAST COAST RAILWAYS.

DUKERIES ROUTE.

Commencing on MONDAY, March 20th,

THROUGH

MIDLAND TRAINS

WILL RUN BETWEEN

MANSFIELD

AND

EDWINSTOWE

in connection with L. D. and E. C. Trains as below:—

The New Service will place the Towns of Nottingham, Derby, Birmingham, Burton, Leicester, &c., &c., in DIRECT COMMUNICATION with EDWINSTOWE, (L. D. & E. C. R.), the centre of

SHERWOOD FOREST AND THE DUKERIES.

A—Mondays excepted. B—Bank Holidays excepted. C—On Monday mornings leaves at 2.34. D—On Saturdays leaves at 3.58 p.m.

For particulars of Fares, etc., apply to the Station Agents.

February, 1899. BY ORDER.

Bemrose & Sons, Limited, Printers, Derby and London.

Left: On 16 November 1896 the LD&ECR opened Warsop Junction 'box initially to control their connection to Warsop Main Colliery. The LD&ECR had originally envisaged a branch to Mansfield, but abandoned the scheme after the MR agreed to running powers to an LD&ECR-built goods depot in Mansfield. However, this idea was also dropped and instead the Warsop Curve was constructed to connect the MR just to the north of Shirebrook Station with the LD&ECR at Warsop Junction. Opened to traffic on 9 January 1899, goods commenced on 16 January which allowed the MR to introduce a passenger service to Edwinstowe on the LD&ECR. Commencing on Monday 20 March 1899, this poster was issued to advertise the trains. Services began from Mansfield at 7.15 am, with subsequent departures at 9.40am, 1.0pm, 6.30pm and a Saturdays only 10.10pm. Departures from Edwinstowe were at 8.55am, 10.55am, 3.10pm, 7.20pm and on Saturdays 10.45pm; there was no Sunday service. Direct Mansfield to Sheffield trains also used the curve but this entailed time-consuming running round at Warsop or Edwinstowe, often causing delays. This led the MR to seek powers to build further connections with the LD&ECR. The Down line left the Worksop line immediately north of the Warsop Curve opposite Shirebrook Junction 'box, and climbed at 1 in 65 before curving round to join the LD&ECR at Langwith Junction East. The Up line left the LD&ECR east of the bridge over the MR and descended at 1 in 63 to join the line from Worksop at Shirebrook Junction. Brought into use on 1 October 1904, the connections allowed direct running from the MR to the LD&ECR at Langwith Junction, and on to Sheffield via the LD&ECR Beighton Branch. ***(Author's collection)***

Left: The opening of the "The New Found Out" connections had required an extension to the frame in the existing 'box, but to fulfil the requirement for more levers for the Welbeck Colliery Branch (opened 1929), an extension to the box itself was needed. The new section is at the steps end, which can be clearly seen on the photo. ***(Pete Churchman)***

Left: Stanier 2-6-4T 42588 passes Shirebrook Junction with a Nottingham to Worksop train in this undated 1960s photo. Previously allocated to Chester, Bangor, Bury, Neasden and Kentish Town, it became a 16A Nottingham loco during the four weeks ending 30 September 1961. Reigning there for just over three years, it was condemned during the week ending 24 October 1964. The passenger service ended 14 days earlier, thereby dating the photo to that three-year period. ***(Author's collection)***

Right: June 1960 was a notably rare warm month of the 1960s, most summers in that decade being poor by then recent standards. On a sunny 25 June the signalman has the windows and door open to permit a breeze through the 'box as 8F 2-8-0 48552 takes the Warsop Curve with a loaded coal train, most likely heading for Mansfield Concentration Sidings. ***(Author's collection)***

Above: On another warm day WD 2-8-0 90448 takes the Warsop Curve at Shirebrook Junction with a train for High Marnham, comprised of specially-built HUO 24.5-ton hoppers for High Marnham Power Station traffic. The 'box and lamp cabin in front have recently been repainted. ***(Bill Taylor)***

Right: Stanier 2-6-4T 42618 passes Shirebrook Junction with a four-coach Worksop to Nottingham train in 1962. Allocated to 16B Kirkby in Ashfield from 13 November 1961, the loco was loaned to 55H Neville Hill on 12 March 1964, before moving to 55G Huddersfield Hillhouse on 7 June 1964. Withdrawal came on 12 July 1965. Comparisons with the earlier photo will show that the two single lines up to the LD&ECR have been lifted. ***(Author's collection)***

Below: 13 years later, little has changed apart from the 1974 reinstatement of the former Down single line to the LD&ECR, now only serving the W.H. Davis wagon works. Class 45 No. 45129 is seen with the diverted 1M28 14.10 Sheffield to London St. Pancras on Sunday 30 March 1975. ***(John S. Gilks)***

Below: DRS 20315+20313 leave the single line from the W.H. Davis wagon works on 23 May 2008 with 4Z06 09.40 Shirebrook Davis & Son to Crewe, comprising two flat wagons. Apart from vegetation growth and the 'box receiving another repaint, the main change has involved the area's resignalling and subsequent loss of the semaphore signals. This was carried out over Saturday and Sunday 17/18 January 1998 when Shirebrook Station 'box closed, and after that date Shirebrook Junction began working direct through to Kirkby Summit 'box. ***(Author)***

Top: In 1974 Bridge No. 37, where the LD&ECR crossed the MR was condemned. This is the view looking east towards Bridge 37A and Warsop Junction, with the MR in the cutting below. Rather than replace it, it was decided to make a new connection between the two lines.

Above: Looking south from the MR line cutting, work starts to cut away the cutting side. The track has been slewed to allow the machinery to cut away the limestone sides.

Top: Viewed looking north from track level, the former LMS Welbeck Colliery Branch cutting is on the extreme right. The signals are Shirebrook Junction No. 33 Outer Home with Shirebrook Station "A" Distant beneath.

Above: The new cutting is now complete, and Bridge No. 37 was dismantled soon after. ***(All Derek Talbot)***

Below: The signalling notice issued on 10 November 1974 shows all the new connections, and the re-laid Down Siding that connects to W.H. Davis. ***(Author's collection)***

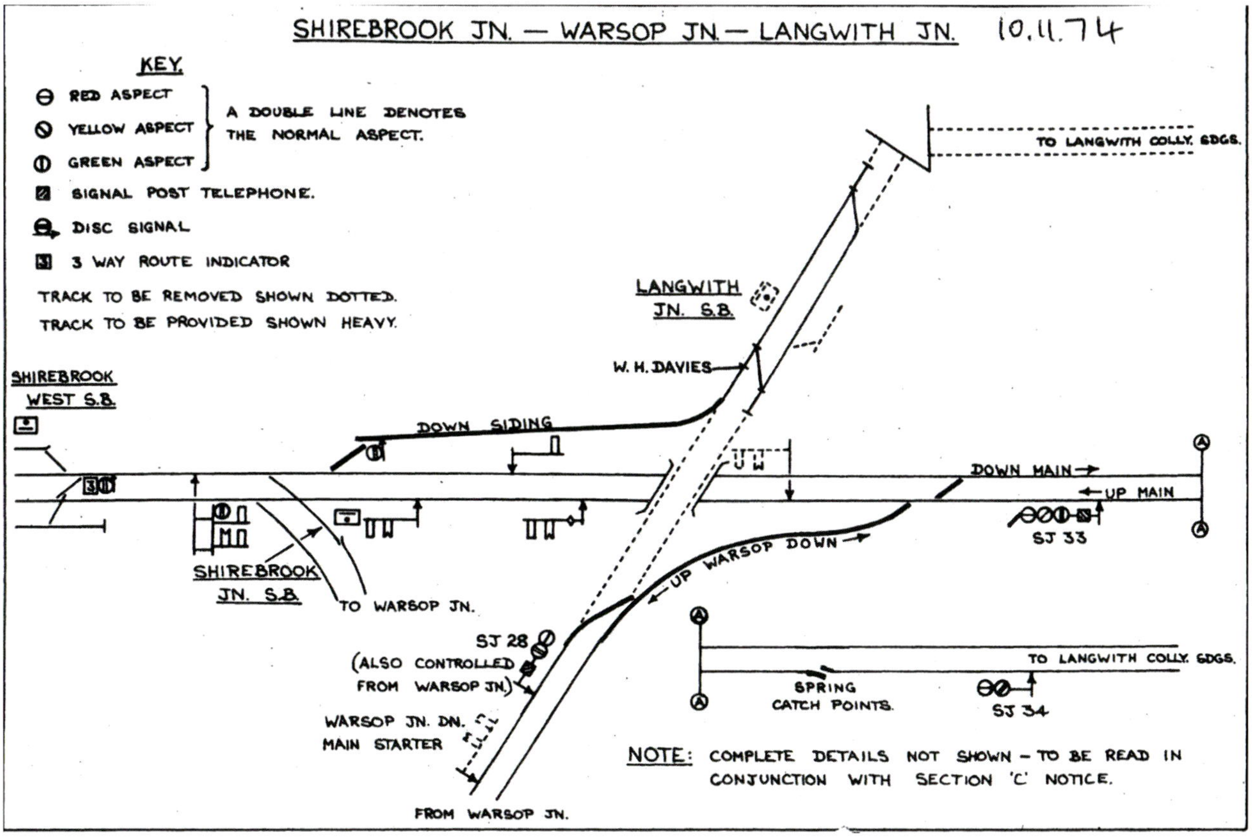

Shirebrook Station

Above: Shirebrook Station was opened for goods traffic in April 1875 and to passengers on 1 June 1875, and is seen here just after opening. The Warsop Curve, on the other side of the overbridge in previous photos, had not yet been built. Notice the MR lower quadrant signal just the other side of the bridge, which would have been worked by the original Shirebrook 'box.

Left: The station received the suffix "West" in 1951, despite being on the eastern edge of the village – purportedly to "avoid confusion" with the other stations in and around Shirebrook. The LD&ECR's Langwith Junction was renamed Shirebrook North in 1924 despite not actually being in Shirebrook, and the GNR's Shirebrook station (on their Langwith Junction to Nottingham Victoria line) was actually in southern Shirebrook so correctly given the "South" suffix. A tender first 4F 0-6-0 clanks into the station with a five-coach Worksop to Nottingham train. Notice the three-way bracket signal: left (obscured by smoke) is for the Langwith Junction route, the highest for the main line to Worksop, and right for Warsop Junction.

Left: Stanier 2-6-4T 42587 arrives at Shirebrook with an afternoon Worksop to Nottingham service. This loco was only allocated to 16B Kirkby in Ashfield during the week ending 8 March 1963, and left for 8F Springs Branch (Wigan) in the week ending 14 November 1964, thus dating the photo to that period. Notice the left-hand signal for Shirebrook North has been removed.

Below: A LM&SR 3rd Class ticket for Shirebrook to Bulwell, and a 2nd Class Holiday Period Shirebrook (West) to Yarmouth (Vauxhall) via Retford and March. ***(All Author's collection)***

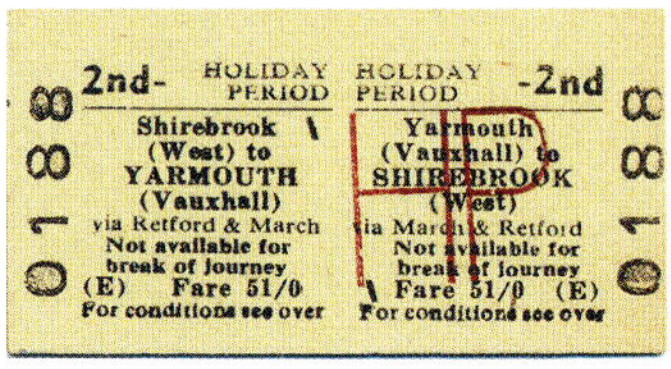

Left: With steam to spare, an unidentified 2-6-4T departs from Shirebrook West for Nottingham around 1964. Of interest in the photo is Shirebrook West Diesel Depot under construction in the former goods yard, just in front of the goods shed which, at that time, was in use as a temporary diesel servicing shed. ***(Author's collection)***

Above: An LNER parcels sticker. ***(Author's collection)***

Left: The station has closed with the platform edges removed, and 41J Shirebrook West Diesel Depot is in full operation. Opened on 14 June 1965, the depot is passed almost ten years after opening by 45020 on Sunday 30 March 1975, whilst working the diverted 1S27 08.50 Plymouth to Edinburgh. Shirebrook Station 'box can be seen to the right of the train. ***(John S.Gilks)***

Right: Former "Alphaline" silver-liveried 158863, by now part of the Central Trains fleet, calls at the reopened station on 22 May 2009 with 2D14 13.38 Worksop to Nottingham. As a result of the 1998 resignalling, the semaphore signals at the end of the platform have been replaced by a single colour light with "feather".

Right: East Midlands Railway 170418 pauses at Shirebrook on 21 December 2021 with 2W13 12.25 Nottingham to Worksop. The diesel depot closed on 28 September 1996 and is now in industrial use; although the building is still in situ it is now just a memory to the enthusiasts who once visited. ***(Both Author)***

Left & below: Shirebrook Station 'box, seen from the top of a lighting pole, opened on 28 January 1890 and replaced an earlier structure. It closed on 12 January 1998, just 12 days after the photo was taken. Inset: The original MR nameplate from Shirebrook 'box, sold at auction in 2019.

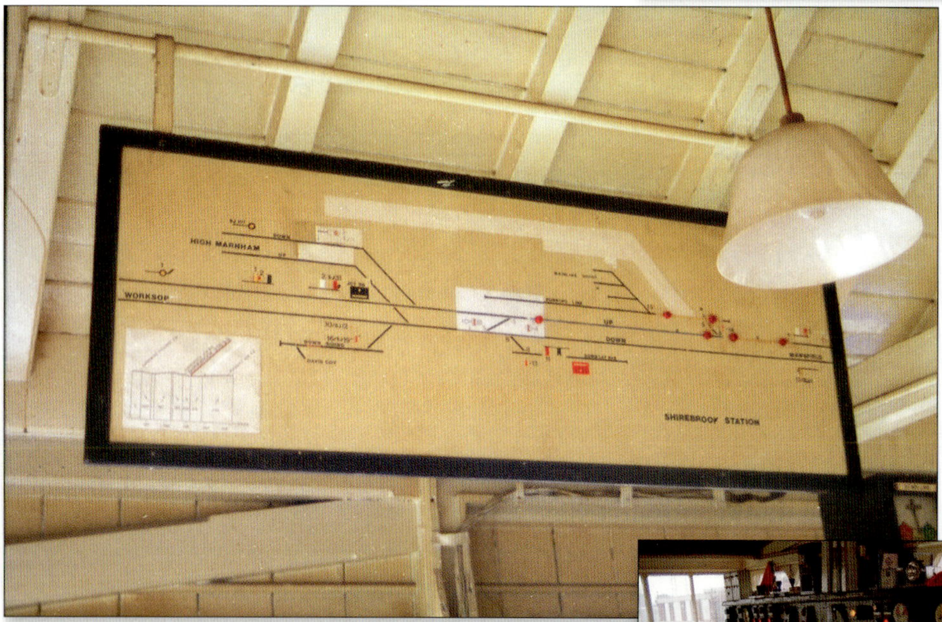

Above & right: The 18-lever frame and diagram inside the 'box. The long white patch covers the details of the MR's Warsop Colliery Branch which, having closed when Shirebrook West Diesel Depot was built, was accessed from the LD&ECR line at Warsop Junction. The MR branch ran alongside the depot building and was reinstated in July 1976. The smaller patch covers the by-now removed connection into the now-closed diesel depot.

Left: 58024 is seen passing Shirebrook Station 'box with 7A17 Clipstone Colliery to Ratcliffe Power Station on 12 January 1998. The closed diesel depot is off camera to the right. *(All Author)*

Above left: A relaxed Bill Jenkins inside Shirebrook Station 'box in May 1961, the all-important tea making facilities on the table beside him. On a cold December night in 1983 he had left the 'box to free up frozen points; sadly, upon his return, Bill collapsed and died in the 'box.

Above right: A view southwards from the 'box in May 1961. A raft of wagons await further duties in the Down Siding; the former goods shed is on the left. The signals are (top) Shirebrook Station No. 11 Down Home, (bottom) Shirebrook Junction No. 4 Down Main Distant, and (left) Shirebrook Junction No. 7 Down Distant for the Warsop direction. The post on the right would have held a Distant signal for the Langwith Junction line. This bracket was replaced by a single post in 1965. ***(Both Steve Godman collection)***

Above: A view of the Station Masters' house and the Warsop Colliery Branch from across the former goods yard in May 1961. The wagons are for the use of High Marnham traffic. ***(Steve Godman collection)***

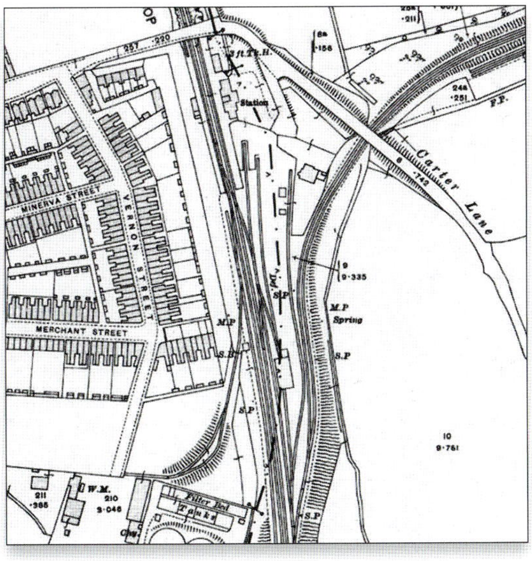

Left: Shirebrook Station 'box also controlled access into the sewage works and the Shirebrook & District Gas Company Siding. This is seen curving round bottom left on the map, with the Warsop Colliery Branch curving top right. The company was incorporated in an Act of 1899 to supply a region that originally covered Scarcliffe and Upper Langwith, part of Pleasley, Nether Langwith, Sookholme and part of Warsop. The Act also gave the company a right of compulsory purchase of land to the south of Shirebrook Station, at the end of Vernon Street and bordering the south of Sookholme Lane. Despite heavy opposition from Warsop Local Authority, the Shirebrook and District Gas Act 1910 was passed, extending the limits to include the rest of Warsop and part of Bolsover. Further acts of 1928 extended limits of supply, and investigations into the purchase of the Southwell and District Gas Co in 1945/6 indicated a desire to expand further, but these plans came to nothing. On nationalisation in 1949, the company was vested in the Chesterfield sub-division of the Notts and Derbyshire's Division of the EMGB. ***(Reproduced with the permission of the National Library of Scotland)***

Shirebrook Depot

Above: In 1962 41J Langwith Junction received its first diesels. However, steam and diesel locos sharing servicing space was not conducive to good clean diesel maintenance. Therefore primitive diesel servicing facilities were provided in the former MR goods shed at Shirebrook West station, where a pit was provided for access beneath the locos, and staging erected for access to bodyside hatches. 41A Sheffield Darnall-based Brush Type 2s (Class 31s) were the first to utilise the new temporary facilities, but by the end of 1963 they were superseded by Brush Type 4s D1702 to D1706 (the Class 48s). 8F 2-8-0 48214 passes the goods shed with two unidentified Class 48s in attendance. ***(Steve Godman Collection)***

Left: During 1962 Shirebrook was also home for a short time to Darnall-allocated D0280 Falcon. It was utilised on coal trains between the area's coalfields and Whitemoor, and later became Class 53 No. D1200. Here it shares depot space with Brush Type 2 D5843 and an unidentified sister. The signal above D5843 protects the end of the Warsop Colliery Branch. ***(Author's collection)***

Right: Fuelling was still initially undertaken at Langwith Junction using railborne tankers, but they were replaced by similar facilities in the old cattle dock at Shirebrook West. The fuelling shed can be seen to the right of Langwith Junction-based Robinson 2-8-0 63850, propelling a brake van through Shirebrook West station. ***(Author's collection)***

Right: By the end of 1963 it became clear that a purpose-built diesel servicing and fuelling depot was required at Shirebrook West. The Eastern Region (ER) was therefore authorised to build a replacement for both Langwith Junction steam depot and the primitive Shirebrook West diesel servicing facility. The two-road depot was of standard ER design constructed with a brick cavity wall to a height of five feet, followed by a steel framework with glass inserts up to gutter level. Its dimensions were 171 feet 6 inches long by 42 feet 6 inches wide, with a total height of 26 feet 6 inches. Inside there were full length pits for maintenance access, capable of attending to four large diesels and two shunters at one time. A sandbox filling point was situated just in front of the depot doors and two fuel tanks holding 60,000 gallons were provided. This is the depot on 24 June 1965, just 10 days after opening. The sand filler points prominent here were soon replaced by a wash plant. Upon the depot's opening, the Warsop Colliery Branch was closed although some of the track was retained as a stabling road, sometimes referred to as No. 4 Road. Notice the clock has now been fitted above the doors.

Right: An internal view taken on 24 June 1965. A pair of Brush Type 4s receive attention, with one of the depot's Class 08 shunters at the back. Only shunting locos were allocated to Shirebrook; all other locos were out-stationed from Barrow Hill, Darnall and later Tinsley. ***(Both Author's collection)***

Above: Brush Type 2 D5692 and two unidentified Brush Type 4s repose inside the depot in 1965. The apron between the two roads has equipment for dispensing lubricating oils. ***(Jim Hatcher)***

Below: The depot shared the code 41J with Langwith Junction, retaining it when the steam shed closed in 1966. Langwith Junction's steam locos received cast shedcode plates but these were not carried over to the diesel fleet; apart from several Class 08s, no main line diesels were allocated there. In 1973 BR introduced the TOPS numbering system; locos were renumbered with five-digit identities, while depots lost their original number/letter combination in favour of a two-letter code. Shirebrook West became simply Shirebrook and gained the code SB. ***(Both Author's collection)***

Left: Clayton Type 1 locos D8604-16 were allocated new to Barrow Hill, some of which made their way to the Shirebrook area on local trip workings. An unidentified example is stabled on the former Warsop Branch. Not regarded as a successful loco, they were soon moved to Scotland to live out their short lives. By the end of 1971, all had been withdrawn with just one survivor. ***(Jim Hatcher)***

Left: Arguably the most colourful and controversial loco of its time, HS4000 "Kestrel" was a prototype high-powered diesel loco built in 1967 by Brush Traction as a demonstrator for potential future British Rail and export orders. The loco number derives from the initials of Hawker Siddeley and the 4000hp power rating of its Sulzer diesel engine, making it the most powerful locomotive built by Brush. The loco was officially handed over at Marylebone on 29 January 1968, and commenced trials on the northern portion of the West Coast Main Line. In the middle of May 1968 Kestrel was allocated to 41A Tinsley and put through its paces on coal workings out of Shirebrook including two round trips a day to Whitemoor, five days a week with coal trains loaded to a maximum of 1600 tons. By mid-August 14,000 miles had been covered with an 88% availability. Testing continued in several locations, and Kestrel performed admirably on freight and passenger duties, despite being overweight; replacement bogies were fitted to reduce the axle loading. In June 1971 the loco was overhauled at Vickers Armstrong works at Barrow, and returned to Shirebrook afterwards. The loco was sold to the USSR railways and shipped to Leningrad on 8 July 1971, and it was scrapped in 1993. The loco is seen here at Shirebrook after working 7J31. ***(Author's collection)***

Left: 58026 and 58040 "Cottam Power Station" receive "A" Exams inside the depot on 6 April 1995. Note the trolley with funnelled containers for dispensing sand into the loco sandboxes; of course, there were once hoppers outside the depot doors for doing just that! ***(Author)***

Left: On 11 February 1991 the train crews from Shirebrook and Barrow Hill depots were transferred to a new train crew depot at Worksop and locos only used Shirebrook for re-fuelling and "A" exams until it closed on 28 September 1996. The building was taken over by Bremick Plastics, but in the early 2000s Bremick Plastics vacated the building leaving it to be totally trashed. By early 2009 the shell of the building looked fit only for demolition, but remarkably yet another chapter awaited. The shell is seen here on 22 May 2009. ***(Author)***

Above: A drone shot of the former depot and station, taken on 14 April 2021. The trees at the bottom denote the route of the long-closed Warsop Colliery Branch. On the far left, the industrial units are on the site of the former gasworks. ***(Ash Edwards)***

Shirebrook Sidings

Right: Shirebrook Colliery Sidings 'box opened in 1897 with a 24-lever frame. Sometime around 1910, two staff members pose for their photo. Midland Railway 5-plank wagon No. 90495 waits to be taken to the colliery to be loaded, the word "Stockport" chalked just above the "M". Meanwhile, behind the 'box, the crew of former LD&ECR Class D 0-6-4T take a breather in-between shunting. The LD&ECR had nine Class Ds; 29–34 were delivered in 1904, and A1 to A3 in December 1906. The GCR renumbered them 1148–53 and 1145–47 respectively. Notice the corrugated iron lamp cabin. ***(John Alsop collection)***

Right: This larger 85-lever frame Shirebrook Colliery Sidings replaced the original 'box on 9 June 1929, but was renamed Shirebrook Sidings before October that year. A busy moment is captured on 12 October 1963 as Fairburn 2-6-4T 42232 hustles past with a Worksop to Nottingham train, while Langwith Junction-allocated 350hp shunter (Class 10) D4069 shunts in the Down Side. In the distance, a light loco is about to pass beneath Wood Lane bridge. Notice a similar lamp cabin to the bottom left. ***(John Peck collection)***

Right: Signalman Jim Small is seen leaning on the 85-lever frame on 12 October 1963. A very busy place in its day, today just a two-track railway passes the forest that has grown up either side of the line here. ***(John Peck collection)***

Left: Another busy moment is witnessed looking north from the 'box. On the far left, an unidentified Class 9F 2-10-0 is ready to depart from Shirebrook Colliery with a raft of 16-ton wagons, possibly destined for High Marnham Power Station. A 350hp shunter, coupled to a brake van, emerges from the colliery neck. To the right, an 8F 2-8-0 heads a motley collection of wagons for Mansfield Concentration Sidings via Warsop Junction. The oil wagons would have been destined for the oil distribution point at Eakring, on the Mid-Notts Joint Line which ran between Farnsfield and Ollerton. ***(Steve Godman collection)***

Above & right: The face of an old-time signalman in Shirebrook Sidings 'box. Bill Jenkins poses for his photo in October 1963 while his tea and cigarette making equipment wait on the table. The clock gently ticks away the afternoon shift at 4.02pm on this sunny October day. A furled red flag waits for any emergencies and the phone hangs silent on its hook. All is quiet – but that would soon change! ***(Both Steve Godman collection)***

Below left: Indeed the quiet didn't last long – the 3.40pm Worksop to Nottingham train was on its way. At 4.04pm the train departed Langwith and a 3-1 bell code would be offered on to Shirebrook Junction, followed by Shirebrook Station, and thence to Shirebrook Sidings. Bill would then have pulled levers 16, 17, 18, 19 and 15 to pave the way for the train. At 4.09pm it left Shirebrook West, and Train Entering Section (2 beats) would be forwarded by Shirebrook Station 'box. Shortly after 16B Kirkby-in-Ashfield allocated, Fairburn-designed (but BR built) 2-6-4T 42089 would come into view, seen here having just passed beneath Wood Lane Bridge. The photographers were standing on the former Shirebrook Colliery Platform, which had opened in July 1901. It allowed miners to arrive for work utilising a workers-only "Paddy train", but had ceased being used before July 1954. The large water tower for replenishing steam loco water tanks looms over the train.

Left: Robinson Class O4 2-8-0 63636 squeals over the pointwork as it arrives at Shirebrook Sidings with a brake van in tow during 1963. This loco was new in 1918 and allocated to Gorton on 23 February 1924. Moving to Langwith Junction on 17 July 1945, it moved to Colwick including a short spell at Annesley. Its final home was Langwith again from 11 May 1952, from where it was withdrawn on 20 December 1964. ***(Both John Peck collection)***

Left: Bill Jenkins was on afternoon duty in Shirebrook Sidings on Saturday 26 June 1971. The 'box closed on Saturday nights, so after his shift ended at 22.00 he locked the box up and went home. In the early hours of Sunday 27 June a fire broke out which destroyed the box. Another signalman, Brian Wragg, tells the story that he was due to pass out as a signalman at Shirebrook Sidings on 29 June 1971, and when he turned up for work he couldn't believe his eyes! So to qualify as a signalman, the "powers that be" hastily cobbled together some flags and equipment to allow Brian to be passed to work this box with a red and green flag, as one signal on the Up and one on the Down, based in the adjacent plate layers cabin. The remains of the 'box are seen a few days after the fire. By now a freight-only railway, trains were kept moving by hand signalling them past the signals held at danger. A few days later, arrangements were made to erect a small GF, and use the wooden plate layers cabin for shelter. Eventually a replacement 'box was provided, just in front of the plate layers cabin seen here. ***(Steve Godman collection)***

Left: Interior of the replacement 'box, – a far cry from the original with its 85 levers! With the closure of Shirebrook Colliery on 7 May 1993 there was no real requirement for the 'box and it was switched out of circuit for long periods. It closed on 2 June 1996, with control of the section of route passing to Kirkby Summit and Shirebrook Station. Not long after closure the 'box was purchased by a Shirebrook driver and is still doing sterling service as a garden shed! ***(Author)***

Right: After the 'box burned down, the track layout was rationalised. Since the colliery access was south-facing, traffic for the colliery from the north had to perform several manoeuvres. On 14 February 1991, 58034 "Bassetlaw" has passed the sidings on the Up Main line, and has set back into No. 1 Up Reception via a set of points operated by a two-lever GF. It will run round using No. 2 Up Reception and propel back out onto the Up Main, before heading north into the colliery. ***(Dave Peachey)***

Right: After the colliery's closure, the sidings were used to store HAA and HEA wagons. At privatisation, the wagons became the property of EWS, and a decision was made to transfer them to Warsop Sidings. Vandals and thieves had done their worst to the wagons and signalling, and it was necessary to top-and-tail the wagons to move them. They also had to run wrong line from Shirebrook Sidings to Shirebrook Station, where there was a crossover. 31407 is seen here waiting the next move on 11 May 1995, 31552 being the other loco used on the day. ***(Author)***

Pleasley Junction

Left: Pleasley Junction 'box viewed south from Northfield Lane overbridge on 3 May 1964. Situated 1 mile 388 yards south of Shirebrook Sidings 'box, the main line to Mansfield heads off straight ahead and the line to Pleasley and eventually Tibshelf diverges off right. There are four sidings on the Down side which could accommodate 126 wagons, and served a spur to Pleasley Junction Quarry, which is off camera right. In the distance No. 10 signal has been cleared for a train. Pleasley Junction 'box dates from 18 April 1886 when the new connection to the Pleasley line was opened. It contained a 12-lever frame, but was closed on 2 March 1964 when the section of line between the junction and Pleasley Vale Sidings was closed. The houses are on Mapletoft Avenue in Mansfield Woodhouse. ***(Transport Treasury PY10080P)***

Left: Viewed north on 12 October 1963, the Saturdays only 1.30pm Worksop to Mansfield train, with Stanier 4MT 2-6-4T 42587 is passing beneath Northfield Lane bridge. The Pleasley and Tibshelf route diverges left. Today the branch trackbed here is occupied by a road to a quarry, and the bridge has been replaced by a steel footbridge, although the original abutments on the left and right have been retained, the centre one has been removed. ***(H.B. Priestley/ Transport Treasury)***

Below: A view of the quarry and lime kilns in the early years. Behind the hand crane on the right is a 10-ton Thomas Smith Steam Goliath steam-operated crane (Works No. 2628 of 1879), supplied new to the quarry. ***(Inspire Picture Archive)***

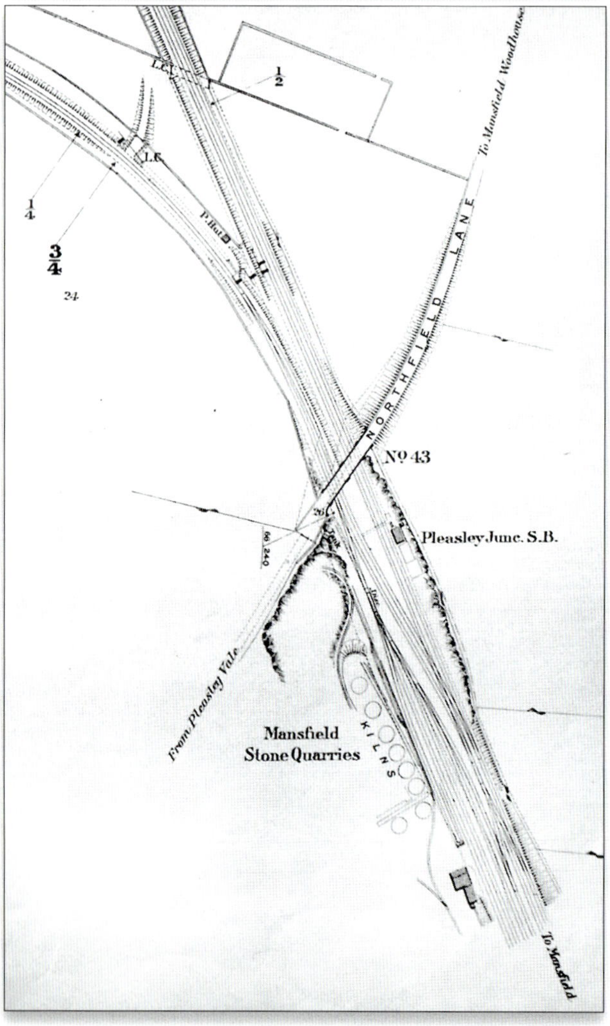

Left: Pleasley Junction diagram in the MR Tibshelf to Teversall & Pleasley Extension & Skegby Branch plan book. Bridge No. 43 (Northfield Lane) is prominent across the railway. Mansfield Stone Quarry, otherwise known as Sills Quarry, was owned by William Sills who operated his own wagons. By March 1897 it had at least 22 wagons, of which it is known that Numbers 17–18 were eight-ton capacity painted "lead colour" and ordered from Bute Supply Works but built by Charles Roberts of Wakefield. Another two were registered by the Midland Railway (MR) on 5 March 1897, built by Edward Eastwood of Chesterfield. The quarried limestone was processed on site in the bank of eight lime kilns seen on the plan. Sills Pleasley Junction Quarry telephone number is listed in 1945, but not 1948; Sills died in 1945 so it is reasonable to assume quarrying ceased at the end of WW2. The company "W. Sills Quarries Ltd" aka "Mansfield Quarries" continued until the very early 60s at their Chesterfield Road site. ***(Dave Phillips collection)***

Mansfield Woodhouse

Above: Mansfield Woodhouse station opened to goods on 18 January 1875, and passengers on 1 June the same year. It was described as "a model of a station, the building is entirely of wood and is relieved with some very pretty ornamentation. A kind of entrance hall, one side of which is nearly all glass, leads into the ticket office, an apartment which unlike many of its kind has not been erected with special facilities to let the wind in. The ladies waiting room is a little gem tastefully furnished and carpeted and the whole aspect of the place is a pleasant contrast of the dreary, disheartening den built in the earlier days of railway enterprise". The station is seen soon after opening when Joseph Harrison was Station Master, in charge until 1899. Notice in the distance the goods shed and Mansfield Woodhouse Station signal box with its protecting signal. This 'box opened with the line but was replaced with another which opened on 26 February 1895. The station was not provided with a footbridge and the 17 February 1916 edition of the Nottingham Evening Post ran the following headline:

KILLED ON THE LINE.
"FOOTBRIDGE WANTED AT MANSFIELD WOODHOUSE".
"A verdict of 'Accidental death' was returned at an inquest at Mansfield Woodhouse this afternoon [17th February 1916] on the body of Samuel T. Smith, aged 69, of Serutt's yard Mansfield Woodhouse, a munition worker, who was killed on Tuesday morning [15th February 1916] by being knocked down by a goods train passing through Mansfield Woodhouse Station. The jury added to their verdict that as representations had already been made by the Urban Council to the Midland Railway Company asking them to provide a footbridge for passengers, they regretted that nothing had been done, and recommended the Deputy Coroner to make further representations to the company". The status quo remained until the station closed.

Right: A 1953 view of the station, which has been brightened up with a repaint, some flower beds and advertisement posters. The former all-timber platforms have been rebuilt in stone. The second Mansfield Woodhouse Station 'box is now in the view; notice the bracket Distant signal next to the 'box for the Pleasley line. ***(Both Author's collection)***

Above: Complementing the early image of the station is this one of the goods shed and the first Mansfield Woodhouse Station signal box, which dated from the line's opening. Particularly noteworthy are the signal's lamp at a lower level to its arm, the inside keyed track (the MR moved to outside-keyed track in 1882) and the employee opening the goods shed door. Just visible inside is the crane for lifting heavy goods in and out of wagons. When the Robin Hood Line was opened, the goods shed formed part of the new station. ***(Inspire Picture Archive)***

Below left to right: The goods shed interior would have been similar to that at Coalville, the hand crane being similar to that visible through the door. The larger Wellingborough Goods Shed had two cranes, which are still in situ today. ***(Author's collection/Creative Commons Attribution 4.0 International License)***

Right: Hand crane inside the goods shed at Kibworth on 7 August 1967. ***(Nigel Tout Creative Commons Attribution-Share Alike 4.0. www.nigeltout.com)***

Right: Mansfield Woodhouse on 6 June 1962, as seen from a Worksop-bound train. Of note are the lamp post complete with BR maroon "totem" (see photo below) the platform barrow piled high with parcels, and No. 3 signal "off" for a Nottingham-bound train – beyond which is Sherwood Colliery Sidings North 'box, showing the signal boxes' proximity to each other. ***(Bill Taylor)***

Left: Stanier 3P 2-6-2 40146 arrives at Mansfield Woodhouse on 9 September 1956 with a Worksop to Nottingham train. The bracket Distant signal for the Pleasley branch has gone, replaced by Pleasley Junction Down Distant beneath Mansfield Woodhouse's No. 14 Down Second Home. ***(Author's collection)***

Below: Special Instructions relating to Mansfield Woodhouse Station signal box. ***(Author's collection)***

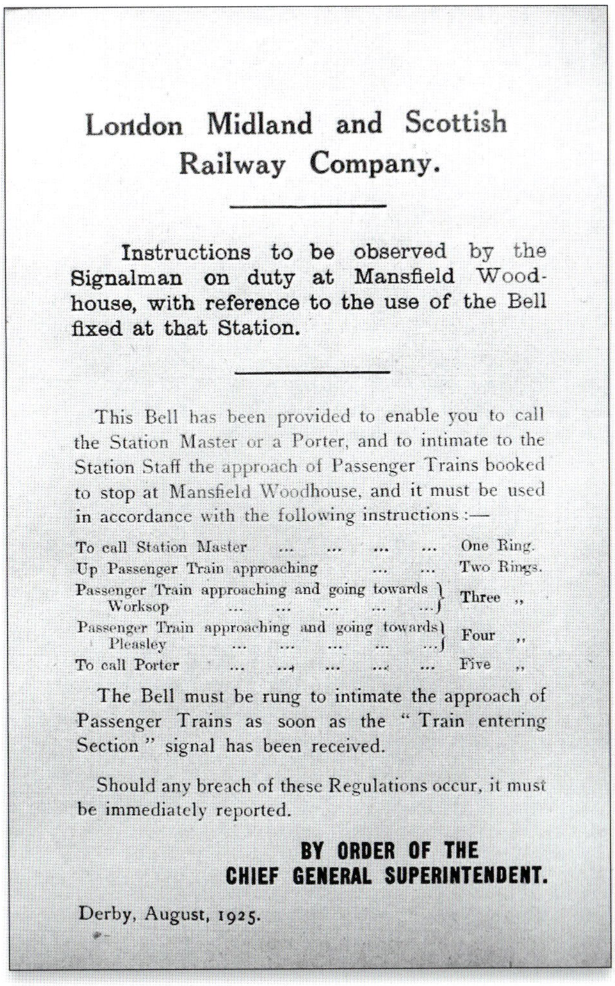

London Midland and Scottish Railway Company.

Instructions to be observed by the Signalman on duty at Mansfield Woodhouse, with reference to the use of the Bell fixed at that Station.

This Bell has been provided to enable you to call the Station Master or a Porter, and to intimate to the Station Staff the approach of Passenger Trains booked to stop at Mansfield Woodhouse, and it must be used in accordance with the following instructions:—

To call Station Master	One Ring.
Up Passenger Train approaching	Two Rings.
Passenger Train approaching and going towards Worksop	Three ,,
Passenger Train approaching and going towards Pleasley	Four ,,
To call Porter	Five ,,

The Bell must be rung to intimate the approach of Passenger Trains as soon as the "Train entering Section" signal has been received.

Should any breach of these Regulations occur, it must be immediately reported.

BY ORDER OF THE
CHIEF GENERAL SUPERINTENDENT.

Derby, August, 1925.

Above: A selection of tickets: a GCR Third Class ticket dated 21 April 1906 and issued for Mr Patinson's party, who were travelling from Mansfield Woodhouse to London Marylebone and were specially routed via Kiveton Park. An LM&SR Third Class Pass for Mrs Stowell to travel to Hanley on 30 April 1945. A First Class single ticket for a journey from Mansfield Woodhouse to Mansfield Town, costing 9d (around 80p today). The equivalent Standard Class (First Class not available) journey today is £2.20. ***(Author's collection)***

Above: A Mansfield Woodhouse "Totem" which sold at auction in 2021. ***(Courtesy Simon Turner GWR Auctions)***

Left: 8F 2-8-0 No. 48143 passes with an Up coal train on 26 March 1964. Mansfield Woodhouse had a 17-lever frame, and closed on 4 June 1967. ***(Transport Treasury PY10141)***

Right: Saturday 10 October 1964 was the last day of passenger services on the line, and photographers were not officially allowed to stand on the platforms thereafter. Mansfield Woodhouse station would be locked up to await its fate and, apart from the odd diversion and excursion, freight traffic would be the sole user as illustrated by 4F 0-6-0 44401 trundling a southbound Class K mixed freight. Pleasley Junction's Down Distant signal has now been removed from the post. ***(Colour-Rail 95566)***

Left: On the same day, 4MT 2-6-4T 42588 pulls into Mansfield Woodhouse with an afternoon service (indicated by the shadows) – possibly the 4.15pm, the small crowd most likely making use of the service for the last time. The last southbound train left Worksop at 7.51pm, calling at Mansfield Woodhouse at 8.23pm. That was the end; the line became freight-only for the next 30+ years. ***(Colour-Rail 95567)***

Above: After closure the station became a magnet for vandals who soon set about smashing windows. These views of the main station building on the Up platform, and smaller Down side building, were taken in 1965 before the whole station was demolished. The former station and goods yard site was sold to Highway Equipment Manufacturing Co. Ltd (HEMCOL), who incorporated the goods shed into their factory. ***(Jim Hatcher)***

Below: 30 years later, Stage 2 of the Robin Hood Line necessitated a new station at Mansfield Woodhouse. By then HEMCOL had moved on, but part of the site was still in use by Flowline Hydraulics who had to be relocated. Fortunately, the former goods shed remained in situ buried inside a larger building, and it was therefore decided to incorporate the shed into the plans. A new island platform was built on the Up side north of the original station, and incorporated the goods shed as a passenger shelter. The coloured postcard shows an artist's impression of the shed with an added wooden lean-to, while the later photo shows the HEMCOL building and the remains of the cobbled goods yard in 1993. ***(Postcard from a painting by Peter Lyons, others Ash Edwards)***

Above: After the demolition of the HEMCOL and Flowline Hydraulics' buildings, Morrison Construction Ltd began work to convert the shed, and in this May 1994 view the land has been excavated to remove contaminants for processing elsewhere; this became a new walkway. The shed works involved cleaning and removal of the arched ends and replacement by a high steel beam, effectively becoming an overall roof for a new bay platform (Platform 3). The work here cost £1.1M, and this turnback facility allowed trains to terminate at Mansfield Woodhouse during Stage 2. After Stage 3 had opened to Worksop, Mansfield Woodhouse enjoyed half-hourly services for Nottingham. ***(Ash Edwards collection/Robin Stewart Smith)***

Left: The new island platform is beginning to take shape as 58035 passes on 18 February 1995 with 7A08 Welbeck to Toton. The goods shed arches have been replaced by the steel beam. ***(Robin Stewart Smith)***

Right: Works on the platform and building are complete, with just the lamp tops to fit. ***(Ash Edwards)***

Below: 17 November 1995 – Stage 2 opening day, and 150018 breaks through a ceremonial banner on arrival from Nottingham. ***(Ash Edwards)***

Left & below: A selection of tickets issued to guests and the public.

Above: Following completion of Stage 2, trains terminated at Mansfield Woodhouse so only Platforms 2 and 3 were finished. The goods shed-cum-shelter hosts 150104 in Platform 3. The "Robin Hood Line" arrow logo in the platform surface, seen to good effect, was a feature of all the stations. Notice the former spoil heap of Sutton Colliery on the right in the top photo. As yet there is no Down side platform for Worksop services; this was constructed under Stage 3 and required a new disability compliant footbridge for access – the first time the station had been graced with a footbridge! ***(Both Author's collection)***

Below: The station received two opening ceremonies. On 10 November 1995 it was formally opened by Transport Secretary Sir George Young, and after the ceremony the party travelled to Nottingham in 150018 + 150022. This was followed on 17 November 1995 when Mansfield District Council undertook a ceremony where Councillor Mrs Mavis Hall and Eric Etherington, the final porter at the original station, unveiled a plaque to commemorate the event. Regional Railways Mansfield Woodhouse station sign, complete with Robin Hood Line logo on one end and Mansfield District Council (MDC) heraldic device on the other. ***(Ash Edwards)***

Above & below: On 19 November 1995 Railtrack held a Robin Hood Line Gala Day prior to the full service commencing, during which the services were well patronised. 150109 forms the 12.13 Mansfield Woodhouse to Nottingham. Stage 2 fully opened from Nottingham as far as Mansfield Woodhouse on 20 November 1995. The colourful timetable leaflets issued for the new service showed a Class 150 exiting Kirkby Tunnel, a theme that was carried on in the summer 1997 edition. The times from that timetable are shown below. ***(Author/Author's collection)***

Rail Timetable From Mansfield Woodhouse to Nottingham

1 June 1997 until 27 September 1997

·ROBIN·HOOD·LINE·

Mondays to Fridays

Mans Woodhouse	Dep	06.28	07.32	08.02	09.17	10.18	11.17	12.19	13.17	14.14	15.17	16.05	17.07	18.13	18.42	20.10	20.47	21.54
Mansfield		06.31	07.35	08.05	09.20	10.21	11.20	12.22	13.20	14.17	15.20	16.08	17.10	18.16	18.45	20.13	20.50	21.57
Sutton Parkway		06.37	07.41	08.11	09.26	10.27	11.26	12.28	13.26	14.23	15.26	16.14	17.16	18.22	18.51	20.19	20.56	22.03
Kirkby in Ashfield		06.40	07.44	08.14	09.29	10.30	11.29	12.31	13.29	14.26	15.29	16.17	17.19	18.25	18.54	20.22	20.59	22.06
Newstead		06.47	07.49	08.19	09.34	10.35	11.34	12.36	13.34	14.31	15.34	16.22	17.24	18.30	18.59	20.27	21.04	22.11
Hucknall		06.52	07.53	08.24	09.39	10.40	11.39	12.41	13.39	14.36	15.39	16.26	17.28	18.34	19.03	20.32	21.09	22.16
Bulwell		06.56	07.58	08.28	09.43	10.44	11.43	12.45	13.43	14.40	15.43	16.31	17.33	18.39	19.08	20.36	21.13	22.20
Nottingham	Arr	07.08	08.10	08.40	09.55	10.56	11.55	12.57	13.55	14.52	15.55	16.48	17.47	18.51	19.20	20.48	21.26	22.37

To make enquiries about the Robin Hood Line call Nottingham (0115) 924 0000

Nottinghamshire County Council

Graphic Design Group 11545

Saturdays

								*	*																
Mans Woodhouse	Dep	06.37	07.40	08.12	08.43	09.13	09.44	10.15	10.45		13.46	14.15	14.47	15.16	15.48	16.19	16.48	17.19	17.48	18.21	19.05	20.09	21.20	21.54
Mansfield		06.40	07.43	08.15	08.46	09.16	09.47	10.18	10.48	*AND	13.49	14.18	14.50	15.19	15.51	16.22	16.51	17.22	17.51	18.24	19.08	20.12	21.23	21.57
Sutton Parkway		06.46	07.49	08.21	08.52	09.22	09.53	10.24	10.54	AT	13.55	14.24	14.56	15.25	15.57	16.28	16.57	17.28	17.57	18.30	19.14	20.18	21.29	22.03
Kirkby in Ashfield		06.49	07.52	08.24	08.55	09.25	09.56	10.27	10.57	THESE MINUTES	13.58	14.27	14.59	15.28	16.00	16.31	17.00	17.31	18.00	18.33	19.17	20.21	21.32	22.06
Newstead		06.54	07.57	08.29	09.00	09.30	10.01	10.31	11.02	PAST	14.03	14.32	15.04	15.34	-------	16.36	17.05	17.35	18.05	18.38	19.22	20.26	21.37	22.11
Hucknall		06.58	08.02	08.34	09.04	09.35	10.06	10.36	11.06	EACH HOUR	14.07	14.37	15.09	15.39	16.09	16.40	17.09	17.40	18.10	18.43	19.27	20.31	21.41	22.16
Bulwell		07.03	08.06	08.38	09.09	09.39	10.10	10.40	11.11	UNTIL	14.12	14.41	15.13	15.43	16.13	16.45	17.14	17.44	18.14	18.47	19.31	20.35	21.46	22.20
Nottingham	Arr	07.16	08.18	08.49	09.21	09.53	10.20	10.52	11.22		14.23	14.53	15.27	15.55	16.24	16.56	17.26	17.56	18.26	18.58	19.43	20.49	21.58	22.37

Rail Timetable From Mansfield Woodhouse to Nottingham

1 June 1997 until 27 September 1997

·ROBIN·HOOD·LINE·

Mondays to Fridays

Mans Woodhouse	Dep	06.28	07.32	08.02	09.17	10.18	11.17	12.19	13.17	14.14	15.17	16.05	17.07	18.13	18.42	20.10	20.47	21.54
Mansfield		06.31	07.35	08.05	09.20	10.21	11.20	12.22	13.20	14.17	15.20	16.08	17.10	18.16	18.45	20.13	20.50	21.57
Sutton Parkway		06.37	07.41	08.11	09.26	10.27	11.26	12.28	13.26	14.23	15.26	16.14	17.16	18.22	18.51	20.19	20.56	22.03
Kirkby in Ashfield		06.40	07.44	08.14	09.29	10.30	11.29	12.31	13.29	14.26	15.29	16.17	17.19	18.25	18.54	20.22	20.59	22.06
Newstead		06.47	07.49	08.19	09.34	10.35	11.34	12.36	13.34	14.31	15.34	16.22	17.24	18.30	18.59	20.27	21.04	22.11
Hucknall		06.52	07.53	08.24	09.39	10.40	11.39	12.41	13.39	14.36	15.39	16.26	17.28	18.34	19.03	20.32	21.09	22.16
Bulwell		06.56	07.58	08.28	09.43	10.44	11.43	12.45	13.43	14.40	15.43	16.31	17.33	18.39	19.08	20.36	21.13	22.20
Nottingham	Arr	07.08	08.10	08.40	09.55	10.56	11.55	12.57	13.55	14.52	15.55	16.48	17.47	18.51	19.20	20.48	21.26	22.37

To make enquiries about the Robin Hood Line call Nottingham (0115) 924 0000

Nottinghamshire County Council

Graphic Design Group 11545

Saturdays

								*	*																
Mans Woodhouse	Dep	06.37	07.40	08.12	08.43	09.13	09.44	10.15	10.45		13.46	14.15	14.47	15.16	15.48	16.19	16.48	17.19	17.48	18.21	19.05	20.09	21.20	21.54
Mansfield		06.40	07.43	08.15	08.46	09.16	09.47	10.18	10.48	*AND	13.49	14.18	14.50	15.19	15.51	16.22	16.51	17.22	17.51	18.24	19.08	20.12	21.23	21.57
Sutton Parkway		06.46	07.49	08.21	08.52	09.22	09.53	10.24	10.54	AT	13.55	14.24	14.56	15.25	15.57	16.28	16.57	17.28	17.57	18.30	19.14	20.18	21.29	22.03
Kirkby in Ashfield		06.49	07.52	08.24	08.55	09.25	09.56	10.27	10.57	THESE MINUTES	13.58	14.27	14.59	15.28	16.00	16.31	17.00	17.31	18.00	18.33	19.17	20.21	21.32	22.06
Newstead		06.54	07.57	08.29	09.00	09.30	10.01	10.31	11.02	PAST	14.03	14.32	15.04	15.34	-------	16.36	17.05	17.35	18.05	18.38	19.22	20.26	21.37	22.11
Hucknall		06.58	08.02	08.34	09.04	09.35	10.06	10.36	11.06	EACH HOUR	14.07	14.37	15.09	15.39	16.09	16.40	17.09	17.40	18.10	18.43	19.27	20.31	21.41	22.16
Bulwell		07.03	08.06	08.38	09.09	09.39	10.10	10.40	11.11	UNTIL	14.12	14.41	15.13	15.43	16.13	16.45	17.14	17.44	18.14	18.47	19.31	20.35	21.46	22.20
Nottingham	Arr	07.16	08.18	08.49	09.21	09.53	10.20	10.52	11.22		14.23	14.53	15.27	15.55	16.24	16.56	17.26	17.56	18.26	18.58	19.43	20.49	21.58	22.37

Mansfield Woodhouse – Mansfield – Sutton Parkway – Kirkby in Ashfield – Newstead – Hucknall – Bulwell – Nottingham

Above: A large viaduct was required to take the railway north of Mansfield, the building of which entailed widespread property demolition. Construction began in 1870 using stone dug from the cuttings near Langwith. Although ready for use by 1872, the viaduct stood idle until the remainder of the line opened in 1875. In this view northwards towards Mansfield Woodhouse, the 15-arch viaduct strides majestically across Mansfield. Mansfield Station North signalbox opened on 24 July 1892, just before the new "Back platform" (Platform 3) opened on 4 September 1892. ***(Record Office for Leicester, Leicestershire &Rutland/Image Leicestershire; L2408)***

Below: The length of the viaduct can be appreciated in this photo taken by a drone at 07.00 on 12 April 2021. The station is just visible on the left edge. ***(Ash Edwards)***

Above: Mansfield was originally the terminus of the Mansfield & Pinxton Railway which opened in 1819, but a new station was required for the MR's extension of the line to Worksop. Built by contractors C. Humphreys to the designs of the MR Chief architect John Holloway Sanders, the new station was opened on Friday 1 March 1872. Comprising of two platforms beneath an overall roof, facilities in the main station building on the Down platform comprised of a booking hall, Ladies First Class waiting room, Gentlemen's First Class waiting room, Ladies Second Class waiting room, and booking and parcel offices. On one side of the building was the porter's room and lamp room, and at the other end was a fish house, and carriage and horse dock. On the Up platform was a boiler room to provide hot water for foot warmers, a Ladies waiting room, and the office of the stationmaster Joseph Somers, who reigned until 1876 when replaced by William Henry King until 1909. The Down platform was 105 yards long but the Up was 67 yards longer to accommodate Southwell trains. In 1892 a third platform outside the roof was opened, effectively turning the Up Platform into an island. This view of the frontage shows what looks like a military contingent on the left side, with miners returning from their shifts at Langwith and Shirebrook Collieries on the right. Could the photo have been taken during World War I?

MANSFIELD, WORKSOP RETFORD, AND SHEFFIELD.

Week Days.	1 & 3 class.	1 & 2 Gov	1 & 3 class.	1 & 2 Gov	1 & 3 class.	1 & 2 Gov
London ......dep.			5 15		11 30	
Leicester			9 30		2 35	
Birmingham			8 55		1 20	
Derby..............			10 25		3 13	
Nottingham	6 0		10 40		4 5	
Mansfield......dep	7 10	10 35	11 45	3 30	5 20	8 15
Mans-Woodhouse	7 15	10 39	11 50	3 34	5 25	8 19
Shirebrook.........	7 23	10 47	11 58	3 42	5 33	8 27
Langwith	7 28	10 51	12 3	3 46	5 38	8 31
Cresswell	7 35	10 55	12 10	3 50	5 45	8 35
Whitwell	7 40	10 59	12 15	3 54	5 50	8 38
Worksop ... arr.	7 50		12 25	4 4	6 0	8 48
Worksop ... dep.	7 55		12 30	4 10	6 1	8 55
Retford	8 10		12 45		6 15	
Shireoaks		11 8		4 15		9 0
Kiveton Park......		11 16		4 21		9 8
Woodhouse		11 27		4 32		9 19
Darnall		11 35		4 38		9 26
Sheffield...........		11 45		4 5		9 34
Manchester		2 30				
Liverpool		3 45				
Gainsborough ...	9 0		3 4		7 48	
Great Grimsby ...	10 35		4 38		9 25	
Hull	10 55		4 55		9 45	

Week Days.	1 & 3 class.	1 & 2 Gov	1 & 3 class.	1 & 2 Gov	1 & 2 Gov	1 & 3 class.
Hull	6 0		10 50			2 10
Great Grimsby ...	6 20		11 0			2 40
Gainsborough ...	7 54		12 36			4 6
Liverpool				11 15	3 35	
Manchester		6 45		12 30	5 0	
Sheffield...........		8 55		2 0	6 50	
Darnall		9 1		2 4	6 56	
Woodhouse		9 10		2 11	7 5	
Kiveton Park......		9 22		2 21	7 17	
Shireoaks		9 30		2 26	7 25	
Retford	8 50		1 0			6 30
Worksop ... arr.	9 5		1 15	2 31		6 45
Worksop ... dep	9 8		1 20	2 37		6 46
Whitwell	9 18	9 40	1 30	2 47	7 35	6 56
Cresswell	9 23	9 45	1 35	2 51	7 40	7 1
Langwith	9 30	9 52	1 42	2 55	7 47	7 8
Shirebrook.........	9 35	9 57	1 47	2 59	7 52	7 13
Mans-Woodhouse	9 42	10 5	1 54	3 9	8 0	7 19
Mansfield	9 48	10 10	2 0	3 15	8 5	7 25
Nottingham	11 5		3 5			8 35
Derby..............	11 15		4 16			9 55
Birmingham	12 50		7 35			1 55
Leicester	12 26		4 2			10 5
London	2 55		6 30			4 15

An Additional Train on Saturdays only will leave Worksop for Mansfield at 8.10 p.m., calling at Whitwell a 8.20, Cresswell 8.26, Langwith8.35, Shirebrook 8.41 Mansfield Woodhouse 8,48, arriving at Mansfield at 8.55 p.m.

Left: Timetable from the 2 August 1878 edition of the Mansfield Reporter, showing three services per day to Sheffield and Liverpool, and three to Retford and beyond. ***(All Author's collection)***

Right: The return half of a Midland Railway Third Class Weekend Excursion ticket, Mansfield to London St. Pancras, the fare being 11s 3d, and a GCR Retford to Mansfield Third Class with a fare of 1s 10d dated 9 July 1915. ***(Author's collection, and courtesy Midland Railway Study Centre)***

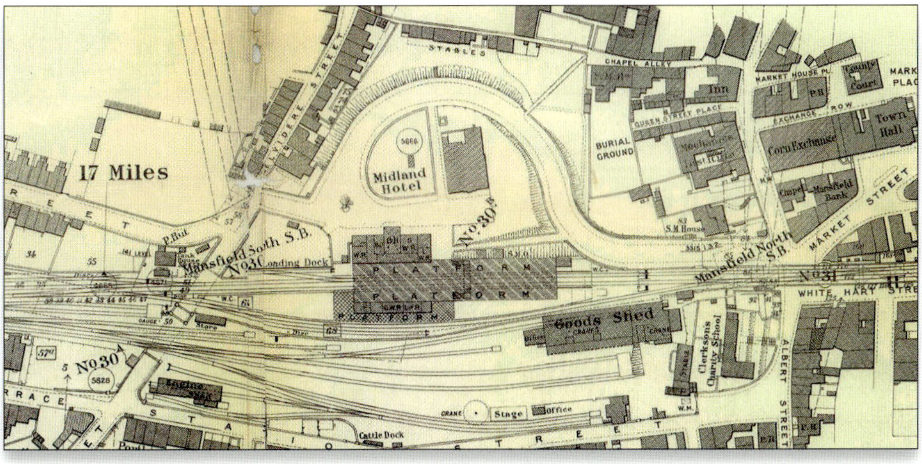

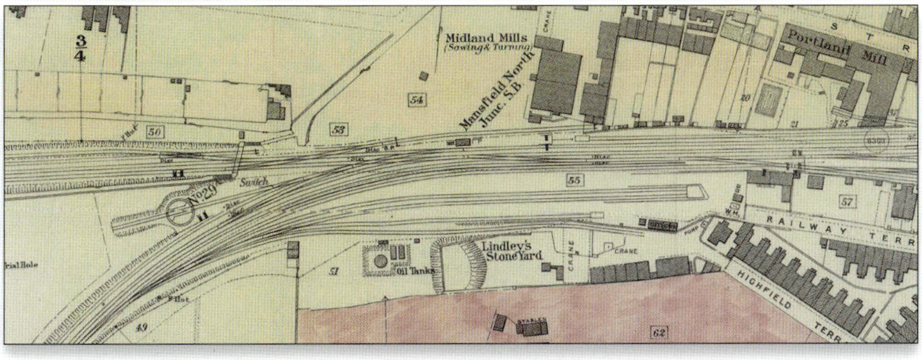

Left & below left: Section of a Midland Railway two-chain plan of Mansfield dated 11 April 1906, prepared to support a claim for Land Tax Redemption. The left plan shows the station area including the original Mansfield & Pinxton Railway Goods Shed. The below left plan shows the North Junction area, with the curve towards Mansfield East Junction and Southwell at the bottom. ***(Courtesy The Midland Railway Study Centre, Derby)***

Below left: Mansfield looking southwards in the 1950s. The station is centre left, with the trainshed and the "back platform" visible extreme left. The goods yard with its shed on the site of the original Mansfield & Pinxton Railway spreads over to the left, and just beyond is Mansfield North curve to the Southwell line. Towards the top of the image are the carriage sidings on the Down side of the line. The white building with a tower is the former Co-operative building on Stockwell Gate, opened in 1922 after the original in the same location was destroyed by fire in 1918. It was extended to twice its size by the Mansfield and Sutton Co-operative Society in 1935 and was latterly Beales department store until closure in 2020. ***(Author's collection)***

Right: Looking towards Mansfield East Junction and the Southwell branch. Of the tracks curving round, only the second-from-right was the (single) running line – the remainder are sidings. On the diagram, the 55-foot diameter turntable at Mansfield North Junction was, according to the story, little used as it was often easier for drivers to turn their locos on the complete triangle than to use the turntable. ***(Unknown)***

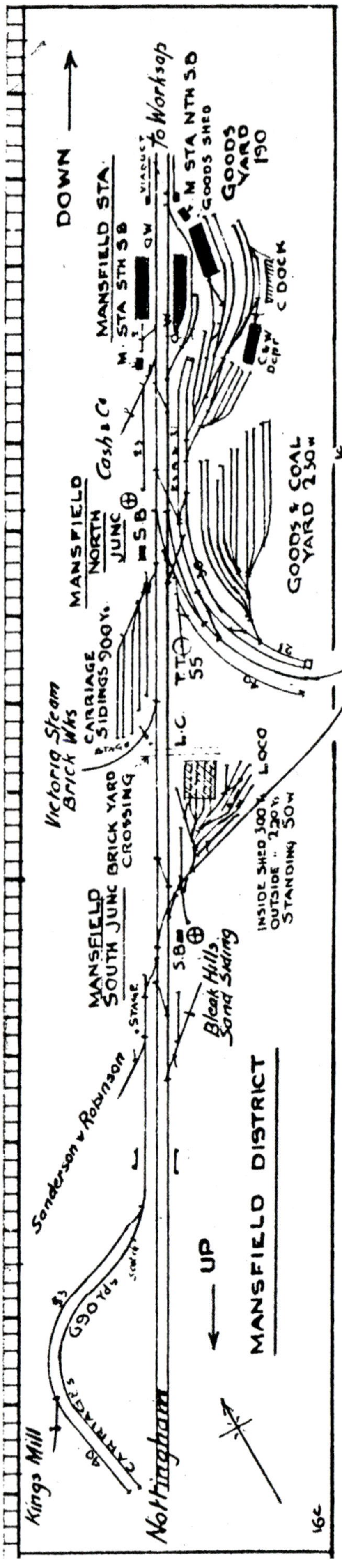

Above: A view inside the trainshed from Platform 2, showing the curved footbridge and a train just departing for Nottingham.

Left: The Mansfield District in its heyday.

Above: A selection of Mansfield tickets: An LM&SR Parking Ticket for a Motor Car or Three Wheeled Vehicle, registration No. JJ5363. An LM&SR Navy, Army & Air Force On Duty ticket for Mansfield to Derby via Nottingham. A BTC Platform Ticket for Mansfield Town. A British Railways Early Morning return, still stating Mansfield (LMS).

Above: Fowler 0-6-0 44168 trundles through the station at 5.25pm with a short freight working, watched by a group of staff with a parcels trolley on the opposite platform. *(All Author's collection)*

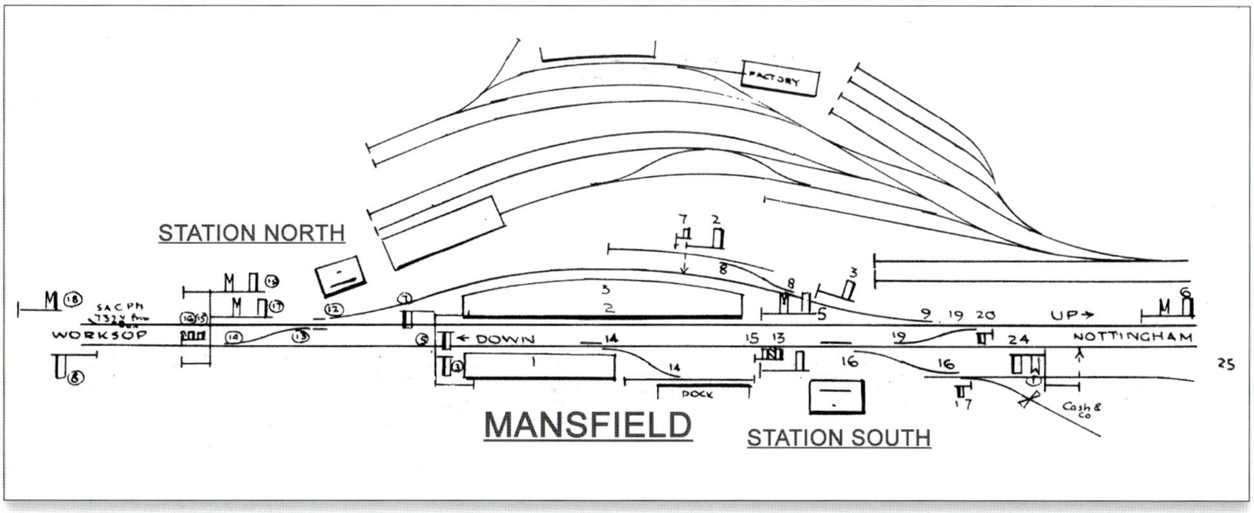

Top: 4F 0-6-0 44416 comes off the viaduct and slows for the station with a Worksop to Nottingham train one afternoon in 1954. The signal box coal bunker seems to be well stocked! ***(Frank Ashley)***

Above: Track layout diagram of Mansfield Station North and Mansfield Station South in the 1950s. ***(Signalling Record Society)***

Right: Mansfield Station North closed on 22 December 1963, but is seen here with windows still intact in April 1964. ***(Mike King)***

Left: With steam to spare and admired by a group of trainspotting lads, Fairburn 2-6-4T 42618 pauses at Mansfield Town with a Worksop to Nottingham service on 20 October 1962. Notice the British Railways Karrier Bantam lorry on the loading dock to the left. ***(Larry Fulwood/Transport Treasury LF FM38-3y)***

Right & above right: Examples of Mansfield LNER and Midland Railway luggage labels. ***(Author's collection)***

Below: Stanier 8F 2-8-0 48114 trundles through the station with a short train of sheeted wagons, possibly containing sand from one of the nearby quarries. ***(Author's collection)***

Right: Fairburn 2-6-4T 42080 pauses with the 3.47pm Worksop to Nottingham train on 5 May 1962. This loco began its career on the Southern Region new to 73A Stewarts Lane on 12 January 1951, but moved to 73B Bricklayers Arms in May 1951. It transferred to 14D Neasden in December 1959, to 16B Kirkby in Ashfield in November 1961. It had further spells at 1A Willesden, 5D Stoke, 12C Barrow in Furness and 9E Trafford Park before seeing withdrawal on 14 January 1967. ***(Milepost 92½)***

Above: Johnson 3F 0-6-0 43727 pilots an unidentified 8F 2-8-0 on an Up Goods train through Mansfield Station in 1955. ***(H.C. Casserley/ Stations UK)***

Left: 16A Nottingham-allocated "Mickey Mouse" 2-6-0 46444 pauses with a Worksop to Nottingham train on 23 August 1963. Notice that track rationalisation has begun; to the left, Mansfield Station South's No. 14 points and trackwork into a dock have been removed. ***(Bill Taylor)***

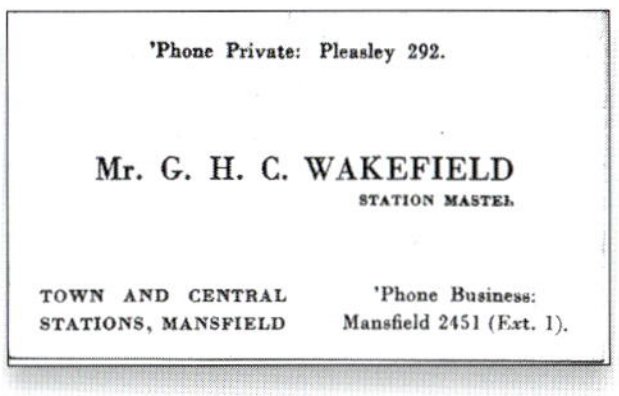
'Phone Private: Pleasley 292.

Mr. G. H. C. WAKEFIELD
STATION MASTER

TOWN AND CENTRAL STATIONS, MANSFIELD

'Phone Business: Mansfield 2451 (Ext. 1).

Above: Business card of Mr G.H.C. Wakefield, appointed Station Master of the Mansfield Town and Central Stations in May 1957. ***(Author's collection)***

Left: The 25-lever frame Mansfield Station South 'box dated from 4 September 1892, replacing an earlier example. It is seen here from the loading dock on 31 January 1961. The two ground discs on the left are Nos. 13 and 15, which apply to the two routes through No. 16 points into two sidings, and the main signal is No. 12. It closed on 5 June 1966. ***(H.B. Priestley)***

Left: Mansfield North Junction 'box on 8 August 1964, looking from an adjacent footbridge. Dating from 28 February 1904, it replaced an earlier structure. With 44 levers, it controlled the junction with the Southwell line together with the carriage sidings and goods yards. The Southwell line connected with the south curve at Mansfield East Junction. In 1961, opening hours of the Mansfield 'boxes were from 4.10am Monday through to the passage of the last train on Saturday night/Sunday morning, or as directed by Control. On the left, the Co-op warehouse building had its own siding beyond the signalbox; the building further away is the Portland Mill. ***(Transport Treasury PY10078M)***

Left: It is difficult to believe this is the same spot. 56020 passes the site of Mansfield North Junction box on 28 March 1979 with a train for Ratcliffe Power Station. Mansfield North to Mansfield East Junctions had been designated as a through siding from 28 November 1965, and closed completely from 11 December 1966. North Junction 'box closed at the same time and, apart from the Up and Down Main, before long all the sidings in this area were removed. The Co-op warehouse was still extant at the time of the photo, but has since been demolished. ***(Malcolm Rush)***

Right: A signalling plan of the North Junction showing the line towards East Junction heading off top right. This route opened on 3 April 1871 and Electric Tablet Block Working was introduced on 27 October 1890. It closed to passengers on 12 August 1929 and completely on 11 December 1966, the line being severed at the North Junction due to the condition of the viaduct over the River Maun. ***(Signalling Records Society)***

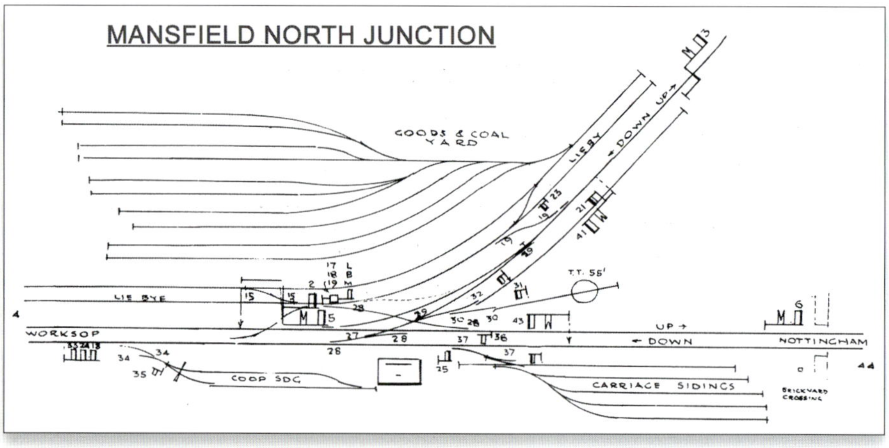

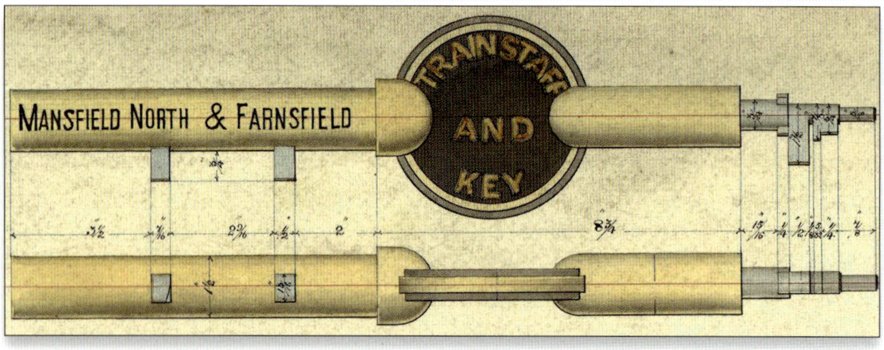

Left: The Mansfield to Southwell Railway was single line and this drawing is for the original MR Train Staff and Key for the Mansfield North to Farnsfield section. ***(Courtesy Midland Railway Study Centre, Derby)***

Above: Mansfield Town Goods Depot, as seen from Albert Street. The building on the left was the original 1849-built Midland Railway Station, and was used until the line was extended to Worksop in 1875. A new "through" station was built off to the right. ***(Steve Godman collection)***

Below: A moment in time in Mansfield Goods Yard is captured sometime in 1975. The driver of Class 25 25244, working on the "Mansfield Tripper", waits for the next command from the shunter. The loco was new to 16A Toton on 3 June 1964 as D7594, and saw spells at 16C Derby, 9A Longsight and D09 Manchester Division. Goods traffic was handled here until 2 June 1975, and the loco was moved to Scotland's Eastfield depot sometime in the two weeks ending 23 August 1975. This dates the photo to the first half of 1975 – but the loco is well outside its normal area as it was seen on 9 March 1975 at Manchester Victoria, then was noted on 30 April at Huddersfield with a parcels train. On 14 June it worked the 09.20 Manchester Piccadilly to Yarmouth with 25086 to Lincoln Central and returned from there with the 09.30 ex-Yarmouth. So what was it doing in the Mansfield area, one wonders?! The loco was withdrawn on 21 July 1986 and later sold to the Swanage Railway Society. In the early 1990s it was transferred to the Nene Valley Railway, but was moved again to the Kent & East Sussex Railway where it has been languishing ever since. ***(Author's collection)***

Right & below right: After passenger services ended on 10 October 1964 the line became freight-only. The station slumbered on until the end of 1968 when the demolition crews moved in. The overall roof and the footbridge were removed and cut for scrap, followed by the platforms. However, the station building remained and acquired listed status in 1978, saving it from demolition. Remaining in a moribund state, it was renovated in 1986 and opened as Brunel's cafe-bar and restaurant on 17 April that year. Here, the scrap men deal with part of the overall roof and a large section of platform has been removed to allow equipment across the tracks, which are protected by sleepers. ***(Both Steve Godman collection)***

Left: Brunel's nightclub saw a decline in fortunes in the 1990s, and the building once again became disused. This is the station building when in use as Brunel's. The gold-coloured Ford Cortina 2.8 Ghia on the forecourt, registration GFE 481Y, was first registered in August 1982. The date of the last V5C (logbook) issued was 3 January 2001, so it was almost 19 years old. Although undated, this image is after the station was reopened for the Robin Hood Line but before it returned to railway use in 2000. ***(Author's collection)***

The changing face of Mansfield, from a bustling railway hub to a two-track railway with a closed station. Photographed on 8 April 1984:

Right: The station buildings, looking from the south end of the former platform area. Notice the Midland Hotel to the left.

Above: The view from the former Down platform, looking south.

Above: The remains of Mansfield North bracket signal that formerly held No. 5 (left) and No. 2 for the curve towards East Junction.

Above: A view from the same footbridge we saw earlier. The bracket signal is still in view, with the station buildings just visible in the distance. ***(All Robin Stewart Smith)***

Above: Having run round at Sherwood Colliery Sidings, a Class 20 trundles southwards over Mansfield Viaduct on 20 June 1979 with wagons for the sand quarry at Berry Hill. The church spire on the left is the Parish Church of St. Peter & St. Paul. ***(Malcolm Rush)***

Left: Another trackside view of the remains of the station, devoid of overall roof and platforms. Notice that the track level has been raised since the station's closure.

Above: A major implication for the station's future reopening was the construction of the inner ring road, which involved the widening of Portland Street. Work began on 17 February 1989 and the Portland Street section was completed in October 1989; the new bridge took away part of the embankment where the future station platforms would stand. ***(Both Ash Edwards)***

The station platforms were rebuilt for Stage 2 of the Robin Hood Line.

Above left: The Down platform under construction on 18 February 1995.

Above right: The new platforms were designed to accommodate a full-length HST but, due to the viaduct, they could not be extended north so had to be extended south instead, which meant placing them along the bridge over Portland Street. At 06.20 on 19 March 1995, during a track possession, the new girders to support the platforms are being swung into place. ***(Both Robin Stewart Smith)***

Left: The new platforms have glass balustrades added, which can be seen over Portland Street bridge.

Left: Access between the platforms was via a new subway. During a nine-day possession in November 1994, 120 metres of the trackbed has been dug away to allow the concrete sections to be installed.

Below left: The first concrete segments have been laid, and the press are descending into the hole to observe proceedings.

Below: The subway entrance was tastefully covered in stone. ***(All Ash Edwards, except where mentioned)***

Left: 150109+153371 work the 12.39 Mansfield Town to Mansfield Woodhouse during the Robin Hood Line Gala Day on 19 November 1995. At that time the station buildings were still in private hands. ***(Author)***

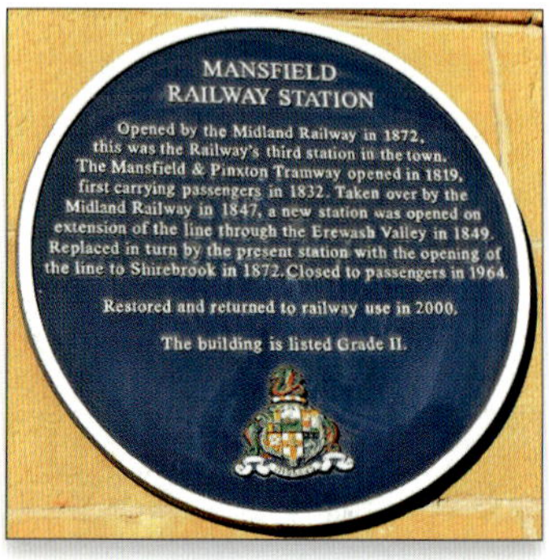

Above right & right: Similarly to Mansfield Woodhouse, Mansfield also had a plaque designed by Ash Edwards (as seen in the drawing) to commemorate the opening day. A blue plaque was also attached to the station in 2000. ***(Ash Edwards/Author)***

Left: The services were initially in the hands of Class 150 DMUs, such as 150128 on a Nottingham service. ***(Author's collection)***

Right: The original style nameboard also incorporated the MDC crest.

Above: The station as it is today, complete with a much smaller canopy compared to the original overall roof. ***(Ash Edwards/Author)***

Above: With Mansfield loco depot peeping above the coaches, Stanier "Black 5" 4-6-0 45253 passes Mansfield South Junction signal box on 8 August 1964 with the 12.41 Saturdays only Skegness to Radford. Notice the zero milepost on the left for the Mansfield to Rolleston Branch. ***(Transport Treasury PY10078M B)***

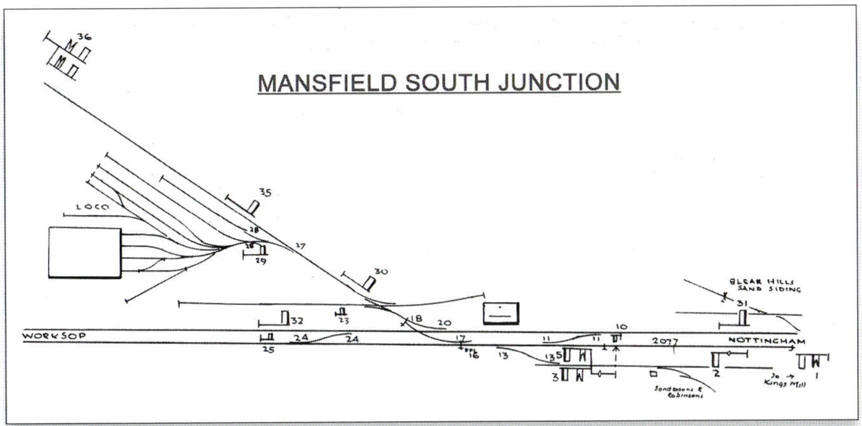

Left: Diagram of the Mansfield South Junction area. ***(Signalling Records Society)***

Right: Looking from the footbridge off the end of Princess Street, 20001 & 20054 trundle past Mansfield South Junction on 27 September 1979 heading north, perhaps to Mansfield Concentration Sidings or Worksop. ***(Malcolm Rush)***

Left: The view from Mansfield South Junction signal box. A pair of Class 37s, 37128 & 37122, are directed by No. 3 signal to take the main line towards Mansfield station with an empty HAA set on 24 May 1979, bound for Sherwood Colliery Sidings.

Below left: 47173 heads 6Z85 Shirebrook Colliery to Ratcliffe Power Station on 2 April 1979. The former Mansfield Engine Shed has received a modern frontage following a change of use, but the original building can still be seen.

Below: Coming off the branch from Mansfield East and passing No. 30 signal, 20076+20195 approach Mansfield South Junction on 8 October 1979 with a Rufford Colliery to Avenue Coking Plant train. This had been delayed because of a previous loco failure. ***(All Malcolm Rush)***

Above, below & below right: The frame and diagram inside Mansfield South Junction, and the Tyers' No. 6 Tablet machine for the single line between Mansfield South Jcn (MSJ) and Mansfield Colliery Jcn (MCJ). The tablet tray is open and one of the tablets can be seen in front of the bell plunger. Clyde Hatter said that "when Mansfield East Junction (MEJ) box was abolished, the S&T transferred this instrument with pattern 'C' tablets (triangular hole in the middle) from MEJ into this box, replacing one with pattern 'B' tablets (square hole in the middle). This operation apparently took four men not-inconsiderable effort, and the tablets then had crude amendments over-stamped onto the pattern 'C' tablets, extending their validity from MEJ to MSJ. However, as far as can be ascertained from subsequent involvement with similar instruments, all that was really required was to swap the tablet tray!" ***(Above, below left Clyde Hatter, below right Malcolm Rush)***

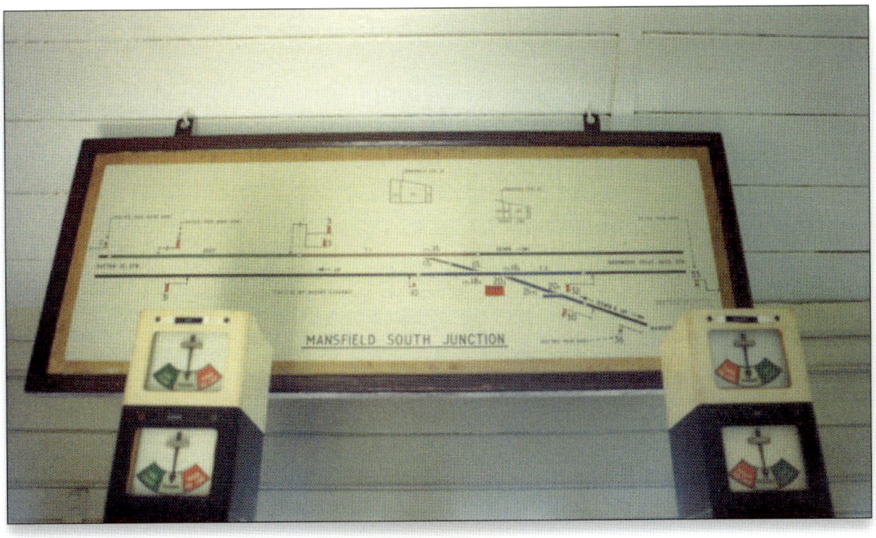

Left: A fibre tablet for the section between MCJ and MEJ. "East" has been over-stamped and "South" applied. ***(Author's collection)***

Mansfield Shed

Left: Mansfield Shed was a brick-built, four-road, single-ended building which opened on 9 October 1862. According to the Ian Allan Depot Directory: "The shed is on the east side of the Mansfield–Kirkby line south of the station. The yard is visible from the line. Turn sharp left outside Mansfield L.M.S. Station into a short approach road, and turn left into Belvedere Street, changing to Portland Street under the railway bridge. Turn right into Quarry Lane and right into Bradder Street. This is a cul-de -sac and the shed entrance is on the left, off a path that runs across the top of the street. Walking time 15 minutes." It was coded 16D between September 1935 and September 1955, when it became 16C. After closure on 1 April 1960, its allocation was transferred to Kirkby-in-Ashfield. Whitelegg 4-4-2T 2098 reposes on 6 June 1936. It was built for the London Tilbury & Southend lines, and was allocated (but never carried) the BR number 41915. Withdrawal came in March 1951.

Above: Cast 16C shed plate sold at auction in 2022.

Above left: Johnson 3F 0-6-0 43529 is on shed during 1952. This came to 16D Mansfield on 1 January 1948 and was transferred to 15D Bedford in the week ending 11 September 1954.

Left: 16A Nottingham-allocated Stanier "Black 5" 4-6-0 44861 is seen at Mansfield on 5 June 1949. Judging by the reporting number, it has either worked a special to, or is about to work a special from, Mansfield. ***(All Author's collection)***

Below: As mentioned, the shed closed in April 1960 and entered industrial use. It is seen here in 1975 in use by Neville's as a workshop, as an unidentified Class 25 passes. The building is still in use today. ***(Jim Hatcher)***

Bibliography

A Regional History of the Railways of Great Britain, Volume 8 South and West Yorkshire, David Joy, David & Charles 1984

A Regional History of the Railways of Great Britain, Volume 9 The East Midlands, Robin Leleux, David & Charles 1989

An Illustrated History of Mansfield's Railways, Paul Anderson and Jack Cupit, Irwell Press 2000

Britain's Joint Lines, H.C. Casserley, Ian Allan 1968

British Railways Layout Plans of the 1950s Volume 14, John Swift Collection, Signalling Record Society

Brother to the Ox, An Autobiography of a Farm Labourer, Fred Kitchen, J.M. Dent & Sons 1942

Coal Mining in the East Midlands, David Amos and Natalie Braber, Bradwell Books 2017

Forgotten Railways: The East Midlands, P.H. Anderson, David & Charles 1978

Great Central Volume Three, Fay Sets The Pace, 1900–1922, George Dow, Ian Allan 1965

Lost Railways of Derbyshire, Geoffrey Kingscott, Countryside Books 2007

Midland Record Number 4, Wild Swan

Railways in South Yorkshire, C.T. Goode, Dalesman 1975

Regional Railway Handbooks No. 1, The East Midlands, P. Howard Anderson, David & Charles 1986

The Good Olde Days, Martin Weiss, AD Newspapers 2007

The Mansfield–Southwell–Rolleston Railway, Robert Weston, Oakwood Press 2021

The Midland Railway – A Chronology, John Gough, Railway & Canal Historical Society 1989

The Midland Railway: Its Rise and Progress, Frederick S. Williams, Bemrose & Co, 1878

The Railways of the South Yorkshire Coalfield from 1880, A.L. Barnett, RCTS 1978

The South Yorkshire Joint Railway and the Coalfield, B.J. Elliott, Oakwood Press 2000

The Story of the Mansfield & Pinxton Railway, Mansfield & Pinxton Railway Project Group 2019

Transport in South Yorkshire, B.J. Elliott, Local History series Sheffield University 1972

Welbeck And The 5th Duke of Portland, David J Bradbury, Wheel Publications 1989

Websites

Grace's Guide To British Industrial History: *https://gracesguide.co.uk/Main_Page*

British Newspaper Archive: *www.britishnewspaperarchive.co.uk*

Six Bells Junction: *www.sixbellsjunction.co.uk*

Railway Magazine Archive: *www.railwaymagazine.co.uk/archive/*

BR Database: *www.brdatabase.info*

North East Derbyshire Industrial Archaeology Society: *https://nedias.co.uk*

Above: Shirebrook Sidings are full of HAA wagons awaiting use as an unidentified Class 37 passes with 6T23 Toton to Worksop on 26 August 1988. The colliery access heads off centre right. ***(Robin Stewart-Smith)***

Addendum to Railways around Worksop Volume 1

Page 41 Top photo should be credited to Howard Turner
Page 102 Bottom photo should be credited to Alan Smalley
Page 103 Photo two should be credited to Alan Smalley
Page 136 Bottom photo should be credited to Alan Smalley

Above: The single line tablet holder can be seen disappearing into the cab as 20174+20185 pass Mansfield South Junction and take the branch line with 0T76 to Clipstone on 18 April 1979. ***(Malcolm Rush)***

Above: 56081 passes through Mansfield Woodhouse with 5Q49 12.05 Worksop Down Yard to Derby Litchurch Lane on 9 October 2021, consisting of Greater Anglia Class 720s Nos. 720532 & 720578 heading from storage at Worksop to Derby for completion before entering service. ***(Derek Wilson)***